Sport and Social Mobility

Ramón Spaaij is a Senior Research Fellow in the School of Social Sciences at La Trobe University, Australia, and at the Amsterdam Institute for Social Science Research, University of Amsterdam.

Routledge Research in Sport, Culture and Society

Sport and Social Mobility

Crossing Boundaries

Ramón Spaaij

Routledge
Taylor & Francis Group
New York   London

First published 2011
by Routledge
711 Third Avenue, New York, NY 10017

Simultaneously published in the UK
by Routledge
2 Park Square, Milton Park, Abingdon, Oxon OX14 4RN

Routledge is an imprint of the Taylor & Francis Group, an informa business

© 2011 Taylor & Francis

The right of Ramón Spaaij to be identified as author of this work has been asserted in accordance with sections 77 and 78 of the Copyright, Designs and Patents Act 1988.

Typeset in Sabon by IBT Global.

First issued in paperback 2013

Library of Congress Cataloging-in-Publication Data

Spaaij, R. F. J. (Ramon F. J.)
    Sport and social mobility : crossing boundaries / by Ramón Spaaij.
        p. cm. — (Routledge research in sport, culture and society)
    Includes bibliographical references and index.
    1. Sports — Social aspects.   2. Social mobility.   I. Title.
    GV706.5.S6925 2011
    306.4'83 — dc22
                                          2010050804

ISBN13: 978-0-415-84871-8 (pbk)
ISBN13: 978-0-415-87488-5 (hbk)
ISBN13: 978-0-203-81377-5 (ebk)

To my parents, and to the memory of Celia da Cal

Contents

Figures

Tables

Acknowledgments

I would like to express my sincere thanks to all the people whose generosity, stories, experiences, interpretations, feedback and support have helped shape this book. The time spent in Brazil, Australia and the Netherlands for fieldwork has been enormously valuable and enjoyable thanks to a great number of people and organizations. I would like to thank Claudia França, Paul Teeple, Luciene Oliveira, Sergio Martins, Bianca Garcia, Mariana Loiola, Brooke Rosenbauer and all the other staff of the Vencer and A Ganar family for their continued commitment and support. Heartfelt thanks are also due to Ralf Bormans, Arno Smit, Henk Medema and their colleagues at the City Steward Rotterdam Foundation, who were incredibly generous in their support for the research project. I am very grateful to Leon Holt and other representatives of the North Central Football League for their continued support and input. I would like to express my gratitude to all the people who have contributed to my research in urban and regional Victoria in so many ways; they will know who they are. Many thanks go to those who welcomed me into their homes during the fieldwork.

I have been very fortunate to be surrounded by kind and supportive colleagues at La Trobe University and elsewhere. In particular, I would like to thank Yusuf Sheikh Omar, Rowan Ireland, June Senyard, Alastair Anderson, Sandy Gifford, Hans Westerbeek and Aaron Smith for the collegiality, stimulating discussions and incisive comments. Amanda Vargas, Flavia Rocha Pedrosa and Chris Kaimmer provided invaluable research assistance and great company. Special thanks also to Maryann Martin for her editing expertise.

The research upon which this book draws has been supported by a number of fellowships and grants from La Trobe University, notably a three-year Postdoctoral Research Fellowship and a series of small travel grants. This funding also enabled me to present various drafts of the manuscripts at international conferences, symposia and expert meetings worldwide. Academic visits to Loughborough University, Yale University and Utrecht University have been particularly valuable in shaping the ideas presented in this book. I thank Tess Kay, Joe Maguire, Harvey Goldblatt, Maarten van Bottenburg and other staff at these institutions for their generosity and interest in my work. I would like to express my gratitude to Tess Kay, who has offered friendship, collegiality and ongoing conversations.

I want to thank Taylor & Francis for permission to include material from 'The Glue that Holds the Community Together: Sport and Sustainability in Rural Australia', *Sport in Society* 12(9) (2007): 1124–1138, and Sage Publications Ltd for permission to include portions (including Table 7.1) from 'Sport as a Vehicle for Social Mobility and Regulation of Disadvantaged Urban Youth: Lessons from Rotterdam', *International Review for the Sociology of Sport* 44(2/3) (2009): 247–264.

I am grateful to Alison and Ingmar and to the rest of my family for their continued love and support.

Introduction

A boy who played with a ball made of socks, who moved on to play with a professional ball, on professional pitches, in teams that made history. I saw the world, met great people—wonderful people. I never expected to fly so high

(Edson Arantes do Nascimento 2006: 5).

The biography of Brazilian football (soccer) star Edson Arantes do Nascimento, known worldwide as Pelé, is indicative of the advantages professional sport may bring to individuals who grow up in poverty, as well as to disadvantaged communities where sport may provide an important form of organized social activity, identity and excitement. For many poor young people, sport presents "the prospect of escape into a better world, at least a lift out of the direct poverty" (Walvin 1995: 122). The sporting success of athletes from impoverished backgrounds fuels the imagination of young people who grow up in similar conditions and encourages them to aspire to building a better future through sport. Quite apart from the real possibilities of a professional career and the upward social mobility that it offers, however, sport tends to be seen by young males in particular as a means to go abroad and escape the difficult life conditions experienced at home (e.g. Poli 2010).

In reality, upward social mobility through professional sport remains mainly in the realm of myth, but such is the power of this myth that aspirants will go to great lengths to succeed. Sport acts as an opiate of the masses "by perpetuating the belief that persons from the lowest social classes can be upwardly mobile through success in sports" (Eitzen 2000: 372). Research by Poli (2010: 1001–2) shows that upward career paths of football players recruited in Africa to major European clubs "are few and hide the numerous failures, not only sporting ones, which confront players who leave the continent to pursue their ambitions abroad." Although difficult to estimate with any precision, the proportion of footballers coming to Europe for trials and who succeed in signing a professional contract is very low. Moreover, even though the possibility of social advancement through sport exists, it tends to be elusive. Lever (1983: 136) points out that for the vast majority of Brazilian football players, football provides only fleeting social mobility, leaving their educational levels unchanged:

At about age thirty most players find themselves with few work skills, more debts than cash reserves, and only memories of their brief careers. . . . Typically he has trouble adjusting to retirement. He has little choice but to accept a low-level job that is hardly commensurate with his newly acquired middle-class tastes. All too often, players return to the poverty-stricken environment from which they came.

Not only are high-flying careers in professional sport very scarce, but professional sport is also a precarious means of securing a living (Leonard and Reyman 1988; Eitzen and Sage 2003). A serious injury can destroy a player's career, which is limited anyway by age eroding physical abilities and possibly diminishing motivation. This is what actually happened to Pelé's father, Dondinho, whose damaged knee ligaments ended his flirtation with professional football.

In terms of non-professional forms of sport, however, many policymakers point to significant social, health and economic benefits, both in western societies and in developing countries. The following statement by the United Nations Inter-Agency Taskforce on Sport for Development and Peace (2003: 1–2) might be seen as typical of the claims made for sport:

> Sport—from play and physical activity to organised competitive sport—has an important role in all societies. Sport is critical to a child's development. It teaches core values such as co-operation and respect. It improves health and reduces the likelihood of disease. It is a significant economic force providing employment and contributing to local development. And, it brings individuals and communities together, bridging cultural or ethnic divides. Sport offers a cost-effective tool to meet many development and peace challenges, and helps achieve the [Millennium Development Goals].

In contemporary political discourse, sport is being analyzed not only in terms of its economic impact but also in terms of its potential to promote tolerance, intercultural dialogue and peace, social cohesion and social inclusion, as well as to combat crime, poverty, homelessness and unhealthy lifestyles (e.g. Sport England 1999; Coalter et al. 2000; Morris et al. 2003; UNICEF 2006; Coalter 2007; Nichols 2007; Sugden and Wallis 2007; Kay et al. 2008; Ministry of Health, Welfare and Sport 2008; Levermore 2008; Levermore and Beacom 2009a; Sherry 2010). Researchers and policymakers tend to emphasize the multidimensional nature of sport's social impact, which has been summarized by its advocates in a single phrase: the global "power of sport" (International Sport for Development and Peace Association 2010).

The idea that sport might be directed toward wider social objectives is central to the development of modern sport. Many of the aspirations that are currently voiced in relation to sport and social policy can be traced, in one form or another, through the history of modern sport. In the nineteenth century, several European states were concerned with the physicality of their agents and the general population, not only in preparation for war, but also for hygiene and health. Sport has also been central to social movements such as muscular Christianity (MacAloon 2006; Booth and Tatz 2000), the *mens sana in corpore sano* ethos and "rational recreation" interventions in the late nineteenth century (Giulianotti 1999; Kidd 2008), and to the establishment of organizations such as the YMCA (Saavedra 2009). However, as Kidd (2008) notes, the contemporary manifestation of the "power of sport" movement is different, *inter alia*, in the rapid explosion of the agencies and organizations that are involved and the extent to which it has been championed by the United Nations and other international governing bodies and transnational NGOs. This movement has been gaining momentum to the extent that, at least for football, it arguably has "the potential to transform the role and perception of the world's most popular sport" (Fleming 2009: 9). Given this, Fleming (2009: 14) asks whether football, in its evolution from disorganized beginnings to a social phenomenon and global industry, can now become equally successful and renowned in the field of social development. To realize this ambition, some advocates argue, sport as a global "social project" needs to be carefully designed (e.g. Beutler 2008).

The battle lines of the "power of sport" debate are yet to be drawn. At present, two seemingly contradictory tendencies hold sway. The first tendency refers to the ways in which research into the social impact of sport tends to be organized and conducted. The challenges of conceptualizing, measuring and explaining social outcomes of sport are plenty, and the existing body of research is generally poorly equipped to meet these challenges. Presumed social benefits of sport remain under-explored empirically (Long and Sanderson 2001; Bailey 2005; Tacon 2007; Bloyce and Smith 2010), with most studies failing to gather the necessary evidence to demonstrate such outcomes and to make a rigorous assessment (Collins et al. 1999; Donnelly et al. 2007). Coalter (2007: 2) rightly notes "the absence of an understanding of processes and mechanisms which either produce, or are assumed to produce, particular impacts and outcomes": what works, what processes produce these effects, for which participants, in what circumstances, and what are their limitations? These are fundamental questions that require increased methodological and empirical rigor. Moreover, Tess Kay makes the important point that many studies are narrowly focused, project-specific and concerned primarily with unpicking how immediate behavioral impacts are affected by program delivery processes. Systematic analysis of contextual influences lies outside the scope of most studies, and so too does consideration of the longer-term impacts of sport participation.[1] There is thus a need for greater and more sustained engagement with empirically grounded research and innovative methodologies that enable the collection and analysis of high-quality data (Kay 2009).

A second, related tendency of the "power of sport" debate is its predominantly functionalist and utilitarian underpinnings, with many of its proponents viewing sport as an antidote to a variety of social problems. In this view, sport is an inherently wholesome, harmonizing and cohesive force which has enormous potential in relation to the promotion of the "collective good." In its contemporary manifestation, the "power of sport" movement has for the most part been devoid of critical and theoretically-informed reflection (Black 2009; Darnell 2010). However, sociologists of sport have been critical of functionalist and utilitarian interpretations of sport, and rightly so. Hargreaves (1986: 3) makes the important point that:

> Sports activity . . . can never be adequately explained purely as an instrument of social harmony, or as a means of self-expression, or as a vehicle for satisfying individual needs, for this ignores the divisions and conflicts, and the inequalities of power in societies, which if we care to look more closely, register themselves in sports. Nor can their social role be explained simply as a means whereby the masses are manipulated into conformity with the social order, capitalist or otherwise, for to do so is to regard people as passive dupes, and it ignores their capacity to resist control and to stamp sports with their own culture.

As Patriksson (1995: 128) observes, sport (like most other activities) is not a priori good or bad, but has the potential to produce both positive and negative outcomes. Indeed, Eitzen (2006: 29) asserts that although sport has a unifying function to some degree, for the most part sport reinforces the social inequalities in society: "the losers in sport have been and continue to be the poor, racial minorities, and women." A sociological understanding of the social impact of sport, then, requires a critical approach which examines both "winners" and "losers," and which reflects more critically on its own values and socio-historical locations.

A key proponent of a critical sociological approach to sport, Maguire (2005) notes the degree of involvement on the part of many people who investigate or write about its social impact. According to Maguire, "power of sport" advocates tend to be firmly embedded in the global sports industrial complex. Studies are often funded, commissioned and/or supervised by organizations that have a vested interest in demonstrating the social benefits of sport, particularly those studies which involve contract evaluation research. Due to their actual involvement in sport circles and/or their quest for status, funding and academic/professional advancement, researchers often appear unwilling or unable to exercise sufficient detachment, opting instead for varying forms of involved advocacy in the "sport for development and peace" movement.

The importance of detachment to counter-balance problems of involvement is well established in the social sciences. Norbert Elias's (1987) notion of detachment refers to a disciplined, qualified exercise in self-distancing, that is, the individual stands back from reflected objects of thought in order to see them afresh. The aim for sociologists, then, is to recognize and understand their involvement and to distance themselves, as much as possible, from their own values in their research. This approach, Elias argues, would facilitate a better, more reality-congruent understanding of the issues related to the area of research. In other words, the "sociologist-as-participant" must be able to stand back and become, as far as possible, the "sociologist-as-observer-and-interpreter" (Maguire 1988).

The involvement-detachment debate and the related (though not synonymous) notion of reflexivity provide an orientation that is of practical and ethical relevance to the entire research process. At the very least, they sensitize researchers to the fact that their orientations are shaped by their socio-historical locations, including the values and interests that these locations confer upon them. This orientation presents "a rejection of the idea that social research is, or can be, carried out in some autonomous realm that is insulated from the wider society and from the biography of the researcher" (Hammersley and Atkinson 2007: 15). It also highlights that the production of knowledge by researchers has consequences which are not neutral in relation to what are widely felt to be important values, nor are they necessarily desirable. This orientation offers an important corrective to some of the de-contextualized, romanticized generalizations about the "power of sport" that continue to hold sway.

Although this orientation appears at odds with the aforementioned call for greater research engagement, both orientations are in fact highly complementary in that they can keep one another in check through simultaneous processes of *self-involving* (i.e. deep engagement with the object of research) and *self-distancing*. In other words, they enable researchers to cultivate a critically engaged position. Both orientations should be kept in balance: too much self-involving can lead to over-rapport and diminished reflexivity, whereas too much self-distancing can lead to under-rapport and speculative theorizing, inviting criticisms of elitism. In this book, this twofold orientation is used to produce critical sociological engagement at three levels:

- *Theoretical-conceptual.* Are the (western) social science concepts we use universally applicable or situationally specific? Are some historical or cultural conditions not so different that these conceptual categories are analytically inappropriate and reductionist? In other words, what are their analytical uses and limits in different socio-historical locations? In this book, these questions are addressed in relation to the key conceptual categories used, notably the notions of social mobility, social capital and cultural capital.
- *Political-ideological.* Is the social change produced in and through sport ephemeral or durable? Is the "power of sport" not a form of "false consciousness," to borrow Marxist terminology; that is, isn't the social impact of sport superficial and self-defeating rather than "real" and profound? Is there a danger that the "power of sport" discourse reproduces rather than resists or transforms the existing social order and attendant social inequalities, while disorganizing and fragmenting subordinate groups? In this book, I explore an intriguing paradox of social development through sport: while sports programs aimed at wider social objectives tend to be highly regarded

by disadvantaged youth and their families, such programs tend to construct disadvantaged young people as a social problem, and their ulterior political-ideological aim is often to discipline and "civilize" the target group rather than enhance their agency and autonomy. Little research has explored the idea of development through sport as a form of social control due in part to the aforementioned degree of involvement on the part of advocates of the "power of sport" discourse. However, as this book will show, the issue of social control is of great import for fully grasping the complex and at times contradictory outcomes of participation in sport.

- *Methodological.* There is a need for greater and more sustained engagement with empirically grounded research and, as part of this, with methodologies that enable the collection and analysis of culturally sensitive, high-quality data. There is also a need for flexibility and creativity in the exploration of under-examined or unanticipated avenues of inquiry, for example by incorporating new social media into the analysis. It is also of vital importance to actively engage with research participants and their communities to enhance the usefulness of the research results and to ensure that all voices are fairly heard and represented.

Building on this orientation, this book provides a critical examination of the ways in which sport contributes to, or inhibits, upward social mobility of disadvantaged people in different social contexts. Clearly, social advancement through sport should be understood in its particular social contexts. The nature and meanings of sport participation and its impact on people's lives vary significantly depending on the social setting and can be better understood when they are compared in relation to two or more meaningfully contrasting cases or situations. Specificities in time and space matter; social practices are always inherently spatial in character, and they are also bound by and constructed over time (Field 2005: 103–4). The approach taken in this book, then, is one that treats social relationships and behavior as constituted by social agents in specific circumstances and with access to unequally distributed assets. It uses a comparative design to improve theory development in regard to sport participation and social mobility, building on a comparison of four cases with the aim to produce nuanced understandings of the lived experience of sport in different social contexts.

ON METHOD

Scholars are uncertain not only about the potential social impacts of sport but also about the capacity of research to reveal them (Kay 2009). Successive attempts to establish a statistical, causal relationship between sport and singular outcomes "can be seen as a rather crass effort to bang square pegs into round holes" (Crabbe 2008: 31). This approach, Crabbe rightly asserts, "ultimately represents a staged attempt to validate the benefits of sporting programmes rather than providing a more valid and complete account of what is actually involved in the process." This critique highlights the need for new and innovative modes of empirical investigation. According to Kay (2009), reflexive qualitative studies that capture authentic local knowledge can help address these issues. She argues that:

> Qualitative investigations may . . . help capture the complex and multi-faceted process through which individuals experience beneficial social outcomes from sport. This means that it is important that concern with "rigour" in sport-in-development research does not lead to too narrow a concentration on positivist methods that deliver the 'hard facts' be-loved of policymakers. We must be cautious about privileging positivist forms of knowledge by valuing research primarily for its contribution to policy and organization effectiveness. Efforts to understand the so-cial impact of sport are unnecessarily limited if we study human be-haviour (e.g. behavioural and attitudinal change) only *as a product of policy implementation*. This leads to limited consideration of broader contextual influences (Kay 2009: 1188; italics in original).

Kay's (2009: 1190) argument that reflexive forms of research provide "a mechanism for the expression of local understandings and knowledge" that are crucial to the assessment of the social impact of sport informs the methodological orientation developed in this book, which is characterized by a deep concern for lived experience, meaning and process. Through in-depth qualitative investigation, the book captures the voices, experiences and meaning-giving processes of the people being studied. However, the intent here is not to dismiss quantitative research methods out of hand. In some instances it may be useful to develop mixed-methods research by combining qualitative and quantitative approaches for complementary purposes. As this book demonstrates, qualitative and quantitative research can be carried out simultaneously or sequentially in a single study (see also Sale et al. 2002).

The book features a comparative case study design. Where cases are chosen strategically, the data from the multiple cases can strengthen the case study results and make the interpretations and explanations more robust (Yin 2004: xv). The comparison may itself suggest concepts that are relevant to the emergent theory (Bryman 2001: 53). Each case is sought to be understood individually and in as much depth as possible. Once such understanding is produced, the principal purpose becomes one of devel-oping cross-case comparisons which illuminate patterns of similarity and difference as a basis for theory development. The multiple-case design is based on "theoretical replication" (Yin 1994; Eisenhardt 1989) involving four cases which fill theoretical categories and provide examples of polar types, as shown in Table I.1.

Case selection draws on the ideal-typical distinction between "sport development" and "sport-for-development" (or "development through sport") (Coalter 2007; Bartlett and Straume 2008; Levermore and Beacom 2009b). This distinction refers to the ways in which sports activities are organized, practiced and experienced. The former implies the development and diffusion of sport itself, whereas the latter implies using sport as a tool in social development initiatives. There is likely to be a significant differential in impact between well-designed, targeted programs that use sport as a vehicle for social and personal development, and more facility-based approaches in which traditional sport development objectives of increased participation and the development of sports skills are emphasized (Coalter 2007; Hylton and Bramham 2008). The latter may be less effective for reaching target groups in disadvantaged urban and rural areas or in addressing complex issues of social exclusion (Collins and Kay 2003; Waring and Mason 2010). Longer-term positive social outcomes are particularly associated with programs that actively engage specific target groups, such as disadvantaged or disaffected young people (Sandford et al. 2006; Bailey 2005; Crabbe et al. 2006). The distinction between sport development and sport-for-development is also useful for grasping differences in participant expectations: in the latter social outcomes are explicitly sought, whereas in the former they may be unintended by-products.

Within each category—sport development and sport-for-development—two cases are compared, a research strategy which is particularly instructive when external conditions are thought to produce much variation in the phenomenon being studied (Yin 1994: 50). The within-category cases can be viewed as polar types that represent markedly different social settings in terms of the forms and degrees of economic and social disadvantage experienced by the communities being studied. These social settings offer important explanatory factors for understanding how and under what conditions sport participation contributes to, or inhibits, social mobility. This is theorized in terms of social agents' "portfolio" of capital in and outside of the field of sport, and in relation to the social inequalities which affect access to capital resources.

As Table I.1 shows, the first case analyzed in this book is the Sport Steward Program (SSP) in Rotterdam, the Netherlands. SSP seeks to contribute to the objective of socio-economic advancement of unemployed young people with low educational attainment and uses sport as a vehicle to effectuate this process. The second case is the Vencer ("to win/succeed") program, a team sports partnership model for youth employability in Rio de Janeiro, Brazil. By focusing on both economic and social development, Vencer seeks to use sport as an educational tool that can be accessed by disadvantaged youth regardless of their athletic skill. The third case, Melbourne Giants Football Club (MG),[2] was founded in Melbourne, Australia, in the late 1990s with the aim of providing sporting opportunities to African refugees, particularly Somalis. MG is a grassroots initiative that receives

Table I.1 Selection of Cases Based on a Replication Logic

	SSP	Vencer	MG	NCFL
Category	Sport for development	Sport for development	Sport development	Sport development
Objective	Enhancing the socio-economic status of unemployed and poorly educated young people in deprived urban areas in Rotterdam	Improving the employablitliy prospects of young people aged 16–24 in poor communities in Rio de Janeiro	Providing football activities for members of the Somali community and other local residents	Providing sporting competitions and facilities for residents of small rural towns
Executing agency	City Steward Rotterdam Foundation (previously Sport Steward Promotion)	Instituto Companheiros das Américas; Partners of the Americas	Local residents; community workers	Local sports clubs and regional leagues
Location	Rotterdam, the Netherlands	Rio de Janeiro, Brazil	Melbourne, Australia	Northwest Victoria, Australia

limited institutional support. The final case is the North Central Football League (NCFL), which is located in the northwest of the state of Victoria in Australia. Rural Victoria has a rich history of organized sporting competitions in a variety of forms. The NCFL encompasses three sports: Australian football, netball and hockey. However, the NCFL study also includes cricket and tennis for the reason that several Australian football, netball and hockey participants are also actively involved in these sports as part of their multiplex sporting relations, which are often seasonally based (see Spaaij 2009b). A thorough discussion of the four cases will be carried out in Chapter 2.

The research conducted at the four sites between 2008 and 2010 combined multiple complementary data collection methods: interviews, focus groups, direct observation, surveys, online blogging and area studies. Interviewing offered the flexibility to react to the respondent's situation, probe for more detail, seek more reflexive responses, and ask questions which are relatively complex or personally intrusive, especially in situations where participants feel comfortable and where reciprocal trust has been established. Key informants at each of the research sites were interviewed up to eight times at regular intervals, which produced rich data on their life trajectories and their evolving experience of sport. Repeated interviews also allowed me "to keep a check on continuities and changes during the various stages of research" (Griffiths 2002: 199).

In total, 53 former Vencer participants were interviewed (35 females and 18 males), and a further 43 interviews were conducted with members of staff, local stakeholders and community residents. In the SSP case study a total of 51 interviews were conducted: 27 interviews with former and then-current participants (16 men and 11 women), 11 interviews with members of staff and 13 interviews with other stakeholders. In both case studies, some of the interviewees were recruited through members of staff. Methodologically, this strategy is potentially problematic since it may yield skewed results if program representatives have a vested interest in putting people forward who they believe will shed a positive light on the program and its achievements. For example, on several occasions staff introduced me to former participants who were deemed "success stories." Thus, although this sampling strategy may be the most practical means of selecting respondents, it can lead to a situation where alternative voices are under-represented or even purposely excluded. To counter-balance this problem, research participants were also recruited independently through snowball sampling, which allowed me to tap people's social networks. Interviews were conducted with 39 players, club officials and other volunteers (34 men and 5 women) associated with the MG. In addition, 12 local residents and community workers were interviewed. The NCFL study included 35 interviewees who were involved in one or more of the five sports as players or volunteers. Twenty-one respondents were men and 14 were women. A further 10 interviews were conducted with representatives of relevant institutions (e.g. local government) and 6 interviews with non-playing residents.

Focus group discussions were conducted to complement the individual interviews. A focus group enables the researcher to study the interaction within the group and the collective construction of meaning, in particular how people respond to each other's opinions and build up a view out of the interaction that takes place within the group (Bryman 2001: 336). The dynamics of a focus group can produce data that would not arise from an interview in which particular questions have been scripted by a researcher (Morgan 1988: 21). A total of seven focus groups were held, each comprising between 4 and 13 participants.

Field visits to the research sites provided the opportunity for direct observation. Observation enables the researcher to obtain impressionistic information concerning sports activities and participants' engagement with these activities. It can contribute to an understanding of how individuals interact and to the assessment of different approaches and activities (Coalter 2002: 51). More generally, it is a means for obtaining a "feeling", albeit a restrained one, for what it is like to be in a particular social situation. On the basis of such experience the researcher is more able adequately to make sense of what people have to say and the ways in which they describe and interpret their social world (Marsh et al. 1978: 119). Access to the SSP and Vencer sites was granted by the two programs owing to their strong interest in being the subject of an academic investigation, which was regarded as an opportunity for evaluation, institutional learning and public exposure. Direct observations were made at sport and classroom activities, teacher and board meetings, workplaces where (former) participants were employed and relevant social activities and institutions in the local areas. In the MG and NCFL cases, research access had to be actively negotiated with club representatives and local residents. Initial contacts with local gatekeepers were central to the early stages of the research, providing guidance, support and insight. Community residents were generally very hospitable and generous, inviting me to numerous public and private gatherings, including family visits, dinners, community meetings and social activities organized by local sport clubs and other community groups. Issues of trust were paramount to the process of developing rapport, which were negotiated in large part through physically being there, listening carefully and respectfully and demonstrating genuine concern for research participants and their interests.

The MG study is unique in that it subsequently developed into a multi-sited ethnography (Marcus 1995). After closely following a group of young players for almost two years, a large proportion of this group moved to other clubs in search of a new team. The fieldwork was expanded to include the players' experiences at their new clubs, which brought a unique within-case comparison to the case study that provided valuable comparative data on social capital, potential barriers to participation and so on.

A survey was conducted among former participants of the Vencer program with its purpose to gather standardized data on program impacts. This data source was added in consultation with the implementing NGOs, who viewed the questionnaire as a helpful method to collect a quantifiable measure of participants' experiences and program impacts, which in turn could benefit institutional learning and future fundraising efforts. The Vencer survey comprised 20 questions, half of which were multiple-choice questions. The survey was applied by the research assistant, an 18-year-old female who lived in one of the communities being studied. A total of 129 completed questionnaires were received, which corresponds to a sampling fraction of 10% (N = 1,286) and a response rate of just below 52%. Respondents were randomly selected and invited to participate either by telephone or face-to-face. The questionnaire was administered directly due to its more personal approach, its greater flexibility and its potential to generate more thorough opinions from respondents in comparison with mail surveys. The gender balance of the survey sample was representative of the sampling frame (61% of respondents were females). A further 92 completed surveys were received from then-current participants of a female-specific version of Vencer, called Vencedoras (see Chapter 2), which corresponds to a sampling fraction and response rate of 77% (N = 120). The survey instrument method was also applied to program staff and other relevant stakeholders to gather their perspectives on the delivery and the impact of Vencer, as well as on local social issues more generally. Twenty-eight completed surveys were received and analyzed, consisting of a sampling fraction of approximately 55% (N = 50).

The significance of online blogs and chats as a data collection method in the Vencer study arose during the research. An online component was added in order to access a wider range of young people who maintain virtual communities through sustained interaction by digital means. Social networking sites and tools like Orkut and MSN are extremely popular among the Brazilian youth being studied. Although most of them do not own a personal computer or laptop, they tend to have at least irregular access to the Internet via LAN Houses (cybercafés) or via computer rooms at local NGOs. The online component of the Vencer study progressed principally through snowball sampling. A major advantage of this method was that it could persist more or less indefinitely and that it was not restricted by constraints of time and travel (Hammersley and Atkinson 2007: 138). Blogging also offered the flexibility to react to changes in the respondent's life and to probe for more detail. For example, participants regularly posted comments on new events and experiences in relation to the program or chatted to me on an individual basis to discuss a job opportunity, a conflict with a loved one and so forth. This communication at times set off a digital exchange in which events were discussed in greater detail.

ON LANGUAGE

Language impinges both on the research exercise and on the social and personal aspects of fieldwork (Devereux 1993). Learning what people mean when they use particular words or phrases is important "not only for understanding what they are telling the researcher but also, at a deeper level, for enhancing trust" in the relationship between researcher and researched (Feldman et al. 2003: 54). A major question that researchers engaging in cross-cultural research are confronted with is whether they can afford the time and intellectual energy required to become competent in a foreign language. This question was relevant to the two languages which I had not mastered at the outset: Brazilian Portuguese and Somali. Early on I decided to gain advanced comprehension of Brazilian Portuguese through intensive language tuition over a period of twelve months prior to the fieldwork in Rio de Janeiro. This decision was driven not only by the expected personal and professional benefits of language-learning, but also by the fact that I generally find learning other languages stimulating and fairly easy and by my fluency in Spanish, which would provide a useful foundation for learning Brazilian Portuguese. Because I aimed to collect data mainly from face-to-face interviews and observation over a considerable period of time, it was important to learn the vernacular as intensely as possible (Leslie and Storey 2003). By achieving advanced comprehension of Brazilian Portuguese, I was able to conduct the fieldwork without an interpreter. I did, however, work alongside local research assistants, who shared a mother tongue with respondents, to avoid miscommunication and inadequate interpretation of data. Their local knowledge was essential at times in deciphering the distinctive *carioca* (Rio de Janeiro) dialect of the people being studied.

Acquiring a robust comprehension of the Somali language was considered more problematic. I initially considered working with an interpreter from the Somali community. However, community leaders objected that using a Somali interpreter would not offer much confidentiality to respondents due to the small and close-knit nature of the community (cf. Laws et al. 2003: 257). They also argued that the research could well progress without the assistance of an interpreter since most Somalis residing in Melbourne have good English language skills, especially the younger generation which tends to be fluent in English and often less well versed in Somali.[3] The research was therefore conducted in English, and along the way I picked up some knowledge of the Somali language. Overall, this approach was moderately successful, as discussed further in Chapter 5.

OVERVIEW

This book offers a comparative analysis of the ways in which participation in sport facilitates or inhibits the accumulation of different types of resources, the composites of which may create paths for objective and/or subjective social mobility in the four settings being studied. The book starts by formulating the theoretical and conceptual frameworks which guide the analysis. Chapter 1 conceptualizes participation in sport as a potential vehicle for the development of social, cultural and economic capital from which certain benefits can be derived that enable social agents to improve or maintain their social position. It is argued that multiform capital should be viewed as a set of unequally distributed resources to action which are a basis for social exclusion and inclusion. Access to and command of these resources can place individuals in positions of greater status and power, enhance their sense of autonomy and agency and, in some cases, produce considerable, if not life-altering, social advancement. However, they may also serve to bolster and reproduce inequality and privilege, acting as powerful social barriers to the social inclusion and upward mobility of subordinate groups.

Following on from the conceptual analysis, Chapter 2 provides a thorough discussion of the four settings being studied, with particular attention to the social and organizational contexts of sport in these communities. It is shown that social and economic disadvantages are experienced very differently across the four settings and that context specificity is therefore of great import if we are to develop nuanced understandings of the factors and processes which affect the lived experience and social impact of sport. It is also argued that in each of these settings people strive to be proactive social agents, meeting the challenges associated with social and economic disadvantage with agency, not as passive victims. With regard to the provision of sport, the chapter discusses how the SSP and Vencer programs use sports activities as part of their broader social and professional development agendas, whereas MG and NCFL are principally concerned with providing accessible sports activities in order to enhance people's sport-specific skills, guide them to improved performance, develop a positive lifestyle and create a focal point for community life.

In Chapter 3, the attention shifts to the political and educational contexts of sport in the communities being studied. Focusing on the political-ideological discourses within which the provision of sport is situated enables us to further de-mythologize the "power of sport" argument. The chapter identifies patterns of similarity and difference in the degree to which sport is viewed in an instrumental and utilitarian way, and it explores the tension that may exist between the objectives of using sport as a means to an end versus providing sport as an end in itself. I argue that sport is used directly or indirectly as a form of social control by state and other institutions, and I discuss how this is reflected, in varying forms, in the four cases. The chapter proceeds by examining the educational and pedagogical approaches that underpin the sports activities, highlighting that while in SSP and Vencer these approaches are explicit and formalized, in MG and NCFL there tends to be a vaguer and more bounded understanding of education in and through sport. It is also shown how particularly in SSP and Vencer relationship building is perceived as underpinning the outcomes of the programs and as a fundamental component of developing social capital.

Following the charting of the social, political and educational contexts of the sports activities and programs being studied, Chapter 4 analyzes the ways in which participation in sport facilitates or obstructs the development of "bonding" and "bridging" social capital. It is shown how sports activities serve as a context for meaningful social interaction, and how social relationships in the field of sport can help cross or break down social boundaries and provide a valuable source of social support and social leverage. However, social capital created in the sports context is also boundary-creating and maintaining, and it has the potential to reproduce or reinforce certain social divisions which may result in social exclusion and act as a barrier to or liability in social advancement. Particular attention is paid to the significance of social markers such as gender, class, race and geographical location in the accumulation, maintenance or diminution of bonding and bridging social capital.

The discussion of the association between sport and social capital continues in Chapter 5, which shifts the focus toward "linking" social capital and the role of institutional agents. The chapter examines if, how and under what conditions participation in sports activities or sport-for-development programs enables the creation of linking social capital and durable bonds with institutional agents, as well as the types of resources that accrue from such social connections. The chapter proceeds by arguing for the significance of family-level effects of social capital, that is, the transmission of social capital beyond the level of the individual within (extended) families. It then explores the distinction between productive and perverse social capital as it relates to the Vencer program and the impact of social violence, building on the idea of social capital as a basis for exclusion.

Chapter 6 addresses the relationship between participation in sport and the accumulation and transmission of cultural capital. In each of the four settings sport is perceived to contribute to the development of knowledge and skills in a number of ways which are transferable to other spheres of life and can serve to alleviate disadvantage. However, it is also argued that the extent, impact and longevity of cultural capital gains are mediated by contextual factors and institutional structures outside of the realm of sport, notably family and school environments. These environments are explored in depth in order to illuminate some of the main structural constraints that affect people's ability to get ahead in life through participation in sport.

Following on from the examination of social and cultural capital in and outside of the field of sport in the communities being studied, Chapter 7 focuses on the theme of economic capital and assesses the prospects and possibilities for social mobility through non-professional forms of sport. It analyzes the multiple ways through which participation in sport may generate economic capital for individuals and their families, and it identifies the main contextual and individual obstacles in this respect, including those that emanate from other social fields such as the economy, education, politics, judicial field and family. It is shown how compared to the mostly implicit accumulation of economic capital in MG and NCFL, individual socio-economic advancement is sought more deliberately and explicitly in the SSP and Vencer programs as part of their efforts to enhance participants' employability prospects. The chapter concludes with the finding that participation in sports programs and activities certainly has the potential to bring about social advancement in people's lives through the accumulation and conversion of economic, cultural and social capital. Nonetheless, objective social mobility in terms of durable occupational advancement is not widespread, and where it does take place, it is at a personal and, to a lesser degree, family level rather than at any structural level. It is also argued that relationship building and skill development in the sports context should be regarded as longer-term, non-linear processes that are profoundly affected by events outside of the realm of sport and which can provide or obstruct future pathways to social mobility.

The concluding chapter draws together and reflects upon the insights from the preceding chapters by delineating a series of contradictory tendencies which reveal the myriad of ambiguous and inconsistent processes that shape the multi-faceted social impacts of participation in non-professional forms of sport. It is argued that these contradictory tendencies, which are identified at four levels of analysis—social systems, governance, group life and collective experience and the individual—are mutually constitutive yet in constant tension.

1 Sport and Social Mobility
Untangling the Relationship

This chapter outlines an analytical framework for investigating the relationship between non-professional forms of sport and social mobility. It unpacks the different components of this relationship and defines the key concepts and associations posited. Sport participation is conceptualized as a potential vehicle for the creation, accumulation and conversion of different forms of capital (economic, cultural and social) from which certain benefits can be derived that enable social agents to improve or maintain their social position. In other words, multiform capital is regarded as a "resource to action" which can form a basis for (or a liability to) social mobility.

The impact of non-professional forms of sport on an individual's social position is analyzed in terms of the effects of sport participation (in playing or non-playing roles) on different forms of capital and the ways in which these capitals are converted and transferred to other social spheres. In short, investigating how, and the extent to which, social agents create, use and convert capitals through sport participation enables us to assess more adequately and accurately the relationship between sport and social mobility.

The associations posited in this chapter are *not* intended to represent the kind of linear causalities on which quantitative analyses of social mobility are grounded. The application of the analytical framework operates in terms of guiding principles for research, rather than a model of testing. The approach taken in this book is to develop theory through systematic empirical investigation. It is principally qualitative, as reflected in its aim to analyze not only how people act, reflect on or think about sport and mobility, but also the complexity of the sequences of cause and effect in human lives. Quantitative data usually do not give a clear scientific indication of process and causation even where the evidence of a strong relationship is compelling (Overton and Van Diermen 2003).

The concepts and relationships elaborated in this chapter serve a modest purpose, namely, to provide a set of "thinking tools" for substantive investigation. The posited framework raises a range of significant questions for research, such as: how is the accumulation of capital in sport influenced by processes of social inclusion and exclusion? How are the different forms of capital generated in the sports context converted, and how do they create the possibility of the formation of each other? To what extent is the capital created in and through sport directly transferable to other areas of social life? How does capital generated through sport interact with social inequalities? Under what circumstances can sport participation contribute to upward social mobility? These questions are located within contemporary debates surrounding the work of French sociologist Pierre Bourdieu and other relevant social scientists. Before turning to these questions, however, it is important to specify what is meant by "sport".

WHAT IS SPORT?

The term "sport" includes a wide range of activities that differ from one another in the ways in which they are played, organized and consumed. Sports can be defined as institutionalized, competitive and ludic physical activities. Three elements in this definition are of particular import in relation to the central themes of this book. First, sports are *institutionalized* in the sense that they are governed by rules that relate to time and space. These rules may be manifest in a variety of ways, including the dimensions of playing fields, time limits on games and codes of conduct. The most formal forms of sport are also institutionalized in the sense that they have expansive and increasingly complex organizational structures and policies (Giulianotti 2005; Houlihan 2008). Second, sports are *competitive*. Competition can best be conceptualized as a continuum that ranges from recreational to elite both between and within sports (Hinch and Higham 2001: 48), but in all instances they are sites of contest and conflict. In sport, opponents are defeated, and records are broken; there are winners and losers. Indeed, when the competitive nature of sport results in people not "making the grade", these individuals may subsequently become disillusioned by and alienated from sport (Crabbe 2000: 390).

The third aspect of sport that is highlighted in the above definition is its *ludic* nature. The term "ludic" is derived from the Latin word "ludus", meaning play or game. Sport is rooted in (although not exclusive to) play and games. This derivation carries with it the ideas of "uncertainty of outcome" and "sanctioned display" (McPherson et al. 1989: 17). The uncertainty of the contest's outcome lends a unique excitement to sports, while sanctioned display gives participants "an opportunity to exhibit attributes valued in the wider social world," such as physical prowess, knowledge, intelligence, courage and self-control (Goffman 1961: 68). Although play may not necessarily be the most important aspect of sport when compared to other motives or considerations (e.g. financial gain, status), "the ludic impulse is, nevertheless, always present to some degree at least, existing in tension with disciplined, organized aspects of sporting activity" (Hargreaves 1986: 11). These tensions will become apparent in the discussion of the social uses of sport in Chapter 3.

Using a precise definition of sport has important advantages for analytical purposes. However, when we focus our attention only on institutionalized competitive physical activities there is a danger of privileging the activities of select groups, while marginalizing those who have neither the resources to play organized sports nor the desire to make their physical activities competitive (Coakley et al. 2009: 6). There are cultural differences in how people identify with sports and include them in their lives, and the data presented in this book serve to exemplify this, problematizing some of the key components of the proposed definition of sports when applied to international development contexts. The data highlight that at the grassroots level sports may be played in modified forms to fit local circumstances. These adaptations are driven either from the bottom up by participants themselves or more top-down as part of physical education curricula. Thus, while the street football games played by bare-footed youth in Brazil's *favelas* (shantytowns) may be shaped by a lack of resources (playing fields and materials), people working with sports programs in these neighborhoods may also deliberately modify the rules of games to reduce their competitiveness, to foster participatory learning and to vary the physical and emotional demands of the activities.

In this book, the main focus will be on team sports, especially football (soccer). Three of the four case studies feature football as the main sporting activity offered to and played by young people. This reflects the fact that football, "the global game", is by far the most used sport in sport-for-development programs worldwide (Levermore and Beacom 2009b). The fourth case study looks at sport in rural Victoria, Australia, and indicates that a much wider range of sports may serve as vehicles for personal and social change. In rural Victoria, sports such as Australian football, netball, cricket and hockey accrue major social significance and constitute the most played, watched and reported sports.

SOCIAL MOBILITY

Social mobility research continues to be highly objectivist, particularly in the English-speaking world. In general, research in this area tends to take a quantitative and extremely aggregated approach to social mobility (Miller 1998, 2001). However, as Strauss (1971: 9) already observed four decades ago, on the margin of social mobility research exists an important strand of qualitative studies which touches directly or indirectly on social mobility, even though its researchers tend to be quoted less frequently in the "mainstream" mobility literature. The central concerns in these studies are usually social issues such as the intersections among poverty, race, gender and delinquency. Ethnographic studies of marginalized or low-income groups such as Donna Goldstein's *Laughter Out of Place* (2003) and Loïc Wacquant's *Body and Soul* (2004), as well as sociological classics such as Herbert Gans's *The Urban Villagers* (1962), are highly relevant to the research orientation developed in this book. At a conceptual level, the work of the French sociologist Daniel Bertaux also stands out as an important addition, or corrective, to the highly objectivist nature of most social mobility research. Before exploring this work in detail, however, it is necessary to define more precisely the different dimensions of social mobility.

Social mobility refers to the movement of individuals or groups between different positions within the system of social stratification. More specifically, social mobility can be described as changes in an individual's social position which involve significant alterations in his or her social environment and life conditions. There are two principal types of social mobility: horizontal and vertical (Sorokin 1959). *Horizontal* social mobility refers to the transition of an individual from one social group to another situated on the same level. When changes involve a significant improvement in or deterioration of the social position, this is called *vertical* social mobility— upward or downward, respectively. Upward social mobility exists in two principal forms: as the rise of the individuals of a lower stratum to an existing higher one; and as a creation of a new group by such individuals, and the insertion of such a group into a higher stratum instead of, or side by side with, the existing groups of this stratum (Sorokin 1959: 133–4).

Two further distinctions are relevant for the present purpose. The first is between structural and non-structural mobility. *Structural mobility* refers to movements made possible by transformations in the occupational structure within a particular society, that is, changes in the social stratification hierarchy itself (Jary and Jary 2000: 570). For example, historical circumstances or labor market changes through processes of (post)industrialization and/or urbanization may lead to the rise or decline of an occupational group within the social hierarchy. *Non-structural mobility*, on the other hand, refers to any movements which do not involve such changes and can be a result of factors such as education, experience, knowledge and individual relationships. In advanced capitalist societies, social mobility depends primarily upon individual, non-structural modifications instead of structural transformations. In such cases, mobility tends to depend upon an exchanging of positions (*circular mobility*), where some rise and others descend in the social structure (Pastore 1982: 5). In this book, I will focus particularly on sport's contribution to non-structural forms of social mobility since it is assumed that the social impact of sport is to be found principally at this level (although one might argue that sport has contributed to some form of structural mobility through the rise of a global sports industrial complex; see Maguire 2005).

The second relevant distinction is between intergenerational and intragenerational mobility (Sorokin 1959). *Intergenerational mobility* refers to the difference between the social positions of individuals at particular points in their adult life and that of their parents. *Intragenerational mobility*, on the other hand, involves the more short-term mobility within a single generation. In this book, the focus is predominantly on the latter. However, as we will see, there tends to be a strong relationship between the social positions of parents and those that their children subsequently occupy (Breen and Goldthorpe 1999; Hasenbalg and Silva 2003; Giddens and Diamond 2005). This relationship will be explored in regard to the intergenerational transmission of capital, for example the ways in which parents mobilize economic, cultural and social resources to increase their children's chances of educational success and occupational advancement (e.g. Devine 2004).

Individual social mobility can be measured in terms of "hard" indicators such as changes in the level of occupation, income or educational attainment. These indicators can be viewed as the objective dimension of social mobility, but such indicators alone provide insufficient insight into how changes in life conditions are actually experienced by individuals. As Bertaux and Thompson (1997: 15–6) argue, "objective resources . . . and constraints . . . are so much mediated by the *perceptions* young people have of them that they remain ineffective and almost unreal as such." However, it is possible to identify a number of indicators of subjective awareness of social mobility, such as perceived changes in emancipation, personal development, skills and identity (e.g. Veldboer et al. 2007a: 9). Social mobility thus comprises objective as well as subjective dimensions.

Incorporating both objective and subjective dimensions allows us to study sport's relationship to social mobility in a more precise manner. A major advantage of this approach is that it can make visible potential discrepancies or contradictions between objective and subjective social mobility. For example, upward social mobility in the objective sense may not necessarily be positively perceived even when it was initially explicitly sought. Strauss (1971: 188–90) observes two problematic consequences of upward mobility. The first is "the existential disappointment of arriving where you dreamed of arriving and then being disappointed at not finding it at all" as it was supposed to be. Strauss identifies several sources of dissatisfaction, among them being when the novelty of the higher position and its rewards (material and/or symbolic) wears off, and when the new lifestyle proves restricting or actually runs against the grain. The second problematic consequence of upward mobility is a possible sense of discontinuity with one's past and one's enduring identity, a feeling that "can appear with movement at any social level, with regard to any amount of distance traversed and with respect to any mode . . . of mobility" (Strauss 1971: 189–90). In such cases, upward mobility can cause a deep rupture to one's habitus, to use Bourdieu's (1984) terminology, which can generate a profound sense of social uneasiness.

Another major advantage of such an approach is that it can reveal the *processes* of social mobility, the particular strategies that people develop to improve their social position and the meanings they give to these processes and strategies. In other words, it allows us to analyze how people act, reflect on or think about mobility. One way to elucidate these issues is the biographical method advocated by Daniel Bertaux (1974, 1977, 1980, 1981). This method has been applied to both intragenerational and inter-generational mobility, most famously in his studies of family transmissions and heritage among French bakers (e.g. Bertaux 1983). For Bertaux, life stories bring home the complexity of the sequences of cause and effect in human lives. He emphasizes the evolving interconnection between individ-ual actors and broader structural constraints:

> In choosing particular courses of action, structural constraints such as economic needs interact with value orientations, moral obligations, self-determined goals, and the individual's own perception of the situ-ation and choices ahead. The actor's subjectivity, and the subjectivity of others in close relationship, are part of the objective situation. . . . Thus the more closely one examines the sequence of events in a life, the further one is forced to move away from the linear causalities on which quantitative data analysis is grounded (Bertaux and Thompson 1997: 17).

Bertaux (1983: 34) argues that life histories are uniquely placed to enable us to "penetrate the solid-looking façade of the present" and "to reintro-duce the crucial role of human action in weaving a present which is also history-in-the-making."

Finally, and arguably most importantly, taking into consideration sub-jective experiences of social mobility is crucial at the level of epistemol-ogy. It is questionable whether the concept of social mobility, which tends to be conceived of in a positivist and deductive fashion, can be applied in any time and place (cf. Connell 2007). My research in Brazil suggests that although most Brazilian social scientists are strongly influenced by western approaches to social mobility (on this issue, see e.g. Briceño-León 2010), residents of the favelas tend to have a partially different interpre-tation of social mobility. For the latter, social mobility is not a narrowly defined or fixed concept which focuses exclusively on objective changes in occupational or educational attainment. Rather, they often construe upward social mobility in more philosophical terms as increased agency and control over their own lives. In contrast, they tend to equate pov-erty with a sense of powerlessness (cf. Melo 1999: 19). Their mobility aspirations are often characterized by a desire to acquire more freedom and not to simply move up the socio-economic ladder. This interpretation of social mobility resonates with Amartya Sen's (1999) thinking about development, which emphasizes the importance of developing what he calls "substantive freedoms" (or "capabilities") to choose a life one has reason to value. From this perspective, social mobility may be concep-tualized in broad terms as "the removal [or reduction] of shortfalls of substantive freedoms from what they can potentially achieve" (Sen 1999:

350). The discussion regarding the trans-cultural application of social science concepts is continued later in this chapter in relation to the analytical categories developed by Pierre Bourdieu.

Social mobility is not merely an individual affair. Rather, it is affected by a range of factors that act in combination with one another in mutually reinforcing ways. Education and family (i.e. home environment, educational attainment of parents) are two of the most important variables influencing relative social mobility (Nunn et al. 2007). Broader economic, political and social conditions also affect opportunities for social mobility; for instance, people are limited in their desires by the structural restrictions of the labor market (Pastore 1982: 20). Liveability, community safety and service provision also appear to be important conditions for upward mobility to flourish (Veldboer et al. 2007a; Wacquant 1998). These issues highlight the interrelationships between sport and other social fields. As will be shown in later chapters, while sport is a relatively autonomous field (Bourdieu 1978, 1984), it cannot be viewed in isolation from other social spheres such as the family, education, labor market and politics.

Analytically, adopting an individualistic perspective to sport and social mobility may lead to the under-estimation or failure to appreciate other relevant units of analysis. Robert Miller (2001) identifies families as a core of social mobility, arguing that the family can be considered as a single unit rather than just a confluence of individuals. For Miller, simply measuring the family's social location by one of its members (i.e. the father alone) is too restrictive; at best, it is a proxy for depicting more complex household processes (cf. Savage 1997: 311). One relatively straightforward possibility for analysis would be to broaden the traditional view of intergenerational mobility, that is, father to son mobility, to include other (intergenerational) pathways within the family, such as female pathways of mobility (Miller 1998: 155). Taking a family-level perspective, Miller argues, leads to a re-conceptualization of the effects of social origins, particularly with regard to educational attainment (see also Silva 2003).

This proposed re-conceptualization of the effects of social origins on social mobility bears close similarities with Bourdieu's work on social reproduction, in which households feature as key actors of reproduction and transformation. His conceptual toolkit enriches, and can be enriched by, the type of social mobility research advocated by Bertaux (e.g. Bertaux and Thompson 1997). But despite Bourdieu's influence on mobility researchers such as Daniel Bertaux in France and Carlos Hasenbalg and Jailson Souza e Silva in Brazil, the impact of his analyses on the study of social stratification has generally been rather limited. Most research in social stratification fails to take up Bourdieu's challenge to understand the nature of social and cultural reproduction. Taking up this challenge would require a more temporally dynamic approach which focuses on processes and strategies of social mobility. It would also require "paying attention to cultural as well as material factors, and to the differentiation of fields and problems of the conversion of capital" (Calhoun 2000: 723). It is to this approach that I will now turn.

CULTURAL CAPITAL

The term "capital" is usually associated with the economic sphere and monetary exchange; that is, as capital that can be readily transformed into money and that can be institutionalized in terms of property rights. Bourdieu's use of the term is broader: it signals "the intention of addressing differential resources of power, and of linking an analysis of the cultural to the economic" (Schuller et al. 2000: 3). His purpose is to extend the sense of the term "capital" by employing it in a wider system of exchanges whereby assets of different kinds are transformed and exchanged within complex networks within and across different fields (Moore 2008: 102). Bourdieu's notion of multiform, convertible capital is important not only because it provides researchers with a rich analytical toolkit but also because of its critical edge. As Thompson (1991: 31) rightly notes, Bourdieu's "relentless disclosure of power and privilege in its most varied and subtlest forms, and the respect accorded by his theoretical framework to the agents who make up the social world which he so acutely dissects, give his work an implicit critical potential."

Cultural capital has been a prominent concept in cultural sociology and in the sociology of education since the early 1980s. Social capital, on the other hand, has more recently come into vogue. Both concepts have come to assume a range of sometimes contradictory and incompatible meanings and have been applied in a variety of contexts, including sport. Social capital in particular has come to constitute a highly specialized and densely populated research area in sport management and the sociology of sport. This development has had two major consequences, as outlined below.

First, like cultural capital, the concept of social capital has been lifted from the context in which it was originally developed. Clearly, this is not necessarily problematic if the distinctive features of the concept are preserved (Lamont and Lareau 1988: 161). This means that, in the study of sport, the micro-political dimension should be preserved by examining mechanisms of social and cultural exclusion. Second, contemporary studies of social and cultural capital in sport tend to apply these concepts in isolation from one another, with little regard for the ways in which economic, social and cultural capital intertwine and are mutually constitutive. Although Bourdieu (1986) formally distinguishes these three forms of capital, he emphasizes that economic, cultural and social capital are inextricably inter-related. The possession of any form of capital can reinforce the power of another or the capacity to acquire another (Young 1999), as the work of Coleman (1990) has also shown. This raises all sorts of important analytical questions regarding the "transaction costs" of conversion, the investment efforts people make to enhance their volumes of capital and the fungibility (transferability) of capital. To study social or cultural capital in isolation from other species of capital is to turn a blind eye to these fundamental questions.

The concept of cultural capital has enriched our understanding of the processes through which social stratification systems are reproduced. The concept was first developed by Pierre Bourdieu and Jean-Claude Passeron in the 1970s. Bourdieu sensed that, in the prosperous post-war societies of the West, cultural capital was becoming a major determinant of life chances and that, under the cloak of individual talent and academic meritocracy, its unequal distribution was helping to conserve social hierarchies (Wacquant 2008a: 262). Bourdieu and Passeron (1977, 1979) contend that the function of education is to produce a social hierarchy, and that this conflicts with the ideal of a "truly democratic" system that would enable all students to have access to skills leading to school success (Reed-Danahay 2005: 49). Educational institutions, they argue, are not socially neutral institutions but reflect the experiences of the dominant classes, and therefore tend to reproduce existing social relations and inequalities. Whether children and young people succeed in education and feel "at home" in schools is dependent to a large extent on the "cultural habits and dispositions inherited from the original milieu" (Bourdieu and Passeron 1979: 13). In *The Inheritors*, Bourdieu and Passeron (1979: 17) write:

> Not only do the most privileged students derive from their background of origin habits, skills and attitudes which serve them directly in their scholastic tasks, but they also inherit from it knowledge and know-how, tastes, and a "good taste" whose scholastic profitability is no less certain for being indirect.

In Bourdieu's work, cultural capital has been used at a range of analytical levels, for example as an informal academic standard, a class attribute and a power resource. Lamont and Lareau (1988: 156) note that "the idea of cultural capital used as a *basis for exclusion* from jobs, resources, and high status groups is one of the most important and original dimensions of Bourdieu and Passeron's theory." The power exercised through cultural capital is, first and foremost, a power to shape other people's lives through exclusion and symbolic imposition. The notion of power is neatly captured in the definition of cultural capital proposed by Lamont and Lareau (1988: 156): "institutionalized, i.e., widely shared, high status cultural signals (attitudes, preferences, formal knowledge, behaviours, goods and credentials) used for social and cultural exclusion, the former referring to exclusion from jobs and resources, and the latter, to exclusion from high status groups." This definition leaves room for individual biographies by taking into consideration variations in how individuals use their cultural capital (Lareau and Weininger 2004). The everyday processes and micro-level interactions in which individuals and their families put their cultural capital to work to gain access to social settings or attain desired social outcomes is an important theme which is congruent with the approach to social mobility advocated by Bertaux. This approach also allows us to take into consideration how these processes are influenced not only by social class but also by gender and race (e.g. Hasenbalg 2003a).

Cultural capital, then, broadly refers to forms of formal and informal knowledge, educational qualifications, linguistic aptitude, competencies and skills which a social agent possesses. Cultural capital can exist in three forms: in the embodied state, in the form of long-lasting dispositions of the mind and the body; in the objectified state, in the form of cultural goods (books, dictionaries, instruments, etc.); and in the institutionalized state, notably educational qualifications (Bourdieu 1986: 243). Cultural capital is developed in the contexts of learning within family and early childcare settings, formal education, workplace training and informal learning. In this book, I have adapted Bourdieu's concept of cultural capital to fit the context of education in and through sport, drawing also on Reay's (1998) study of home–school relationships and Field's (2005) work on lifelong learning. In doing so, I have developed a list of seven main components of cultural capital:

- Educational knowledge;
- Skills (social, cultural, professional, life skills);
- Educational qualifications;
- Knowledge of the educational system;
- Social confidence and "self-certainty" (Bourdieu 1984: 66);
- Material resources for learning and teaching; and
- Available time to invest in extra-curricular education.

In the next section, I turn to the related concept of social capital.

SOCIAL CAPITAL

There has been considerable debate in recent years concerning the signifi-cance of conceptual understandings of social capital for sport development and policy (e.g. Seippel 2006; Burnett 2006; Coalter 2007; Walseth 2008; Nicholson and Hoye 2008; Kay and Bradbury 2009). The term "social capital" has gained enormous popularity in academic and policy circles, particularly in response to the work of political scientist Robert Putnam (1993, 1995, 2000). However, the term itself does not convey new ideas. Its core idea, that social relationships can have positive consequences for individuals and community, resonates strongly with classical sociological problems—for example, Emile Durkheim's (1893) emphasis on group life as an antidote to anomie. In recent years, the broadening of the notion of social capital has resulted in its merging into broader ideas of social cohesion and development (Blokland and Savage 2008). In the process, the concept has lost much of its distinct meaning and "risks becoming synonymous with each and all things that are positive in social life" (Portes 2000: 3). As Fine (2006: 559) notes, social capital "has become something of a cliché, deployed by all and sundry in whatever way that suits."

Bourdieu's (1980, 1986) conceptualization of social capital—albeit sketchy—is particularly useful not only for re-asserting what is distinctive about this form of capital, but also for analyzing the linkages between social capital and other forms of capital. The concept of social capital is different from economic and cultural capital in at least two ways: first, it is relational rather than being the exclusive property of any one individual; and, second, it is produced by investments of time and effort but in a less direct fashion than is economic or cultural capital. Bourdieu defines social capital as "the sum of the resources, actual or virtual, that accrue to an individual or a group by virtue of possessing a durable network of more or less institutionalized relationships of mutual acquaintance and recognition" (Bourdieu and Wacquant 1992: 119). Social capital resides in social connections, group membership and, in the most general sense, interaction with others. However, Bourdieu is quick to point out that his concept of social capital conveys far more than simply "connections":

> [B]y constructing this concept, one acquires the means of analysing the logic whereby this particular kind of capital is accumulated, transmitted and reproduced, the means of understanding how it turns into economic capital and, conversely, what work is required to convert economic capital into social capital, the means of grasping the function of institutions such as clubs or, quite simply, the *family*, the main site of the accumulation and transmission of that kind of capital, and so on. We are a long way, it seems to me, from common-sense "connections", which are only one manifestation among others of social capital (Bourdieu 1993: 32–3; italics in original).

Bourdieu (1986) emphasizes the material or symbolic benefits that accrue to individuals by virtue of their access to, or participation in, particular kinds of social networks, groups or communities that permit them to appropriate the material or symbolic profits that flow from group membership (see also Portes 1998). For Bourdieu, social capital refers to a kind of unequally distributed "resource to action" that is produced by, and invested in, social relationships by social actors for their individual and mutual benefit (Hogan and Owen 2000: 81). The actual or potential benefits (material or symbolic) which accrue from group membership are the basis of the solidarity which makes them possible. However, this does not mean that they are consciously pursued as such. Social capital does not necessarily arise because people make a calculated choice to invest in it, but also as a by-product of activities engaged in for other purposes, as Coleman (1988) notes. In relation to sport, Seippel (2006: 171) observes that, to a large extent, social capital benefits are "probably the unintended consequences of instrumental, normative and/or expressive actions."

Lin (2001: 19–20) suggests four social mechanisms through which social connections may constitute a resource to action: information, influence, social credentials and reinforcement:

- Social relations located in certain strategic locations and/or hierarchical positions work by facilitating the flow of *information* for the individuals or groups involved, including useful information about opportunities and choices otherwise not available;
- Social connections may exert *influence* on those (e.g. recruiters or supervisors of an organization) who play a critical role in decisions involving the social agent;
- Social ties may be conceived as certifications of the individual's *social credentials*, "some of which reflect the individual's accessibility to resources through social networks and relations" (Lin 2001: 20); and
- Social relationships may *reinforce* identity and recognition, providing not only emotional support but also public acknowledgment of one's claim to certain resources.

Bourdieu's emphasis in this respect is on long-term investment in durable social networks rather than on weaker forms of association. He insists that the (re)production of social capital depends on the institutionalization of social exchange centered on mutual acquaintance and recognition. For Bourdieu, investment in sociability is necessarily long term and therefore costly. Social capital is not constituted once and for all by an initial act. Rather, it is "the product of an endless effort at institution . . . which is necessary to produce and reproduce lasting, useful relationships that can secure material or symbolic profits" (Bourdieu, 1986: 249). Like Coleman (1988), Bourdieu recognizes the family as a key institution for the accumulation and transmission of social capital.

Group membership can confer access to social capital, but it is not long-term or formal membership itself that constitutes social capital. The requirement for network density for the utility of social capital is not necessary (Lin 2001). Rather, it is the pattern of social relationships that social agents participate in that provides access to social capital. Access to social capital resources will be influenced in part by the particular qualities of the social relationships between agents as well as by the particular qualities of the contexts in which social interaction takes place (Hogan and Owen 2000). Onyx and Bullen (2000) argue that social capital can be produced through participation in voluntary associations and community organizations as well as in the workplace, through public institutions and through informal networking among friends and neighbors. Moreover, expansive or diffuse social networks characterized by the salience of weak ties (Granovetter 1973) can also contain opportunities to access social capital resources. In contemporary social life, social interactions also need to be understood "in terms of their decentralized, diffuse, and sprawling character which depend on multiple and myriad technological, informational, personal and organizational networks that link locations in complex ways" (Blokland and Savage 2008: 5).

Social Capital as a Basis for Inclusion and Exclusion

In the work of Putnam and his followers, social capital is a largely unproblematic, functional concept. They view social capital formation to be almost entirely positive in terms of its outcomes, despite some peripheral discussion of the "dark side" of social capital (Putnam 2000; Putzel 1997). A major limitation of Putnam's interpretation of social capital is its failure to adequately address issues of power and structural inequalities (Schuller et al. 2000; Blokland 2002). In Putnam's analysis, "social capital becomes divorced from other forms of capital, stripped of power relations, and imbued with the assumption that social networks are win-win relationships and that individual gains, interests, and profits are synonymous with group gains, interests, and profits" (DeFilippis 2001: 800). Bourdieu (1980, 1986), on the other hand, offers a more critical perspective which focuses on social inequalities and their reproduction. Bourdieu's usage of social capital is designed to address "the way in which social capital is part of a wider set of structural relations and subjective beliefs that are bound up with inequalities of resources, and hence with inequalities of power" (Field 2005: 19). For Bourdieu, social capital is not a benign force working equally in the interests of each and all. Rather, it is "a means by which the powerful may protect and further their interests against the less powerful" (Arneil 2006: 8). Thus, like cultural capital, social capital serves as a *basis for exclusion* from the social mechanisms described by Lin (e.g. Stanton-Salazar 1997). Social capital can promote inequality in large part because access to different kinds of social networks is very unequally distributed. Social capital tends to be positive for network members but serves to bolster and reproduce inequality and privilege in the wider world (Field 2008: 85); in short, "social capital for some implies social exclusion for others" (Harriss and De Renzio 1997: 926).

In social capital debates this point has been positioned as merely a critical aside. Recent studies, however, re-emphasize the need to relate social capital to matrices of power and inequality (Morrow 2004; Onyx et al. 2007; Blokland and Savage 2008). Blokland and Savage (2008: 13) make the important point that social capital research "needs a wider acknowledgement that social capital is border-creating and maintaining, hence exclusionary and laden with power." It is important to recognize, for example, that access to social capital "depends on the social location of the specific individuals and groups attempting to appropriate it" (Edwards and Foley 1997: 677), and that the social location of social capital itself affects its value as a resource to action. These arguments are pertinent also to sports research, which has systematically under-valued social capital as a basis for exclusion, despite some minor references to negative sides of social capital (e.g. Nicholson and Hoye 2008). It should also be recognized that social capital may be experienced differently according to gender, sexuality, religion or ethnic background (Stanton-Salazar 1997; Morrow 2001; Arneil 2006; Van den Berg 2007), as scholars such as Elling (2002) and Walseth (2008) found in relation to sport.

Aspects and Outcomes of Social Capital

Bourdieu's (1986) work enables us to develop an in-depth analysis of the exclusionary and inclusionary mechanisms of social capital. However, I am conscious of the rather sketchy and under-developed nature of his conceptualization of social capital. First, Bourdieu's approach remains rather one-dimensional as it acknowledges principally the social capital of the privileged, that is, the reproduction of elite social capital. In so doing, he fails to fully recognize the importance of social capital to disadvantaged groups (Field 2008: 22). Coleman's (1990) idea that social capital is not limited to the powerful, but can also convey benefits to disadvantaged groups, is an important corrective to Bourdieu, a point I will return to in the discussion of criticisms of Bourdieu's theory. Second, it is possible to add to Bourdieu's approach to social capital by drawing upon recent debates regarding different aspects and outcomes of social capital. This issue is taken up below.

Social capital is a multidimensional phenomenon which is associated with a range of social outcomes. Briggs (1998: 178–9) argues that, as an individual good, there are two outcomes of social capital that should interest researchers and policymakers: social leverage and social support. Social leverage and social support networks can work in tandem or in tension to allow or preclude day-to-day survival and social mobility (Domínguez and Watkins 2003). *Social leverage* refers to social connections that improve opportunities for upward social mobility and "getting ahead" through advice, contacts or encouragement, such as access to job information, a recommendation for a scholarship, a loan or start-up financing (Briggs 1998: 178). This outcome is essentially about access to power and influence. *Social support* refers to social relationships that help individuals to "get by" or to cope with difficult situations. This can include child minding, being able to get a ride, confiding in someone or obtaining a small cash loan in case of an emergency. Briggs (1998: 178) argues that social support is especially vital to the chronically poor as it can substitute for things that money would otherwise buy. Social support networks may provide not only material support but also emotional and moral support in difficult times. However, social support networks can also have a restrictive effect on social leverage or obstruct opportunities for upward social mobility (Portes 1998; Young 1999). For example, Wacquant (1998: 27) argues that "affiliative ties and bonds of obligation with friends and associates in the ghetto constitute a resource for survival, but they create impediments and obstacles when attempting to move up and into the official labor market." In a similar vein, Domínguez and Watkins (2003) assert that social support networks can inhibit social mobility by enforcing time-consuming and professionally limiting expectations on women. In such instances, social capital can create downward leveling pressures that thwart attempts to get ahead (Portes and Landolt 1996, 2000).

Like many social capital scholars, Briggs (1998: 188) notes how dispersed ties to a range of different kinds of people tend to be more important to get ahead than are strong ties to kin and close friends, which are more suited for mobilizing social support. This argument is reflected in the distinction between bonding and bridging social capital which was popularized by Robert Putnam (2000). *Bonding social capital* refers to close ties among kin, neighbors and close friends. It is viewed to promote homogeneity and emphasizes the building of strong ties while at the same time being more likely to be inward-looking and less tolerant of diversity. Putnam (2000: 22) notes that bonding social capital "is good for undergirding specific reciprocity and mobilizing solidarity." *Bridging social capital* refers to more distant ties with like persons, such as loose friendships and work colleagues. This type of social capital is usually associated with resources that help individuals to get ahead or change their opportunity structure (Gittell and Vidal 1998: 16–8; Putnam 2000: 22–3). Putnam (2000: 22) considers that bridging networks are "better for linkage to external assets and for information diffusion" and emphasizes that bonding and bridging social capital "are not 'either-or' categories . . . but 'more or less' dimensions along which we can compare different forms of social capital." He asserts that the "right mix" is required for benefits to accrue. Furthermore, bonding and bridging are not interchangeable, and there are often tensions and trade-offs between the two forms.

Social capital also has a "vertical" dimension, which features centrally in Bourdieu's (1986) approach to elite social capital. This is conveyed in the notion of *linking social capital*, which refers to "relations between individuals and groups in different social strata in a hierarchy where power, social status and wealth are accessed by different groups" (Healy and Côté 2001: 42). Linking social capital reaches out to unlike people in dissimilar situations, such as those who are entirely outside of the community, thus enabling members to leverage a wider range of resources than are available within the community (Woolcock 1998). The links in linking social capital also involve individuals' or communities' interactions with agencies of the market and state (Talbot and Walker 2007: 483), notably the capacity of individuals and communities to leverage resources, ideas and information from formal institutions beyond the immediate community (Woolcock 2001). For Talbot and Walker (2007: 490), linking social capital "should form a conduit between the formal infrastructure and the informal loose networks at community level described in bridging social capital." Different combinations of bonding, bridging and linking social capital will produce different outcomes (Field 2008: 46). Woolcock (2001) contends that the poor typically have a close-knit and intensive stock of bonding social capital that they leverage to get by, a modest endowment of the more diffuse and extensive bridging social capital typically deployed by the non-poor to get ahead, and almost no linking social capital enabling them to gain sustained access to formal institutions such as banks, insurance agencies and the courts (cf. Narayan 1999).

Problematic in the distinction between bonding and bridging social capital is the claim that weak, bridging social capital is generally beneficial and benign in allowing connections to be forged between different kinds of people, whereas the exclusionary aspects of social relationships are reserved only for some aspects of bonding social capital (Blokland and Savage 2008: 5–6). From this perspective, a shift from "getting by" to "getting ahead" is automatically seen to entail a shift from bonding to bridging social capital. Although dense social networks and particularized trust can easily form the basis for out-group antagonism and vilification, bonding social capital is also frequently associated with outcomes such as increased educational attainment and reduced costs of job search (Field 2008; Bigelow 2007). Studies in the sociology of migration show that bonding social capital can also facilitate upward social mobility and make very significant contributions to people's efforts to bring about social advancement (e.g. Portes and Zhou 1993). Moreover, bridging and linking social capital are themselves not exempt from exclusionary mechanisms: they can nurture insider networks and thus reproduce inequality. It is therefore important not to draw too sharp a distinction among bonding, bridging and linking ties (Field 2008: 98). A Bourdieuian approach suggests that social capital—in whatever shape or form—is border-creating and maintaining, hence exclusionary and laden with power.

THINKING WITH/AGAINST BOURDIEU: FOUR DEBATES

Only a small part of Bourdieu's impressive *oeuvre* deals directly with sport (Bourdieu 1978, 1984, 1993). However, as I have suggested elsewhere (Spaaij 2009a; Spaaij and Anderson 2010), Bourdieu's conceptual framework is "enormously good to think with" (Jenkins 1992: 11) in the investigation of the social impacts of sport. In this book, I appropriate Bourdieu's sociological orientation as a set of "thinking tools" for substantive investigation (Brubaker 2004: 26). Thus far, I have focused primarily on his notions of cultural and social capital. Before they are put to work to analyze the processes through which resources are accessed, accumulated and utilized, it is necessary to relate these notions to two other key concepts in Bourdieu's work: field and habitus. The interdependent and co-constructed trio of habitus, capital and field is integral to Bourdieu's understanding of the social world. They are mutually constituted and necessarily interrelated, both conceptually and empirically (Bourdieu and Wacquant 1992: 96–7). The aim here, however, is not to give an exhaustive overview of Bourdieu's theory of practice. Rather, I will focus on four debates which are pertinent to the study of sport and social impact, and which enable us to further operationalize the concepts outlined in this chapter. These debates are: social reproduction and social transformation, convertibility and fungibility of capital, universality and cultural specificity, and appropriate units of analysis.

Social Reproduction or Social Transformation?

Earlier in this chapter I argue that Bourdieu's approach to social capital remains rather one-dimensional since it acknowledges primarily the social capital of the privileged and fails to fully recognize the importance of social capital to disadvantaged groups (Field 2008: 22). This argument resonates with one of the more persistent critiques of Bourdieu's work: that it is determinist, or at the very least dwells too much on the process of reproduction and not on social change (Thomson 2008; Savage et al. 2005). Jenkins (1992: 90–1) contends that it remains difficult to understand how, in Bourdieu's theory, social agents or collectivities can intervene in their own history in any substantial fashion: "His social universe ultimately remains one in which things happen to people, rather than a world in which they can intervene in their individual and collective destinies." Is this criticism of Bourdieu's analytical apparatus justified? And, if so, what are its implications for the study of social mobility through sport?

   To answer these questions, it is important to turn to the concept of habitus. Habitus designates the system of durable and transposable dispositions through which we perceive, judge and act in the world and which ensures the active presence of past experiences, an embodied history internalized as a "second nature" (Bourdieu 1990: 56). Bourdieu argues that agents act within socially constructed ranges of possibilities durably inscribed within them (even in their bodies) as well as within the social world in which they move. The habitus "orients" their actions and inclinations without strictly determining them. It gives them a "feel for the game," a sense of what is appropriate in the circumstances and what is not (Thompson 1991: 13). Habitus is acquired in early childhood and evolves through one's lifetime on the basis of new experiences. Bourdieu (1990: 60–1) gives disproportionate weight to early experiences:

[T]he habitus tends to ensure its own constancy and its defence against change through the selection it makes within new information by rejecting information capable of calling into question its accumulated information, if exposed to it accidentally or by force, and especially by avoiding exposure to such information.

In other words, habitus tends to favor experiences likely to reinforce it.

In reply to criticisms of the concept of habitus as being over-determined and over-determining, Bourdieu emphasizes that the habitus can be transformed by changed circumstances, and that expectations or aspirations will change with it:

Habitus is not the fate that some people read into it. Being the product of history, it is an *open system of dispositions* that is constantly subjected to experiences, and therefore constantly affected by them in a way that either reinforces or modifies its structures. It is durable but not eternal! (Bourdieu and Wacquant 1992: 133).

Bourdieu regards habitus as an open concept since actors' dispositions are constantly subjected to a range of different experiences. Habitus is permeable and can allow new forms and actions to arise. It thus allows for a process of continual correction and adjustment (Calhoun 1993: 78). In this sense Bourdieu's concept of habitus is neither static nor over-determining. For example, he argues that "Pedagogical action can . . . open the possibility of an emancipation founded on awareness and knowledge of the conditionings undergone" (Bourdieu 1999: 340).

It is highly unlikely, however, that the deep structure of the habitus is ever completely erased. Changes are likely to be mostly small and incremental. Bourdieu anticipates that most experiences will serve to reinforce the habitus since people are more likely to encounter situations and interpret them according to their pre-existing dispositions rather than to modify their feelings (Bourdieu and Wacquant 1992: 133). He argues that "the conditioned and conditional freedom [habitus] provides is as remote from creation of unpredictable novelty as it is from simply mechanical reproduction of the original conditioning" (Bourdieu 1990: 55). In sum, habitus involves both social continuity and discontinuity:

. . . continuity because it stores social forces into the individual organism and transports them across time and space; discontinuity because it can be modified through the acquisition of new dispositions and because it can trigger innovation whenever it encounters a social setting discrepant with the setting from which it issues (Wacquant 2008a: 268).

Bourdieu's theory is at its best as a theory of social reproduction, but it is arguably weaker as a theory of social change (Calhoun 1993, 2000; Fried-mann 2002). It may nonetheless be possible to elaborate Bourdieu's theory more fully to allow for greater tension and instability in social reproduction than he seems to permit (Savage et al. 2005: 42–3). Friedmann (2002: 302) argues that there are many situations where both individual and collective habitus are altered in a fundamental and/or accelerated way, with major consequences for social life generally. He asserts that although Bourdieu is right to stress its stabilizing role, "the twinned concept of habitus/field is a great deal more malleable than Bourdieu suggests" (Friedmann 2002: 304). In this book, the potential malleability of habitus is addressed in two ways: first, through empirical investigation of sport's contribution to social, cultural and economic capital; and, second, by addressing the impact of pedagogical action in the field of sport in the lives of disadvantaged groups. It thus incorporates the idea of agency and resistance by historically subor-dinated groups (Arneil 2006; Schuller et al. 2000). The related concept of field is discussed below.

Convertible and Fungible Capital?

One of the most original and important features of Bourdieu's theory is his analysis of the differences in forms of capital and the dynamics of conver-sion between them (Calhoun 2000: 714). Bourdieu's notion of multiform capital emphasizes that, with varying levels of difficulty, it is possible to convert one form of capital into another. As noted earlier, the sum of social, economic and cultural resources possessed by individuals or groups may be viewed as their entire portfolio of capital, whose volume and composition vary enormously (Bourdieu and Wacquant 1992; Anheier et al. 1995).

Economic capital is essentially that which is "immediately and directly convertible into money" (Bourdieu 1986: 243), unlike educational cre-dentials (cultural capital) or social capital. Social and cultural capital is convertible, in certain conditions, into economic capital. This conversion can be intergenerational or intragenerational, or both. Bourdieu (1984) demonstrates how the ability of the bourgeoisie to reproduce their social position is not a result simply of their possession of economic capital but is reinforced by their investment in cultural practices and in the educa-tion of their children. This is a way of converting money into cultural capital which, in this form, can be passed on and potentially reconverted into an economic form. Economic capital may also facilitate access to particular exclusive social networks. In this way, the possession of any form of capital can reinforce the power of another or the capacity to acquire another (Young 1999). However, the opposite is also true. Noord-hoff (2008) argues that poor people are often trapped in a vicious circle that starts with having insufficient monetary resources to compensate for shortcomings in cultural capital, and therefore being unable to strengthen their labor market position. He found that single parents living in poverty often need all three forms of capital: social capital to provide for flexible, cheap day care; sufficient cultural capital to get a job which secures an income that is higher than the average welfare benefit; and economic capital to pay for the day care. If they lack any of these forms of capital, their chance to maintain a secure and rewarding position in the labor market is reduced considerably.

Bourdieu's work emphasizes two important issues with regard to conversion strategies: first, that the transaction costs of conversion are far from homogenous across the different kinds of capital and, second, that the conversion of capital requires effort. Capital accumulation has to be reproduced in every generation or it is lost (Calhoun 2000: 714). Bourdieu (1993: 33–4) expresses his dissatisfaction with the treatment of the "conversion problem": "I constantly raise the problem of the conversion of one kind of capital into another, in terms that do not completely satisfy even me. . . . What are the laws governing that conversion? What defines the exchange rate at which one kind of capital is converted into another?" We are unlikely to find general laws governing the conversion of capital since individuals always act in particular historical and social contexts; that is, practice is located in time and space (Jenkins 1992: 69). The "concrete modalities of this conversion and the exact rates at which they are effectuated depend on the particular fields in which they occur" and are thus likely to work in different ways in different fields (Peillon 1998: 219).

The reference to the concept of field is important here. Bourdieu stresses that "a capital does not exist and function except in relation to a field" (Bourdieu and Wacquant 1992: 101). Particular practices or perceptions should not be seen as the product of the habitus as such, but rather as the product of the relation between the habitus and the particular social fields within which social agents act (Thompson 1991: 14). Bourdieu considers society to be a multidimensional space, differentiated into relatively autonomous but structurally linked and overlapping fields (*champs*). Within each field, individuals occupy positions determined by the volume and the composition of capital they possess. A field is, by definition, a field of struggles in which agents are concerned with the preservation or alteration of the distribution of the forms of capital specific to it (Jenkins 1992: 85). Strategies for preservation and upward mobility are, for instance, the reconversion of economic into cultural capital by business elites, protectionism, segregation, discrimination and imitation (Fuchs 2003). Conversion strategies can also be found at the other end of the social spectrum. A professional athlete from an economically disadvantaged background, with a large volume of social and cultural capital specific to the field of sport, may convert this capital into money by signing agreements to endorse products or by opening businesses in which celebrity status in the sporting field may help to attract customers (Calhoun 2000: 714). Thus, even though a field is profoundly hierarchical with dominant social agents and institutions having considerable power to determine what happens within it, there is still agency and change (Thomson 2008: 73).

The relative autonomy of social fields means that the field can produce its own distinctive capital and cannot be reduced to immediate dependency on any other field (Calhoun 2000: 715). Applied to the study of social mobility through sport, this implies that one needs to examine not only the accumulation and conversion of capital within the field of sport but also the extent to which and ways in which this capital is transferable to other fields, such as the labor market and education. There are, however, important homologies (likenesses) between fields. The practices within each field tend to bear striking similarities, as do the kinds of social agents who are dominant in each field. There are also relationships of exchange between fields which make them interdependent. For example, as noted in the Introduction, poor persons desperately seeking careers as professional athletes to enhance their social status may neglect other aspects of their lives, such as educational attainment (see also Sack and Thiel 1979; Mewett 2003).

The issue of relative autonomy raises two complex issues. The first refers to the problem of boundaries: how do we find out where the field effects stop? Bourdieu acknowledges that this is a very difficult question, "if only because it is *always at stake in the field itself* and therefore admits of no *a priori* answer" (Bourdieu and Wacquant 1992: 100; italics in original). Thus, the boundaries of the field can only be determined empirically. The second issue is the problem of the interrelation of different fields. Some fields are dominant and others subordinate. In advanced capitalist societies, the economic field (alongside the political field) is seen to exercise especially powerful determinations. But Bourdieu also asserts that "there are *no transhistoric laws of the relations between fields*" and that "we must investigate each historical case separately" (Bourdieu and Wacquant 1992: 109; italics in original). This remark leads us to another major debate surrounding Bourdieu's theory: does his analytical apparatus work in historically or culturally distinct instances, that is, across time and space?

Universal or Culturally Specific Concepts?

Bourdieu can be credited with crafting a powerful toolkit for sociological research. It is debatable, however, whether his conceptual tools—such as habitus, field and capital—can be applied in *any time and place* (e.g. Connell 2007: 40). According to Calhoun (1993: 65), Bourdieu offers "an inadequate account of how to address the most basic categorical differences among epochs, societies and cultures and corresponding differences in how his analytic tools fit or work in historically or culturally distinct instances." At stake here is whether Bourdieu's analytic apparatus should be understood as applying universally (without modification) or as situationally specific. Brubaker (1993: 220), for example, argues that what Bourdieu offers is not a fixed propositional scheme but a theoretical habitus, a well-defined manner of doing the job of theorizing or "the disposition to think in dispositional terms." Some of Bourdieu's key concepts, such as habitus, may readily fit all social and historical settings. But are his other key concepts altogether trans-cultural? The idea of different forms of capital can arguably be applied anywhere. However, the extent and ease of convertibility will be quite different in different societies, with a high level of convertibility being characteristic especially of capitalist societies: "Where capitalist relations enter, traditional barriers to conversion of forms of capital are undermined" (Calhoun 1993: 68).

What are the implications of this for social mobility research? It could be argued that some historical or social conditions are perhaps so different that Bourdieu's conceptual categories are analytically inappropriate. Two case studies in this book come to mind as potential candidates: Rio de Janeiro's favelas and the Somali community in Melbourne. Judging by the popularity of Bourdieu's conceptual toolkit among Brazilian sociologists working in the fields of social stratification, class relations and education, one can only conclude that his analytic apparatus is highly applicable to the Brazilian context (e.g. Hasenbalg 2003a; Silva 2003). In her moving ethnographic account of the everyday lives of women in the favelas, Goldstein (2003: 35–6) demonstrates the applicability to Brazil of Pierre Bourdieu's analysis, "especially of how concentrations of economic and cultural capital lead to unequal levels of political capital and, ultimately, through an elaborate symbolic struggle between classes, to a legitimation of social differences."

The Somali context is more complex not least because the people under study have migrated to a late capitalist society. Forced migration typically involves a fundamental altering or readjustment of both individual and collective habitus (Friedmann 2002), especially when this migration involves a move between different types of society, for example from a more "traditional" to a late modern society. But this distinction should not be pushed too far. If we accept the argument that a high level of convertibility of capital is characteristic especially of capitalist societies, then we should accept that a fairly high degree of convertibility does exist in modern Somalia. Abdi Samatar (2007: 131) argues that the pastoralist and nomadic nature of Somali society is often misunderstood. Pastoralism, he writes, is a means of livestock production employed under a variety of social and historical conditions. Contemporary Somali pastoralism

> is dominated by a commercial system and the production of exchange values. The commercial system that prevails in the country can be thought of as peripheral capitalism. . . . [A]s Somali society became an integral part of the global capitalist system, beginning in the late 19th century, the forces of the world-system had a transformative effect upon it. . . . Contemporary Somali social structure displays the emblem of capitalist transition, clearly heralding the passing of a way of life (Samatar 2007: 131–2).

This "capitalist transition" is accompanied by a proliferation of relatively autonomous fields. The uncoupling of fields manifests itself in a reduction in the extent to which each field is homologous with the others (Calhoun 1993: 77).

Units of Analysis: Individuals, Families, Communities

Thus far in this chapter social agents have been conceived of primarily as individuals (and their families) in line with the conceptualizations offered by Bourdieu (1986) and Coleman (1988). This approach has been challenged by those who extend the concept of social capital to refer to different units of analysis, including entire communities or nations. In macro-level approaches, the concept is stretched to become an attribute of the "community" itself; social capital benefits accrue not so much to individuals as to the collectivity as a whole (Portes 2000). At the macro-level, social capital is seen to contribute to social cohesion and harmony, economic and social development, lower crime rates and more effective democratic procedures (Field 2008). This conceptual stretch was initiated by Putnam (1993, 1995) in his studies of social and civic engagement in the United States and Italy.

The transition of the concept of social capital from an individual asset to a community or national resource can be criticized on a number of grounds. Portes (2000: 4) argues that "causes and effects of social capital as a collective trait were never disentangled, giving rise to much circular reasoning." At the individual level, the sources of social capital were explicitly associated with a person's social connections, while effects were related to a range of material and informational benefits. These were separate and distinct from the social structures that produced them, as is clear in Bourdieu's analysis. Collective social capital lacks this distinctive separation. Another important criticism of macro-level approaches to social capital is its neglect of the way in which social capital is part of a wider set of structural relations and subjective beliefs that are bound up with resource and power inequalities. As noted earlier, these inequalities are crucial for understanding how different species of capital are generated, accumulated and put to work in particular social contexts. Both Putnam (2000) and Coleman (1988) can be seen to under-value the role of structural inequalities. They also tend to assume rather naively that social capital is inherently a good thing and that more is almost invariably better (Field 2005: 28). A Bourdieuian perspective which views social capital as a positional asset which social agents can use in order to strengthen or maintain their position relative to others enables a more differentiated, micro-political analysis of social capital. Furthermore, as also noted earlier, it is important to acknowledge that (elements of) social capital may be experienced differently according to gender, class, age, religious or ethnic background.

The question remains whether the individual is the most appropriate unit of analysis in the study of sport and social mobility. Tess Kay and I (in press) argue that researchers need to give more consideration to family influences when they study the impacts of sport participation in young people's lives. This argument resonates not only with the approach advocated by social mobility scholars such as Miller (2001) but also with the work of both Bourdieu and Coleman. Coleman (1990) notes that parental investments of time and effort (e.g. shared activities or helping with homework), the affective bonds they create and maintain and the pro-social guidance they offer positively affect a well-supported youth's behavior and educational performance. In Bourdieu's work, the family is both a habitus- generating institution and a key site for the accumulation of cultural capital. He emphasizes the importance of analyzing family processes of intergenerational transmission (Gunn 2005). Bourdieu also offers an account of the gendered differential in expectations and responsibilities between mothers and fathers. In particular, he recognizes the pivotal role mothers play in the generation and transmission of cultural capital (Reay 1998: 57). Bourdieu's approach to family cultural capital has been successfully applied in Brazilian studies of poverty and social mobility (Goldstein 2003; Silva 2003; Hasenbalg 2003a) and, as this book will show, is highly instructive for analyzing sport's contribution to the accumulation, transmission or diminution of cultural capital.

Although the analytical importance of family has also been recognized in relation to social capital, "community" rather than family life has taken center stage in Putnam-inspired social capital research. Edwards (2004a) observes that the place of the family often remains glossed over in social capital debates. She takes issue with the place of families in "social capital lost" stories, which tend to lament "family deficiencies" and the decline of the "traditional" family. What is silenced in these policy-championed accounts of social capital are issues of power and conflict, precisely the issues that Bourdieu sought to uncover. Also absent, she argues, are "conceptions of children as active participants in shaping the nature of family life and caring relationships, and in generating social capital for themselves, parents, siblings and other family members" (Edwards 2004a: 8).

CONCLUSION

This chapter set out to elaborate an analytical framework for investigating the relationship between non-professional forms of sport and social mobility. In addition to offering basic definitions of sport, social mobility and different species of capital, I have sought to examine the relationships among these concepts. The approach laid out in this chapter draws heavily on the work of Pierre Bourdieu, but it is also informed by related sociological perspectives, such as that of social mobility scholar Daniel Bertaux. I have shown that the notion of capital as "all good things" is analytically useless, and that it is more adequate to refer to capital as a set of unequally distributed resources to action which are a basis for social exclusion and inclusion. Access to and command of these resources can place individuals in positions of greater power and status.

For those concerned with assessing the social impacts of sport, Bourdieu's concept of field is of great import because it raises vital questions regarding the complexity of the sequences of cause and effect in human lives. To fully grasp the relationship between sport participation and social mobility, one will need to examine not only the creation, accumulation and conversion of capital within the sporting field, but also the ways in which this capital can be transferred to other fields. Moreover, one will need to investigate the influence of exogenous field effects that bear on the sporting field and that affect people's engagement with sport, as well as the structural constraints that other fields impose on the accumulation and distribution of resources within the field of sport. The weight and the nature of these issues are likely to vary significantly across time and space. As such, they can only be determined through empirical investigation of specific cases. It is to this investigation that I will now turn.

2 Social and Organizational Contexts of Sport

This chapter examines the social and organizational contexts of sport in the communities being studied, and it shows how these sports activities are organized and embedded in particular social settings that are subject to change over time. The four cases analyzed in this book all cater to a specific need. This need is at once personal and collective, and it is voiced not only by individuals, groups and agencies "from above" (i.e. politicians, policy-makers, professionals) but also "from below", that is, by young people and other community members. Before proceeding to an in-depth cross-case comparison, however, it is necessary to explore the nature of this need as a way to situate people's experiences with sport.

Each case analyzed in this book is described in terms of its wider social context and its modes of organization and provision, and what each demonstrates is that social and economic disadvantages are experienced very differently across the four settings. What aligns these diverse cases, however, is that people in each of these communities meet the challenges associated with social and economic disadvantage with agency, not as passive victims. Sport is one social field in which they endeavor to be proactive social agents.

SPORT FOR SOCIAL ADVANCEMENT IN ROTTERDAM

Delfshaven and Feijenoord, the two districts in which the Sport Steward Program has been established in Rotterdam, are characterized as "vulnerable" areas in that Municipal Government's recent Social Index (Gemeente Rotterdam 2008a). Both districts feature comparatively high levels of unemployment and relative poverty. More than 60 percent of households are in low-income groups, and more than one in five households earn less than or equal to the "social minimum", which roughly equates to the social security entitlement in the Netherlands (Centrum voor Onderzoek en Statistiek 2008). Households in these districts have the lowest average incomes in Rotterdam and among the lowest in the country. Local authorities have been particularly concerned about the persistence of long-term unemployment, which is concentrated disproportionately among first- and second-generation migrants from non-western countries (e.g. Engbersen et al. 2005). Delfshaven and Feijenoord (together with Charlois) have the largest proportion of young people in Rotterdam living on social security entitlements (Gemeente Rotterdam 2005) and are characterized by relatively low educational attainment and higher drop-out rates among young people, especially among minority ethnic youth (cf. Kalmijn and Kraaykamp 2003). Youth unemployment in these districts has been associated with a range of by-effects which affect the perceived liveability of the areas, including comparatively high levels of crime, segregation, drug abuse, nuisance and the depravation of housing and shop premises (e.g. Gemeente Rotterdam 2007, 2008a).

In areas such as Delfshaven and Feijenoord, the Sport Steward Program (SSP) has been working toward its objective of socio-economic advancement of its young people. SSP is a partnership among the City Steward Rotterdam Foundation (previously Sport Steward Promotion), two colleges, professional football clubs and local government agencies in Rotterdam. SSP was initially funded through the European Fund for Regional Development and the educational colleges, but since 2008 it has been financed by the Department of Social Affairs of the Municipality of Rotterdam. The program recognizes that many unemployed youth in Rotterdam want to work but lack the opportunities and formal qualifications to obtain secure and rewarding employment. John[4], a program coordinator for SSP who is in his 30s, explains how:

> Many of them are caught up in a cycle and they want to get out, but they can't. That's frustrating for them. Their parents often don't know what they are up to, and they spend a lot of time in the streets, just hanging out, doing nothing. I don't see them as problem cases, but as young people who need a small push in the back, because many of them have a lot of intelligence and many qualities, but they are not developing themselves because they are stuck at home, not studying or working. That's the problem.

His colleague Danny, also in his 30s, adds that:

> There is a lot of potential in this city. But at the same time the gap between demand and supply is too large, and therefore much of this potential goes to waste. We want to change that. [Politicians] usually talk about them as problem youth, thugs, hopeless. We assume the positive in every young person. Every individual has talents, albeit one more than the other. We always approach youth from a positive angle. That's the power of the project.

One area which is particularly relevant in the light of contemporary social issues in Rotterdam is SSP's attempt to enhance local social cohesion. The city council has prioritized ethnically segregated neighborhoods as the most important hurdle to social integration. In districts like Delfshaven and Feijenoord, both of which feature high concentrations of non-western immigrants, the lack of social "mixing" between different ethnic and social groups is believed to put the community under serious pressure, alongside problems of urban decay and unemployment (Gemeente Rotterdam 2003). In Delfshaven, for example, the proportion of residents with non-western backgrounds is 65 percent; the average for Rotterdam is 46 percent (Gemeente Rotterdam 2008b). Research shows that in Rotterdam many residents from different ethnic groups are strongly inward-focused and have limited interaction with members of other ethnic groups (Gijsberts and Dagevos 2005). SSP program staff recognize this issue and are seeking to make a modest contribution to enhancing the social interaction between different ethnic groups in Rotterdam. The majority of SSP participants are first- or second-generation migrants of Antillean, Moroccan or Cape Verdean descent, while there are also some participants from Eastern Europe, the Middle East and Sub-Saharan Africa. However, the program also has a number of participants (approximately 25%) with a non-immigrant background. SSP encourages the participation of young people from all these ethnic groups as part of its strategy to build relationships and to give participants the opportunity to broaden their horizons. Danny explains this challenge as follows:

> Last year we had a group of guys from Spangen [a neighborhood in Delfshaven]. They are very much attached to their own neighborhood. Their social living environment is the neighborhood, with people from mostly the same socio-cultural backgrounds. And you notice that it's quite difficult to present them with alternative world views alongside their own restricted world view. But that's the challenge: to show them that not all white people are bad, and so forth. . . . So you basically try to broaden their reference point and their world view. It's a major challenge but it's also great fun because you notice that once in a while it has an effect, even though these are processes that for most people take longer than the four months they are with us. I believe it's human nature to hold on to what you know and to regard that as normal. . . . Especially when you grow up in an environment where basically everyone has the same background, and no other background is being placed alongside or in opposition to this. When that's the only world you know, it's a process that reinforces itself as you grow older. And so the art is to show them alternatives, which allows them to see or at least to think "hey, this is something I am not familiar with but it's another way of thinking and doing." The challenge is to encourage them to sniff around in a world which has been a bit outside of their gaze.

SSP is aimed specifically at creating an educational platform where youth obtain knowledge of and experience with the profession of sport steward.

The program is delivered by youth workers, teachers and counselors from a range of backgrounds, including local government, education, sport and police. Taught subjects include Basic Instructions Steward, Frisk Training, Traffic Regulation, In-house Emergency Service, Social Abilities and Employment Training, Communication, ICT, VCA (safety training) and Sport and Physical Activity. The program is a certified educational institution and aligns with existing courses provided by local educational colleges and event security organizations as much as possible in order to secure formal qualifications for participants, which is seen as key to increasing their employability prospects. For example, successful participation can lead to formal qualifications in stewarding and crowd management, first aid, traffic control and VCA (safety certificate).

SSP training also involves practical work experience at major sporting events in Rotterdam, which in many cases continues on a (paid) casual basis after completion of the program. The program offers intensive counseling and guidance. A personal, engaged approach based on sustained contacts among participants, teachers, mentors and prospective employers is seen as crucial both during and after completion of the program. This sustained engagement assists participants with any issues that may arise and enables them to access the vast social networks maintained by the organizations and individual staff involved in the program.

SSP attracts participants through a variety of routes, including both formal and informal referrals from social services, youth work, community police, friends and personal initiative. From its inception, SSP has sought to use outreach approaches and loose informal referrals as a means of positive engagement with local youth, for example through distributing flyers and working with community residents. In recent years, members of staff have had to come to terms with the impact of the new Investing in Youth Act (*Wet Investeren in Jongeren*, October 1, 2009) which orders municipalities to offer young people aged 18–27 who apply for social security a job or study program. In other words, young people in this age category are no longer entitled to social security unless they work or are enrolled in education. As a consequence, SSP now needs to negotiate each individual case with social service officials to convince them that SSP is a suitable program for the individual in question. Members of staff indicate that this has heightened the participation threshold and reduced the program's capacity to recruit participants through loose informal referrals. On the other hand, the new legislation gives SSP the opportunity to "enforce" participation more effectively. In the past participation was entirely voluntary and attendance rates were fairly low (approximately 60 percent on average), however staff now have the power to communicate to participants that if they fail to attend the project on a regular basis, their social security entitlements may be revoked. Members of staff are nevertheless conscious of the fact that although this may stimulate participants to attend the program more frequently, whether they actually engage to any real degree is a different question altogether.

Thus far seven groups of approximately 15 young people have participated in SSP. Participants are young males and females aged 16 to 31; most are in their 20s, and approximately one-third are female. The vast majority of participants live either at home, usually with their mother, or in so-called "guidance homes" under supervision of a counselor or case manager. Like their parents, most participants have not completed secondary education. Although demand exceeds supply, SSP staff face significant barriers in regard to maintaining prospective participants' commitment to the program. The first group of participants in 2007 serves as an example. A total of 39 people were initially approached for an intake interview, but 20 dropped out before or after the intake for various reasons including: finding a (temporary) job, not responding to the invitation, not showing up for the intake and pressing financial problems. Of the 19 people who formally committed to participation in SSP, two failed to show up at the start of the training, and a further two people did not return after the first day. None of the remaining 15 people dropped out before completion of the program. The considerable degree of non-participation and drop-out points to the problem of self-selection: those who are intrinsically motivated are most likely to enter and successfully complete the program. It seems clear then that unless young people are motivated and willing to engage, the outcome is likely to be minimal, as SSP coordinator John observes:

> Experience tells us that if someone does not have some kind of intrinsic motivation to do something, for whatever reason, then it's not going to work. It takes a lot of energy to engage such a person, which may eventually have a negative effect on other participants. So you choose what we call the 80/20 rule. You sort of anticipate that you will lose around 20 percent of the people who start the program. You actively try to engage those 20 percent at the start of the program, and if possible you contact their parents or job coaches [appointed by social services]. But if that doesn't work, you don't want to invest too much in those 20 percent but rather in the remaining 80 percent. That's the reality of this type of program, as crude as it may sound.

Formerly and from its inception, SSP made significant efforts to engage individuals who appeared less motivated in the early stages of the program. More recently, however, program coordinators have become more selective due to previous experience and the impact of the new legislation, which has changed the way in which the program is financed. Program funding was initially based almost entirely on the provision of the course. At present, however, 65 percent of the funding is based on a single, narrowly defined outcome: the percentage of young people who find employment or enroll in formal education within 12 months of entering the program. This policy change has resulted in a growing tension between the idealistic nature of the program and economic cost-benefit analysis. Danny expresses this tension as follows:

> We do our jobs with certain idealism. That's how we started the program for this difficult target group. But on the other hand, from a business perspective, we have discussions like "should we keep working with, say, a person with a long criminal record for drug dealing or robbery, who is also cognitively impaired, because the chance that you won't be able to find them a job is relatively large?" Which means that, as an organization, you invest a considerable amount in the education, whereas the chances of successful outcomes [in terms of finding employment], which is the most advantageous for us financially, are small. It's a very difficult dilemma. Personally, I do find that you become a bit more strict and selective.

This tension, which emanates primarily from funding pressures, is also observable in the Vencer program in Rio de Janeiro, as discussed below.

SOCIAL AND PROFESSIONAL DEVELOPMENT THROUGH SPORT IN RIO DE JANEIRO

Although culturally disparate, what aligns the SSP and Vencer programs is their emphasis on the use of sport as a vehicle for social and professional development. Vencer is built on the belief that team sports, and especially football, are an effective tool for motivating disadvantaged youth to participate in vocational training and for teaching employability skills. Vencer uses football activities to create a fluid learning environment for supporting and delivering educational content in an experiential way. Participants play football games with special rules and use football-based texts and lessons to transform sport skills (e.g. teamwork, communication, a focus on results) into marketable job skills. The intended overall program outcomes, then, are demonstrably improved employability skills for participating youth, practical work experience that builds their credentials, and knowledge about how to pursue job opportunities. Vencer coordinators expect that at least 70 percent of program graduates will find formal employment, start their own business or return to the formal education system.

Vencer participants highly value the use of football as a "hook" and a context for learning. They argue that the inclusion of football makes class time (both on the field and in the classroom) more enjoyable and more relevant, and that the intrinsic qualities of football (i.e. its fun and collective nature) provide experiences which allow them to develop skills that equip them to deal with broader issues in their lives (cf. Kay et al. 2008; Kay 2010). Furthermore, they indicate that youth who may not respond in a traditional school setting have a better chance of responding via Vencer. For example, former Vencer participant Paulo, who is in his 20s, notes that sport has specific qualities that make it a suitable context for learning, including for those who may be hard to reach through other social institutions:

> There are youth who are not really interested in doing a professionalization course but have a strong interest in football, in playing sport. Thus, if you don't succeed in getting them into the employability part, you can engage them through sport, that is, through sport they begin to attend classes, new activities, so it becomes one package with sport, classes, theory . . . it comprises all of this. So even those who initially may not be interested in the technical part will end up engaging in the technical part.

To facilitate young people's entry into the labor market, Vencer offers participants practical application of the taught workforce and employability skills. This provides young people with the opportunity to put their training into practice based on the assumption that demonstrated work experience is crucial to obtain future employment. Participants are expected to complete at least 180 hours of on-the-job experience through internships with local business, NGOs or in the public sector.

The objectives of the Vencer program are reflected in the self-reported needs of participants. When asked why they participated in Vencer, only 9% of survey respondents named playing sport as their principal motivation. Finding employment (73%) and developing new skills and professional attributes (72%) were reported as being by far the most important reasons for participation. Participants express similar sentiments in the interviews, notably their desire to take advantage of the employment and learning opportunities offered by the program. For them, getting a job, preferably in the formal sector, is the ultimate goal of their participation in Vencer. For example, 24-year-old former participant Marta reports: "I was unemployed. I have a seven-year-old daughter so I really needed to work to support us, and I entered the program with that as my goal."

Prospective participants are primarily recruited through outreach approaches and loose informal referrals. This recruitment increasingly takes place through word of mouth; several recent participants are family members, neighbors or friends of previous participants. Vencer uses a number of criteria for the selection of appropriate participants. Applicants need to be between 16 and 24 years of age and live in the low-income communities (mainly favelas) in which the program operates. Vencer principally targets young people who have completed 11 years of education (i.e. *Segundo Grau*) or who are in their final year of high school. This criterion is based on stakeholders' experience that organizations in the formal economy are unlikely to hire people with less than 11 years of education. However, approximately 87 percent of participants had not completed secondary education at the time they entered the program. The final selection criterion is personal motivation and drive, which is viewed as crucial to successful participation. Catarina, a Vencer educator in her 40s, describes the significance of personal motivation as follows:

> For me, the most important thing is *vontade*. We look for a young person who says "I want to make my life better, I have a child to feed, I have a mother or sister to look after," or whatever. "I need income, I need to do something. I am looking to work. This is not just a fun program so my father or mother will leave me alone. I am motivated."

To date, a total of 1,286 young people have participated in Vencer, and two-thirds of these participants have been female. The greater educational engagement of young women compared with young men is well documented in the Brazilian literature (e.g. Sansone 2003) and internationally (e.g. Lopez 2003). Stakeholders and participants acknowledge this differential. For example, Rafael, an ICT teacher in his 40s, argues that "girls are much more dedicated than the boys." Boys, on the other hand, are seen to "carry the project in a different way," being more ambivalent about the promises of education. Another reason for this differential appears to be the greater pressure exerted by family members on young males to work from an early age (e.g. as street vendors or manual laborers) to contribute to the family income.

Vencer is part of a wider program, called A Ganar, which commenced as a pilot in Brazil, Uruguay and Ecuador, but has subsequently evolved into an 11-country alliance of several organizations and donors. A Ganar has expanded beyond football to now include educational activities based on rugby, baseball, netball, basketball and cricket. A Ganar was developed and is managed by the international NGO Partners of the Americas (Partners). Vencer is coordinated in Brazil by Partners' affiliate organization, the NGO Instituto Companheiros das Américas (ICA). Sponsored by the Multilateral Investment Fund (MIF) of the Inter-American Development Bank (IDB), A Ganar (Vencer) was originally a $3.6 million pilot designed to train more than 3,100 young people in Brazil, Uruguay and Ecuador. The Nike Foundation subsequently invested $1.99 million in a female-specific version of Vencer in Brazil called Vencedoras. In 2010 the MIF approved a new $3.6 million scale-up of A Ganar, and an additional $1.4 million investment by USAID in 2009 enabled the program to expand to four countries in the Caribbean. Nevertheless, Rio de Janeiro continues to be the largest program site, and it is this location upon which the present analysis focuses.

The aims and impact of the Vencer program do, however, need to be understood within the context of the enormous economic and social disparities in Brazilian society generally, and in Rio de Janeiro specifically. Brazil is a country of great wealth and resources and one of the fastest growing economies (e.g. Winterstein 2009). On the other hand, Brazil has one of the highest income inequality indexes in the world (Barros et al. 2000; Araújo and Lima 2005). The country features high rates of youth unemployment and job insecurity, especially for those with low educational attainment (Hasenbalg and Silva 2003; Noleto and Werthein 2003; Gacitúa Marió and Woolcock 2008), and poor quality of public schooling (World Bank 2001; UNICEF 2009). Overall, persistent poverty is strongly concentrated in the Northeast of Brazil and in the rural and small and medium sized urban areas. This contrasts with the dominant perception that poverty is located primarily in the favelas of the mega-cities of São Paulo and Rio de Janeiro, where it is arguably most visible (World Bank 2001: 5).

Education is a key correlate of income inequality in Brazil (Pastore and Silva 2000). According to the World Bank (2001: 15), "low educational outcomes and attainment among the poor remains the single most important obstacle to reducing poverty and inequality in Brazil." Pastore (2004) shows that although only one quarter of Brazilians has completed secondary education, the vast majority of formal employment opportunities in metropolitan areas are available only to those who have at least a secondary education degree. The remaining three quarters of the population, Pastore argues, remain in the world of exclusion, prolonged unemployment or precarious work. Despite the increased access to primary education for all Brazilians, superior levels of education "continue to be a privilege enjoyed principally by persons originating from more elevated class positions" (Costa Ribeiro 2003: 146). The school-to-work transition tends to be particularly frustrating for young people with low educational attainment. They often experience great difficulty in finding secure employment due to the lack of formal qualification, experience and specialization (Castro and Abramovay 2002; Sansone 2003; International Labour Organization 2008).

In the case of Rio de Janeiro, these general features tell only part of the story. Extreme poverty directly alongside showcases of immense wealth distinguishes Rio de Janeiro as a city of extremes (Goldstein 2003: 70) or, put more graphically, a fractured city. The geography of economic and social disadvantage in Rio de Janeiro is remarkably complex. The Social Development Index (SDI) maintained by the Municipal Government of Rio de Janeiro gives some indication of this complexity. The 2008 SDI used several indicators, including sanitation, housing, household income and educational attainment. The index shows the massive disparity in living conditions across the 158 official *bairros* (neighborhoods) included in the index. The SDI scores of the neighborhoods in which the Vencer program operates are well below the average of 0.596 (Prefeitura da Cidade do Rio de Janeiro 2008).

The SDI scores are, however, averages for entire neighborhoods and fail to provide a more microscopic picture of the inter- and intra-neighborhood differences that characterize the socio-economic landscape of metropolitan Rio de Janeiro. Certain parts of the city have more favelas and higher

favela population densities than others, and favelas also differ considerably according to their proximity to more affluent areas. For example, the
favelas in or near the predominantly middle-class areas of the *Zona Sul*
(South Zone) tend to differ from those in the north and west of the city in
terms of their relative security and the nature of the local labor market (e.g.
O'Hare and Barke 2002). Furthermore, the larger favelas are characterized
by considerable heterogeneity in terms of socio-economic conditions, housing, sanitation, community safety and racial composition (Preteceille and
Valladares 2000). Favelas are not necessarily the poorest neighborhoods;
in fact, comparable or even more extreme levels of economic disadvantage
can be found outside of the favelas in poor neighborhoods located in the
periphery of the city (Telles 2004: Ch. 8; Brandão 2004). Although the
socio-economic composition of the vast majority of favelas is well below
the city's average in terms of household income and educational attainment, we should approach the common association between favela and
social exclusion with caution because favelas do not distinguish themselves
that strongly from other poor areas in this respect (Preteceille and Valladares 2000; Brandão 2004).

In Rio de Janeiro, violent crime is sometimes identified as a major barrier
obstructing the escape from poverty (e.g. World Bank 2001). For example,
Abramovay et al. (2002: 9) report that "the violence suffered by young
people is strongly associated with the social vulnerability in which Latin
American youth find themselves," diminishing their access to opportunity
structures in the spheres of health, education, employment and leisure. The
city of Rio de Janeiro has become significantly more violent since the late
1970s, as have several other parts of the country. In Rio de Janeiro, homicide rates tripled during the 1980s, slightly decreasing and stabilizing in
the 1990s. This rise in homicide rates reflects growing rates of criminality
and especially homicides among young men related to drug dealing and
firearms trafficking (Pinheiro 2000; Zaluar 2007). The increase in violence
in the 1980s and 1990s is not simply the product of poverty, of course,
but of a combination of labor market transformations, corruption in the
judicial and penal systems, political patronage and the rise of the drug
industry (Zaluar 2004, 2007; Leeds 1996). The violence in Rio de Janeiro
is unequally distributed as it affects specific places and persons differently.
Whereas the highest rates of violence are in favelas and poor neighborhoods (UNDP 2001; Goldstein 2003; Dowdney 2003), the government is
generally unable to guarantee the political order necessary to protect the
civil and human rights of residents in these communities (Arias 2004).

The favelas of Rio de Janeiro have come to exemplify violence and immo-
rality as a result of the perverse images disseminated by the media about
crime, drug use and other forms of deviant behavior, generating a pervasive
sense of fear among the middle and upper classes (Velho 2008; Souza 2008).
The increase in urban violence, and the fear thereof among Rio de Janeiro's
middle and upper classes, fuel the demand for repressive policies to control the

poor (Ivo 2005), resulting in a "militarization" of urban poverty (Wacquant 2008b). Evidence suggests that public and private social policy interventions are often designed in an instrumental and reductionist fashion as a means to normalize and civilize the favelas, especially its young residents (Machado da Silva 2006). As a consequence, favela residents suffer what Machado da Silva (2006) calls a "process of silencing," which negates their participation in the public debate as well as their recognition as full citizens.

In this context, Perlman (2006: 167) writes about "the sense of exclusion and stigma that the poor feel as a result of their residence in favelas, a stance expressed in their complaint that they are not seen as people (*gente*) by the middle and upper classes." In other words, their mere place of residence, through its association with poverty and crime, has in itself become a factor in their social exclusion from the labor market, education and social life more generally (Castro and Abramovay 2002; Perlman 2006). The poor in Rio de Janeiro are also increasingly distant from the means to influence political processes (Wheeler 2005: 102). As Ribeiro and Telles (2000: 86) note, the spatial proximity of the two ends of the social structure in Rio de Janeiro's city center, coupled with middle-class fear of the poor, has produced new forms of social segregation in residence and leisure, exemplified by, for example, walled communities, streets patrolled by private police and residential enclaves.

Residential segregation in Rio de Janeiro, however, cannot be accounted for only by socio-economic status; it also has a racial component, albeit to a far lesser degree than in the United States (Telles 2004: Ch. 8; Brandão 2004). Although the favelas are largely nonwhite, there are comparatively high levels of interracial interaction in poor neighborhoods, where whites and nonwhites often live side by side. However, such interaction is much lower in middle-class areas in the South Zone largely because nonwhites "have been kept out of the middle class" (Telles 2004: 214).

Part of the reason that some favelas are not, or are no longer, among the poorest neighborhoods in Rio de Janeiro may be the investments by public agencies, NGOs and local populations as part of urbanization and physical upgrading policies (Preteceille and Valladares 2000). Favelas have been part of the city's landscape for more than a century and have been the subject of numerous policies which have variously sought their removal or their assimilation into the city fabric (Perlman 1976; Pino 1997; Valladares 2005). The policy of favela removal has gradually given way to a policy of regularization and urbanization, as notable in the large-scale Favela Bairro upgrading program, which was launched by the Municipal Government of Rio de Janeiro in 1994 (e.g. Riley et al. 2001). More generally, research shows that social investment programs that foster collaboration among local actors, community organizations, NGOs and municipal governments in poor urban neighborhoods can have positive effects on the social inclusion of the poor (Jacobi 2006). It is this philosophy of "joined-up" governance that also underpins the Vencer program.

The Vencer program has been implemented in seven communities in metropolitan Rio de Janeiro. Six of these communities are favelas, whereas one program site is more accurately described as a poor neighborhood because, unlike the six favelas, it was not founded as an illegal squatter settlement and is relatively new. Although the socio-economic circumstances in these communities are broadly similar, there are some significant differences that affect the local implementation and impact of Vencer. For example, unlike the six favelas the poor neighborhood mentioned above is not *de facto* controlled by drug factions but by a militia which is predominantly made up of former police officers and soldiers. Working in and with these communities requires extensive local knowledge and navigating complex networks of power (e.g. Arias 2006). For this reason, locally embedded NGOs are subcontracted to deliver the Vencer program in their respective communities, with the exception of one community where ICA implements the program. Vencer coordinator Edu explains the rationale for this approach as follows:

> It's essential that we work through existing organizations in those communities, because those organizations have done all the groundwork, have built their relationships with the formal and informal structures that exist there. . . . If you are a community organization that is going to work there, you have to make those connections and, at a minimum, be able to exist without the interference of those kinds of governing bodies. [It's of great import] that they [drug factions and militias] understand that your motives are true, and that they are going to leave you alone or even encourage people to join the program. Whether it's the militias or the drug factions, they have an interest in maintaining good community relations. So it has been important for us to do that.

Since opening its office in the community where ICA implements Vencer, it has taken great measures to become a community-trusted organization. The subtle yet significant inter-neighborhood differences outlined above will be further explored in Chapters 4–6 in relation to Vencer's contribution to the development of social and cultural capital.

FOOTBALL AND THE SOMALI DIASPORA IN MELBOURNE

Whereas the Vencer and SSP programs use sports activities as part of their broader social and professional development agendas, Melbourne Giants Football Club (MG) is principally concerned with providing accessible football activities in order to enhance young people's football skills, guide them to improved performance and develop a positive lifestyle. MG is primarily (but not exclusively) aimed at first- and second-generation Somali immigrants who live in Melbourne's north-western suburbs. The club is supported by a handful of local community organizations which have been instrumental in providing limited funds and whose community workers have invested considerable time and effort into its management. In recent years, the club has been awarded small grants by local government agencies and the Football Federation Victoria, which have helped it to acquire football jerseys and training materials, and to lower its membership fees in order to reduce the cost barrier to participation. MG currently has approximately 60 paying members.

The voluntary contribution of community residents has been instrumental in the management and operation of MG. However, the pool of motivated volunteers is limited. Several coaches and club administrators in the study note the lack of initiative on the part of many parents in terms of the day-to-day management of the club. Only a handful of parents appear to be committed to performing administrative or coaching tasks. For example, Ahmed, a father in his 40s, suggests:

> A major theme in your research should be the lack of co-operation between parents and the coach. Parents like to see their kids play football but they don't have time to be involved themselves. They are too busy working or running the household. It's the children who are pushing their parents to take them to soccer, not the other way around.

Often-heard arguments voiced by parents are that they do not have time to help out due to work and family responsibilities, or that they lack the skills needed to perform these tasks. An underlying reason seems to be that sport has lower priority in Somali culture than in mainstream Australia. The concept of organized sport is relatively alien to many older Somalis or may even be seen as culturally inappropriate. Mohamed, a Somali community organizer aged in his 40s, explains that:

> Sport is very new in Somali society. We didn't have such a formal sport structure. It was very, very weak. We had some football at the national level but it wasn't that popular. It wasn't a matter that attracted parents and the community at large. They were playing at school, different school teams played each other. They used a ball made of socks. Sports did not have such a value or position in Somali society. I think different people have different views. For young people it was fun to play sport, but for older generations it was seen as a waste of time. And some people still view it like that. In a way, I cannot generalize, but sport was also linked to bad behaviour, to modernity, so they believed that it was a negative attitude culture in the eyes of the older generations.

Mohamed confirms Ahmed's observation that parents' involvement in MG is in most cases driven by their children's desire to play football: "they are influenced by their children who actually want to have fun and engage in activities such as sport. So it's coming from the children, who are asking their parents to take them to soccer games." Ayan, a local youth worker in her 20s, subscribes to this view, but she also notes the prospect of change:

> More and more parents are realizing the importance of occupying their kids with sport and being more in touch with their kids' interests, because they are becoming more aware of the impact of issues in terms of identity and fitting into Australian society. They are realizing this more now and therefore they are more supportive and aware of the benefits.

From her own experience, however, Ayan argues that parents' growing support for their children's involvement in football should not be confused with active participation on their part:

> The majority of parents use the club as a baby sitting facility. This is not limited to just the Somali club I found out. But you know there are parents that are really committed and I am hoping to set a good example. I as a parent hope to ... I have my son around at the club and I get my family involved, they get their friends involved. Just invite everyone. But, yeah, the majority are using it as a baby sitting service right now.

Moreover, as Ayan rightly observes, the perceived shortage of active volunteers is not unique to MG. Rather, it appears to reflect community sports clubs more generally. Although these clubs are very dependent on parents as volunteers, "only a very small percentage of parents ... are actively involved in their child's club" (Doherty and Misener 2008: 133–4).

To understand the significance of MG's place in the local community, however, it is important that it be sited within the context of the forced migration and resettlement experiences of Somali refugees. Prolonged violent conflicts between government forces and armed opposition in Somalia culminated in the collapse of the Somali state in 1991 with the overthrow of Siyad Barre's military rule. This resulted in the intensification of conflict between clan-based military factions in many parts of the country. By the end of 1992, more than 500,000 people were estimated to have died, well over 1 million Somalis were internally displaced and 600,000 had fled to neighboring countries (McMichael and Manderson 2004: 90). In a situation of continued factional fighting and fractured government, the numbers of displaced people and refugees from Somalia have risen steadily in the years following. At present, there are approximately 1.4 million internally displaced people in Somalia, whereas more than 560,000 Somalis are living as refugees in neighboring and nearby countries (UNHCR 2010). Today, Somali diaspora can be found virtually worldwide.

Somalis constitute one of the largest refugee populations from Africa currently living in Australia. Somali refugees began to arrive in Australia in significant numbers from the late 1980s, primarily under the Refugee and Special Humanitarian Program. The peak years for Somali arrivals in Australia were between 1994 and 2000 (Jupp 2001: 688). Many of them arrived indirectly via refugee camps in Kenya, Ethiopia, Yemen and Djibouti, which served and still serve as centers or stepping stones for migration to the West (Horst 2002). The 2006 Census of the Australian Bureau of Statistics recorded 4,310 Somalia-born people in Australia, a 17 percent increase from the 2001 Census. To this we should add a further 2,000 people who describe themselves as being of Somali ancestry. Victoria has by far the largest number of Somalia-born people with 2,620 (60.8%, followed by Western Australia (14.6%), New South Wales (13.4%) and Queensland (6%) (Australian Bureau of Statistics 2006). Although Somalis are mostly nomadic pastoralists, in Australia they have become one of the most urbanized groups. Almost all Somalia-born people in Victoria reside in Melbourne (99%), the main concentrations being in the inner northern and western suburbs (Victorian Multicultural Commission 2007). Significant factors in this concentration pattern are the availability of low-cost housing, pre-existing social support networks (family and clan related), chain migration patterns (with later migrants sponsored by earlier ones) and access to mosques (Clyne and Kipp 2005; VICSEG 1997).

Forced migration often involves stressful and challenging processes that profoundly influence the health, well-being and social participation of those who come to a new country to create a better life (Danso 2001; Brough et al. 2003; Bruce 2003; Correa-Velez et al. 2010). Post-migration factors such as socio-economic disadvantage, discrimination and a lack of cohesive social support have been identified as major contributors to anxiety, depression and feelings of social isolation (Pernice and Brook 1996; Correa-Velez et al. 2010). Social networks are considered extremely valuable to refugees, providing much-needed support and assistance (Lamba and Krahn 2003; Williams 2006). However, war and displacement disrupt family ties and erode social relationships and co-receptive trust, and these are not readily restored upon resettlement. The political conflict which provokes displacement will often continue to inform social relationships after resettlement. Furthermore, the conditions of resettlement do not necessarily provide an environment that promotes social capital (McMichael and Manderson 2004).

Research into resettlement experiences in Australia and other western societies reveals some of the key challenges that Somali refugees face. There is a high incidence of disrupted families as a result of the civil war and the stringency of family reunion policies. A large proportion of women have been separated from their husbands and families and often have three or more children to care for. McMichael and Ahmed (2003: 145) report that Somali women in Australia "find that family separation is a primary source of personal sadness and loneliness and causes anxiety about the well-being of others." This is exacerbated by the constraints of humanitarian visa allocations, which make family reunion an unlikely event. According to Omar (2005: 13), more than one in three Somali youth in Melbourne live without one or both of their parents, which may have a negative impact on child development. Several research participants voice a similar sentiment. Abdi, a community leader in his 40s, makes the following remark:

> The majority of the single mothers are people who came here with their kids, without dad. There was this problem of language and difficulties trying to understand Australian culture; how the system was going on in Australia. And on top of that, all the responsibilities coming back to the mother. There's no other partner supporting her with the kids. And she has to take care of the kids, the responsibility of the house, and trying to guide these kids into a proper environment. She doesn't understand the language, the culture, no person to support her.

Abdi's comment points to another common obstacle faced by Somali refugees in Melbourne. Due to years of interrupted education in Somalia and in refugee camps, many older refugees experience gaps in their English language comprehension, which may put them "in a state of communicative isolation" (Omar 2005: 7). Language difficulties are seen by some Somali refugees as the most important obstacle in the early years of resettlement (Danso 2001; Omar 2009). For example, Ayub, an MG representative in his 40s, reports that he did not speak any English when he arrived in Australia in the early 1990s, which was highly frustrating for him: "When I first came here, I heard people speak on the street and they sounded like birds singing. You hear the sounds around you but don't know what they are saying." In contrast, children who arrived at an early age or who were born in Australia may understand their native language but often feel more comfortable expressing themselves in English. This may lead to intergenerational conflict and/or a situation in which parents struggle to engage proactively in their children's education (Omar 2005; cf. Bigelow 2007). This issue will be examined in the discussion of cultural capital in Chapter 6.

Unemployment and under-employment are also viewed as important obstacles to successful resettlement (Omar 2005). There appears to be an above average level of economic disadvantage and poverty in the Somalia-born population residing in Australia due to a combination of gaps in English language comprehension, recency of arrival and the lack or non-transferability of educational qualifications (e.g. White et al. 1999; Nsubuga-Kyobe and Dimock 2002). The unemployment rate among Australia's Somalia-born population aged 15 years and over was 30.8 percent in 2006 compared with 5.2 percent in the total Australian population. However, the 2006 Census does indicate a significant improvement in the unemployment rates, which had decreased from 47 percent in the 2001 Census (Australian Bureau of Statistics 2006).

Although the majority of Somali refugees in Melbourne face the above challenges, two important qualifications need to be made at this point. First, the Somali community "is not a homogeneous mass" (Horst 2007: 280). Somali refugees in Australia come from diverse backgrounds in terms of wealth, social status and region. Prior to immigration, some had lived as nomads and others worked in the cities in business or government; some were educated and others illiterate (McMichael and Manderson 2004: 93). Their resettlement experiences also vary significantly, as we will see in the following chapters. Second, there is a risk that we present Somali refugees as passive victims, whereas in reality they are persons with agency (Horst 2006; Bigelow 2007). The data presented challenge the deficit discourse often associated with refugee communities by showing how, for example, Somali residents in Melbourne create and use social and cultural resources to get by and get ahead (cf. Loizos 2000). The data show that, like other refugee diaspora (Williams 2006; Correa-Velez et al. 2010), members of the Somali community in Melbourne endeavor to be proactive social actors and meet new challenges with agency, not as victims.

Research into the Somali diaspora emphasizes the role of community associations in (re)building community life and a sense of belonging which has been disrupted by displacement. Somali community associations can serve as public vehicles for the articulation of communal interests and identities. However, the Somali associational landscape is highly fragmented (Griffiths 2002), and many Somalis feel marginalized in terms of service provision despite the high number of specifically Somali community organizations that exist (Hopkins 2006). Representatives of African communities in Victoria recognize the importance of strengthening community associations as a means to enhance the provision of recreation and leisure facilities for African youth, including sports clubs and programs (Nsubuga-Kyobe and Dimock 2002). Local NGOs express similar views, arguing that sport can play an important support and service delivery role for young people with refugee backgrounds (Dykes and Olliff 2007). The Melbourne-based Centre for Multicultural Youth (CMY 2007) identifies sport as a priority for refugee youth alongside housing, employment and education, and it recommends that more resources be devoted to it.

This view is shared by many young Somalis who indicate that there are insufficient sports activities for young people in their neighborhoods (White et al. 1999: 30). Research participants also recognize the need for increased sports activities for youth, especially football which is by far the most popular sport among Somalis (Abdullahi 2001: 164–5). When asked about the role of Melbourne Giants in the local community, Yunus, a father in his 40s, says:

> Well, the whole welfare and trying to educate the community, the kids, and also the parents who are not involved with the kids . . . trying to bring the community together. Have that link. Because we don't have,

you know, any association or any activity for the kids, and the kids will not see one another. We are having this club so they are having an awareness of who is who.

MG representatives are conscious of the broader social impact of the club within the local community. They view football as a forum for fostering social connectedness and a sense of belonging. They also recognize the importance of being able to socialize with those with whom one feels comfortable. Somalis may want to play and socialize with others from the same cultural or language background or with those who have similar life experiences. For people going through the difficult process of settling in a new country, playing football in a supportive environment can provide a "time out" from the challenges of resettlement and a space where they can do something they are familiar with (CMY 2007). However, as discussed earlier, MG representatives may find it difficult to convince other adults to become actively involved in the club.

ORGANIZED SPORT IN THE NORTH CENTRAL FOOTBALL LEAGUE

The above shows that the adult Somali community in Melbourne is somewhat ambivalent about the value of sport to their youth. In contrast, in small rural towns in the same state, sports clubs play a pivotal role in social and cultural life (Dempsey 1990; Driscoll and Wood 1999; Bourke 2001; Townsend et al. 2002). A Parliamentary Inquiry into Australian football in rural towns in Victoria reports that "football/netball clubs are, to a significant degree, the 'glue' holding many small rural communities together" (Rural and Regional Services and Development Committee 2004: 50). The inquiry notes a range of positive outcomes associated with organized sport in rural Victoria at both the personal and community levels, such as skill development, increased revenue and tourism, improved health, community pride and social cohesion. This view is also commonly held by players and volunteers in the North Central Football League (NCFL), which is the focus of my fourth case study. For example, Geoff, a resident of a small town in northwest Victoria, explains how sport "is a focal point of the community. It's like the glue that holds the community together and provides a purpose for the community. If you don't play sport in country Victoria well what do you do?" Or, as expressed in a leading local newspaper: "Local sporting clubs in rural and regional areas are integral to the fabric of the community, not only providing opportunities for sport but also providing a focal point for social and community activities" (*The Buloke Times* June 27, 2008).

The NCFL incorporates seven clubs from seven small rural towns which consist of population clusters of 400 to 1,600. Each club is represented in three sports—Australian football, netball and hockey—at junior, senior, male and female levels. Sporting competitions in the NCFL are largely provided through the initiative and voluntary contribution of community residents. Their contribution has been central in all aspects of provision, including the management and operation of sports clubs and organizations (cf. Driscoll and Wood 1999: 7). The NCFL is funded in large part through membership fees, community fundraising and sponsorship from local businesses. The clubs that make up the NCFL also receive minor state and local government funding. The Shire Councils in northwest Victoria appoint a part-time recreation officer who is responsible for the development and maintenance of sporting facilities in the region, and they also provide small subsidies which cover part of the costs associated with the provision of sport, such as water usage and service costs.

The contemporary social significance of the NCFL needs to be understood within the context of profound social and economic changes that have impacted on Australia's rural communities since the 1970s (Spaaij 2009b). These changes have had an effect not only on the social and cultural life of small towns generally but also residents' experience of sports and leisure activities specifically. From the early 1970s, Australian economic policy has gradually changed from one characterized by tariff protection and a focus on socio-spatial equity, to a philosophy of free-market economic efficiency (Talbot and Walker 2007; Tonts 2005b; Alston 2005b). This policy shift featured the reduction of primary industry tariff protection as part of the federal government's efforts to link the Australian economy more tightly into the global economy. This shift also signalled the government's determination to make the economy more responsive to market forces through deregulation in the finance sector and labor market, privatization, reduction in public provision of social infrastructure and services and wider application of the "user pays" principle (Black et al. 2000; Lawrence 2005). The economic restructuring of agriculture, which was also driven by technological changes, has resulted in a situation where farm incomes have steadily fallen, and as a consequence many families have been forced to leave the industry. Indeed, the total number of farms operating in Australia fell from around 201,000 in 1960 to just over 130,000 in 2004, with the country experiencing the loss of 20,000 farms between 1994 and 2004 (*The Age* August 31, 2005).

To compound the impact of these farm closures on the local economy, those families which have left the farm rarely remain in rural areas and tend to migrate to cities or coastal areas (McKenzie 1994). The loss of population from rural communities (through a combination of decreased employment opportunities, farm closures or amalgamations and the removal of services) has resulted in many local businesses and services becoming unviable (Talbot and Walker 2007: 484), leading to their closure and/or relocation from small rural towns to regional centers or major cities. The loss of facilities and services that are deemed essential to the survival and identity of small rural towns—including schools, banks, railway stations, post offices and hospitals—has caused an erosion of the roles and functions performed by these towns (Budge 2007: 56).

Many small rural towns in Australia have experienced a contraction of local economic activity, further outmigration of young adults and families with children and the breakdown of certain local social institutions and networks (Tonts 2000: 52; Stayner 2005: 128). The fundamental problem of population decline, as McManus and Pritchard (2000) note, is that it locks some towns into a vicious cycle where the removal of services not only contributes to population decline but often results in the more entrepreneurial and higher spending residents moving elsewhere in search of better opportunities. Overall, the loss, withdrawal and centralization of government services and private businesses produces a reduction in the pool of professional and semi-professional people who were formerly employed in banks, schools, health services, local government and so on. For several communities, this has created "a leadership vacuum" and/ or a loss of their "tangible skill and expertise base" (Driscoll and Wood 1999: 26).

We should add to this the impact of long periods of drought on agriculture, which has been an integral part of the economic, social and environmental issues facing farmers in rural Victoria (e.g. Alston and Kent 2004). In northwest Victoria, a decade of severe drought has "wrought significant damage on living standards" (Alexander 2008: 4). Drought also affects the maintenance of sports facilities in the region, forcing clubs to implement strategies for sustainable water usage on sports grounds. For example, John, a local farmer in his 50s, describes the impact of drought on the sustainability of the local golf club as follows: "In a drought, golf is the team that suffers because the grass just doesn't get grown, because there's never any rain. If they get half an inch of rain or whatever, but so, golf has gone way back."

The effects of these developments are distributed unevenly across Victoria. There is a growing division between those (mainly coastal, accessible or environmentally attractive) rural areas experiencing population growth and those (mainly inland agricultural regions) experiencing decline. The wheat and sheep belt of northwest Victoria falls into the latter category, with most towns experiencing either a slow or a more rapid decrease in population (Victorian Government 2005; Department of Planning and Community Development 2008). This is accompanied by the progressive withdrawal of local services by commercial agencies and the state (Budge 2007). In some cases the closure of public services has had a significant psychological impact on rural towns, arguably signalling the "death" of the town (McKenzie 1994). Such changes may also affect the sustainability of voluntary organizations such as sports clubs. The rural towns in northwest Victoria have witnessed an accelerated "flight of youth" to seek education, training and employment in regional and metropolitan cities, most notably Melbourne, Ballarat and Bendigo (Rural and Regional Services and

Development Committee 2006). Jane, a local resident in her 60s, explains this process as follows:

> There are more chances for employment for younger people [elsewhere]. There used to be . . . people used to live on their farms, their houses were out there and people worked on the farms and the young ones went to school. But now everybody does VCE [Victorian Certificate of Education], most of them go to tertiary education of some kind and once they get away they get into more interesting things. And there's nothing for them on the farm anyway because the farm machinery now is such that they don't need a lot of people. Farming used to be very labor intensive, but now it's not.

The "flight of youth" affects not only the social structure and amenity of the towns generally but also the supply of able-bodied volunteers for vital community work including health care and sporting events (Martin 2007: 63). This is exacerbated by the increased responsibility for maintaining local community services and infrastructure that is being given to community members who are expected to act as volunteers (Talbot and Walker 2007: 488). Rural communities must provide volunteer labor to ensure that these services are delivered to minimum standards (Driscoll and Wood 1999: 43). Talbot and Walker (2007: 490) note how "the enactment of the efficiency imperative in the rationalisation and privatisation of services was experienced as leaching resources from rural communities." Emerging gaps in service provision are increasingly filled by community development initiatives and local volunteers. However, volunteerism is ultimately "unable to adequately fill the gaps and enhance the increasing inequalities in access to services."

This development has been more profound in some small rural towns than in others. Certain rural towns in northwest Victoria appear to have been relatively successful in retaining or attracting young people, for example through establishing cutting-edge agricultural organizations or by attracting new industries. These organizations have successfully tempted young professionals to move into the area. These young professionals tend to perceive involvement in sport as a way to meet new people and to integrate into the community. Some of them are prominent figures in the management of local sporting competitions. Matt, a teacher in his 30s, reports:

> I have only been in the town for five years. Being involved in hockey and football is a great way to integrate and to get to know people, especially for my wife because she was a school principal in the past so she used to have a large social network.

Atherley (2006) argues that the above-mentioned processes of restructuring have a direct impact on rural sports clubs. She found that the adaptive strategies of sports clubs in Western Australia are a direct result of the clubs being exposed to these processes. Common strategies include amalgamation and the spatial reorganization of sporting competition locations. The extent of these impacts appears to be less pronounced in northwest Victoria, where the loss and amalgamation of sports clubs has been a less frequent but nevertheless significant occurrence in recent decades.[5] In recent years there have been two amalgamations of football/netball clubs in the area as well as an amalgamation of tennis clubs. The loss of a local sports club can impact negatively on existing social networks and community identity, cutting deeply into the pride of the town. Local farmer James interprets the amalgamation of his Australian football club with a club in a neighboring town (with the latter functioning as the club's new home base) as follows:

> The end of the footy club was due to the loss of population, which in turn is due to changes in farming. This has signalled the death of the town, loss of a community hub. Now the club is amalgamated but only in name. It has lost most of its community appeal.

James's comment illustrates how the wider changes in northwest Victoria may also affect local sports activities and their capacity for social engagement. This issue will be examined in more detail in Chapters 4 and 5.

The focus of this chapter has been on the social and organizational contexts of sport in the four cases being studied. These contexts are of great import if we are to develop robust and nuanced understandings of the factors and processes that affect the lived experience and social impact of nonprofessional forms of sport in different social settings. Chapter 3 continues the comparative analysis of the wider contexts of sport provision, focusing on its political and educational contexts.

3 Political and Educational Contexts of Sport

This chapter discusses the political-ideological contexts of sport provision in the communities being studied, with a focus on the interplay between the discourse of sport as welfare and that of sport as social control. The chapter also analyzes the approaches to and perspectives on education that underpin the sports activities in these communities. Finally, the role of relationship building in engendering the social outcomes of the sport-focused interventions is explored.

THE POLITICS OF SPORT: SOCIAL WELFARE AND SOCIAL CONTROL

The political-ideological discourse which portrays sport in instrumental and utilitarian terms as a vehicle of social policies is outlined in the Introduction. Government and sport agencies worldwide have often sought to integrate sport and social policy with much attention drawn to the importance of community sport as a form of social welfare (Hylton and Totten 2008; Bloyce and Smith 2010). This focus is also evident in the case studies. Research participants associated with the sports activities describe how participation in sport enables people to gain a sense of achievement and self-determination and to develop a set of skills which they can apply to other areas of their lives. They also comment on the social significance of sport more generally. As noted in Chapter 2, there are considerable similarities in their responses across the four cases. The following remarks by two interviewees are indicative of this:

> I find sport important principally as a means, because I observe that many young people really like sport and love to do it. They need to learn to cooperate, win and lose, throw and receive a punch. I find that sport is generally undervalued in Dutch society and particularly in education. As a society, you can achieve much more with sport than is currently the case. (Male teacher, 40s, SSP)

> Obviously there are also a lot of health ramifications from being involved physically in sport. Socially it gives people something to do,

something positive to do. . . . There is literally nothing else to do. Definitely you'd be bored. (Female netball player, 20s, NCFL)

Despite the similarities in responses across the four cases, there are also differences in the degree to which sport is viewed in an instrumental and utilitarian way. These differences are broadly representative of the theoretical categories ("sport development" and "sport-for-development") identified in the Introduction. As is to be expected given the programs' stated objectives, SSP and Vencer staff emphasize the wider social uses of sport. This perspective values sport according to its extrinsic significance, for instance its role in fostering social relationships, transferable skills and character building. Renata, a program assistant in her 20s, describes Vencer's focus on "sport as a means" as follows:

There are sport organizations that also do development and there are youth development organizations that use sport as a hook or motivator. A Ganar/Vencer is the latter and we try vehemently to establish ourselves as such. A Ganar/Vencer is not a training program, it is not a sports academy, and is not an athletic feeder for big clubs—it is a program whose top priority is youth development and we have found that sport is the most effective tool to reach youth. A Ganar/Vencer really prides itself in its focus on youth development rather than sports.

Respondents in the MG and NCFL case studies, on the other hand, stress the expressive qualities of sport, notably its ludic element. From this perspective, sport participation is a valued end in itself: people may participate in sport simply because they enjoy playing the game or to learn particular skills directly related to the game (Vuori and Fentem 1995; Janssens 2004). Sophie, the secretary of an NCFL hockey club, feels that being involved in sport is "just all about participation and having fun." In a similar vein, Samatar, an MG volunteer in his 20s, argues:

Sports give [young people in the community] something to concentrate on when they are not doing anything else. Fun is the most important thing; to give them something fun to do, to exercise and to have fun. It should be fun, that's the core. And to have something outside of school and home.

In practice, however, there is a variable degree of overlap between the two perspectives. On a different occasion Samatar tells me that, in his opinion: "Sport can play and does play a great role in integrating people. Sport's a great connector. Anyone can play sport. You don't even have to be good at sport [and] you don't even need language." Similar examples can be found in the NCFL case, where the government representatives interviewed describe how sport provides a unique forum for communicating social messages, for example in relation to drug and alcohol awareness. Local government agencies in northwest Victoria have established partnerships with sports clubs to communicate such messages to residents.

The above reveals some of the tension that may exist between the objectives of using sport as a means to an end versus providing sport as an end in itself. As noted in Chapter 1, the ludic element of sport is inherently irreducible to programming for control (see also Hargreaves 1986: 222). In placing emphasis on instrumental forms of sport participation, the ludic element of sport may be diminished, which may cause some people to disengage from (organized) sport. Tensions of this kind become visible when we consider sport as a form of social control.

Sport is used directly or indirectly as a form of social control by state and other institutions (Eitzen 2000; Hylton and Totten 2008). Community sports initiatives target various categories of potential users, but within the political-ideological discourse discussed earlier its main concern is with the "potentially troublesome"—"at-risk" youth, ethnic minorities and/or the unemployed (Hargreaves 1986: 189). These groups are targeted through programs which use sport as a vehicle to alleviate social problems, enhance community cohesion and generate social order.[6] The social control perspective highlights the existence of a tension between the rights to participate in sport (equity) and concerns to use sport in an instrumental way. Sport is one sphere of life over which people are believed to exercise considerable autonomy and freedom, but this interpretation of sport as freedom is at odds with the notion of social control (Hylton and Totten 2008: 109; Donnelly and Coakley 2002: 4–5). This ambiguity is reflected in the four cases, albeit to varying degrees and in different forms.

The emergence of SSP should be understood within the context of attempts by a coalition of national and local public actors to reduce welfare dependency and generate social order in disadvantaged urban neighborhoods (Spaaij 2009a; cf. Uitermark and Duyvendak 2008). Baillergeau and Schaut (2001) contend that the contemporary practice of social work in the Netherlands tends toward a new balance between change and control at the expense of emancipatory practices focused on marginalized people, especially minority ethnic youth (see also Baillergeau and Duyvendak 2001). Indeed, social workers in disadvantaged urban neighborhoods can be seen to "put in place a system of control and risk prevention as a mix of social work and people policing" (Baillergeau and Schaut 2001: 427). As part of this trend, the Dutch government has increasingly come to recognize sport as a significant element of urban social policy. The Dutch Ministry of Health, Welfare and Sport (2005: 49) views sport as "a highly desirable and effective way of achieving key government objectives," especially in relation to combating anti-social behavior and social polarization. Local authorities in Rotterdam have initiated several strategies for *sociale herovering* ("social reconquest"; e.g. Engbersen et al. 2005) in areas that are deemed prone to poverty, segregation, crime and nuisance, including a range of initiatives which revolve around sport and leisure (Sociaal Platform Rotterdam 2007). In this political context, SSP can be interpreted as a means through which government agencies and their partners seek to regulate and civilize "at-risk" youth, especially those who are unemployed or who have "dropped out" of the education system. Such intervention rests on the belief that sport can be used "as a means to 'motivate' marginal youth," to normalize their behavior (e.g. contingent work, refrain from criminal behavior) and "to 'integrate' them into wider society" (Rijpma and Meiburg 1989: 151). SSP coordinator Danny describes the tacit political uses of programs like SSP as follows:

> Projects usually run for several months. People interact intensively in them, and that produces social ties and social cohesion. That's so interesting about many of these projects: that you have a lot of by-catch the target group is not even aware of. From a governmental perspective, that's the objective you achieve in that way.

The interpretation of sport as social control is also highly relevant to the Vencer case. The Vencer program is largely run from within civil society. The program's affiliation with organizations like the Inter-American Development Bank nevertheless compromises its position as a grassroots campaign. Thus, although Vencer has this large civil society component, the program is driven from both ends bottom-up and top-down simultaneously. Some of the practitioners and social activists associated with Vencer, and/or the implementing NGOs, recognize its potential political use as an instrument of social control. As noted in Chapter 2, the favelas in which the program operates are commonly portrayed by the media, politicians and middle and upper classes as a social problem (Valladares 2005; Perlman 2006; Velho 2008). In this context, social policies and projects that target these neighborhoods can be interpreted as attempts to control and discipline the conduct of favela residents, especially young people (cf. Sposito et al. 2006: 243).

Rodrigo, a local activist in his 50s who is not connected with Vencer, poses the rhetorical question of whether we can read the Vencer program as an attempt to "control the poor," by centering on the alleviation of disorder, violence and the threat of political mobilization (a "revolt of the masses") with the purpose of moving favela residents into the hegemonic capitalist order, rather than opening up alternative realities. In his view, social programs like Vencer not only run the risk of being merely a bandaid solution; there is also a danger of co-optation and, therefore, of de-politicizing and de-mobilizing marginalized groups. This sentiment gives voice to the important critique that sport-for-development programs may "signal to subordinate groups that significant changes in opportunity can be brought about without the need for structural change" (Hargreaves 1986: 198). The causes of deprivation, disadvantage and community disintegration, and of inequality of opportunity in sport, are largely absent from this discourse.

Some members of the Vencer staff recognize these concerns, as well as their own ability to resist the above-mentioned discourse of control and to pursue and realize their own objectives. Bianca, a coordinator in her 40s, argues:

> We cannot prepare people only for that [capitalist] market, because that is not the society we want. We want people to be capable of changing that society, not only to reproduce. . . . My personal point of view is that we have built a society that is not capable of . . . I know that not everybody will be inside, but the way it is only a small part will be inside. So we need to change the way it is. . . . The point is that even if the society is this I can still have an opportunity for myself to have a better life, to improve my life, and also to generate opportunities for those around me. In my point of view we are learning that capitalist society is a staircase and that you need to go step by step. But it's a small staircase, it gets narrower and narrower towards the top, and we can grow together until a certain point where I will need to step over you. And what I am trying to say is that the staircase does not need to be this shape. It can be a staircase that grows wider, where every time you go up you can take two people with you, and the next step you can take two other people up. I am not saying that in the end it will not be very narrow, but there will be much more room in the middle. And it doesn't mean that there are no people who do not want to climb the staircase. Some people really don't want to.

Thus, Bianca emphasizes the significance of critical emancipatory participation to combat inequality in all its forms. She also stresses the importance of education for enhancing people's agency, including its practical uses in providing young people with the tools to increase their opportunities and to foster critical awareness that may enable them to contest and change their social realities. In other words, the key objective of Vencer is to *empower* participants, that is, to enhance their sense of power or control over their lives. Vencer coordinator Edu describes this as follows: "Continually youth say that before the program they didn't know that they could dream. They felt that the only reality for them was what they see daily in their community. We are helping to change that. We don't say what the dream should be, we provide a path for helping them achieve that dream."

The MG and NCFL cases differ from the two cases discussed above, in the sense that they are organized primarily "from below" and therefore less subject to state planning and control. However, the narratives of research participants reveal another aspect of the social control dimension of sport. Several interviewees perceive sport as a welcome form of informal social control aimed at reducing anti-social behavior in their local communities. Hassan, an MG coach in his 20s, articulates this view as follows:

> You try to control the kids and the most dangerous night is Friday night. So we train on Friday nights because we don't want the kids to go out. And Saturday night they have to sleep because Sunday they have a game. So it's a bit of impact to the kids. We have had some kids who started doing some wrong, like stealing. When we heard about it we talked to them and brought them to the club. And they realized they were doing something wrong and they changed their behavior. One of them came to the meeting last week and said "If I leave here where am I going to go?" They know that if they leave the club and go somewhere else, they'll do something wrong.

An identical sentiment is voiced by Jim, the coach of an Australian football team in the NCFL:

> At least while the kids are playing football they are training, they are going to football matches, they are not just standing around the street getting into mischief. . . . We had a child who was seriously running off the rails. He was quite young but he was getting involved in all sorts of petty criminal activity, and it was quite clear that that child was going to have lots of problems. So we brought that kid into the football club, made a fuss of him, made him feel important as a member of the team, and gave him some purpose . . . so that he would be training rather than roaming the streets getting into trouble. . . . In the process he actually got to see how other people behave. And how some behaviour was unacceptable, you know. So it might be cliché but it was a useful tool in helping that kid to learn some life skills.

These examples illustrate how within both MG and NCFL, sport is at times employed as a means to discipline and normalize the behavior of young people deemed "at risk." They also highlight the significance of relationship building as an educational approach to sport. This issue is discussed below.

EDUCATION IN AND THROUGH SPORT

The educational processes and outcomes of the sports activities being studied vary greatly according to the particular circumstances in which they operate. Educational philosophies are explicit and formalized in SSP and Vencer, whereas in MG and NCFL there tends to be a vaguer and more bounded understanding of education in and through sport. In the latter, the focus is on the central role coaches play in developing participation in sport. Key principles underlying coaching strategies are: making sport fun, accessible and safe; providing supportive and instructional feedback; improving sport-specific skills; developing fair play, discipline and respect; enhancing physical fitness and a positive lifestyle; and guiding players to improved performance (Lyle 2008; McCann and Ewing 2006).

One of the issues raised by coaches in the MG and NCFL cases is the need to foster an inclusive sporting environment in which competitiveness and accessibility are balanced. As noted in Chapter 1, competitiveness is inherent to sporting activity. One way in which the competitive nature of sport manifests itself is in what can be called a talent/ability barrier. Those who are less talented may not get the same opportunities to play and often have less social status within a team or club. For example, when in 2009 a father enquired whether his son could join MG, a club representative responded that this would depend on "whether he is a good player or not." On another occasion, a boy who was new to the club had to train with the team for a couple of weeks before a decision regarding his future with the team was made. The coach was not satisfied with the skills and effort the boy demonstrated during training and therefore decided not to include him in the team despite the insistence of the boy's father. Notwithstanding, coaches in the MG study generally demonstrate a commitment to reduce the potentially exclusionary consequences of the talent/ability barrier by promoting an environment in which the focus is less on winning or losing and more on the ludic, friendship and learning aspects of sport. They disagree, however, on how to balance competitiveness and accessibility in practice. The following extract from the MG focus group (male football coaches in their 20s or 30s) articulates this debate.

Asad: Different coaches deal with this in different ways. Some coaches field their best players because they want to win, but others if the kid is very disciplined and he cannot even play they might play him because he might improve. So most coaches either want results or they want to improve someone.

Roble: There is a difference between junior and senior teams, because junior players all need to play.

Yusuf: As a coach [of a senior team], your first priority is to win. But sometimes there is a weak game so you sneak in one or two of the worse players. I know this may not be the right thing to do, but winning is your first priority. If you have an A, B and C team this gives you flexibility.

Roble: I coach a junior team and my priority is to get everyone on the game. You can make as many substitutions as you like so you can put someone on and take him off again.

Asad: With seniors it's very hard because you only have three substitutions.

Mohamed: Exactly, 'coz you only have 14 players so you have to use them well. Usually what I do [as a junior's coach] is to put in the best eleven and then substitute from there. And I encourage them to come to the training. If they only train once a week those guys will probably not play. Otherwise they think they can get away with it and half the team will not show up. So it's important to be very strict.

There is some significant variation with the NCFL case in this respect due in large part to the particularities of sport in northwest Victoria. The shortage of players appears to reduce the talent barrier of sport participation and to enhance the inclusiveness of sport clubs at least to some degree. Several respondents regard the NCFL as very inclusive. Local farmer Jack gives the following example:

> Pretty much everybody is welcome to have a go. I remember when I first got to [this town] there was a teacher here . . . and he was the worst footballer that I have ever seen in my life. He was hopeless. They were fairly short of numbers and they gave him a game every week. Put him on the bench for most of the game. So he was included. He came to this community for his work, he had no other ties in this community but the football club for him provided his social outlook, you know. He was just the worst footballer . . . but the club gave him a run and was inclusive and I think that is a good thing.

But not every respondent subscribes to the view that in the NCFL competitiveness is of less import than accessibility. Claire, a netball player in her 20s, notes that different sports have different social dynamics. In her view, hockey is a very inclusive sport in northwest Victoria due to the shortage of players. Netball, on the other hand, is considerably more competitive:

> Hockey will take anyone, bit more friendly, but netball is really cutthroat and without sounding stereotypical it's because women are involved and men aren't involved. So often it becomes about who likes who. If you're related to who[ever] then you're expected to be good at it and that sort of thing and because it's a smaller team, they've only got 7 places and not 22 so it does make a difference. Netball and football are generally fairly similar, but hockey is different.

Joseph, the vice-president of a local football club, also admits to the existence of a talent/ability barrier, but he stresses that this does not prevent access to sports clubs. When asked whether one has to be talented to be accepted, Joseph replies:

> Of course it helps, yeah, I think in some ways you're right though, the better you are the more accepted you are at times. But we've got examples now of people who are just terrible, can't play at all, but they're still accepted in the footy club, because they still train and having a go.

As long as they are good people, it really doesn't matter about their football skills.

In comparison, Vencer and SSP staff are less concerned with fostering an accessible sporting environment as such and more with establishing and maintaining a supportive *learning* environment aimed at achieving social outcomes beyond sport. Their vision of the potential impacts of their programs is much broader than the narrowly defined objective of enhancing young people's employment prospects. SSP staff regard the educational content of the program as merely one dimension of a broader personal and social development process. For them, relationship building, intensive guidance, helping participants to get a job and post-program assistance are all essential elements of the program. A similar sentiment is voiced by Vencer educators. For example, Ana, a Vencer coordinator in her 40s, describes her ambition as follows:

> The process we're trying to generate is much broader than just finding a job. . . . To make people think "hey, wait a minute, something is different here." That is the effect we're trying to generate. . . . We give them a way to assess reality better, but not to say that they cannot do anything. Rather, we want them to understand that they can make things happen if they plan it right. We are trying to specifically show the way of work. That does not mean that they will work in this way and that's the end, but they can choose many different ways or they can choose one way.

Ana gives the following example of the type of outcome she aims to achieve:

> One supervisor told me she was really disappointed with one girl in the program who was good and who found a job, and she started working and started studying, but then suddenly she decided to stop work and study to get married and be a mother. What I said is "how did that girl make that decision?" If it was under the pressure of her boyfriend or family or others, if she did not find any other way to escape, then that's bad. But if she looked at herself and at her boyfriend and the boyfriend promised to take care of the kids and the house, then that's their agreement. That's good, why not? It's a choice. It's all about the way you choose.

Ana's comments hint at some of the ways in which members of staff seek to incorporate certain elements of the critical pedagogy advocated by Paulo Freire (1972, 1973). Freire stresses the need to develop people's abilities to understand, question and resist the conditions for their poverty. It is Freire's (1972: 12) conviction that all human beings are capable of looking critically at their world in a dialogical encounter with others. Through such an encounter, they can gradually become conscious of their social situation and the contradictions in it, and intervene critically. A critical pedagogy of this kind, Freire (1972: 25) argues, "must be forged *with*, not *for*, the oppressed."

In this vein, Vencer coordinators emphasize the significance of a form of education which empowers young people to develop critical awareness and reflection vis-à-vis the world around them. Moreover, they seek to offer participatory and dialogical learning spaces which facilitate the type of "problem-posing," "co-intentional" education proposed by Freire (1972: 44, 54). Catarina, a psychologist working with the program, explains this approach as follows:

> I have a particular view on education. The majority of schools in Brazil are preoccupied with the content of education, the quantity of information. This quantity of information means nothing to the students. . . . I need to know what I can do with the info, how can I use it in daily life. Our schools don't understand that. The vision that I have of education is first and foremost try to show the young people that they do have opportunities; that these opportunities exist. That they have the qualities within them, and that they only have to work on discovering which positive qualities they possess. Secondly, I try to awaken in them a certain curiosity. It's not easy, but that's my purpose for the program. Why? Because when you are interested in something, what will you do? You go searching, you go investigating. . . . So our objective is, first, that they discover or identify their own talents. And to show them that people respect them. Second, awakening their curiosity in something. Doesn't matter what it is, whether it's curiosity in mathematics, in language, or whatever. Every person has their own interests. Something that drives them forward, that triggers them. The third objective is critical reflection on the world around them and their place in that world.

However, Vencer does not explicitly embrace the most far-reaching implications of Freire's revolutionary pedagogy, which would be to strive for the transformation of the structure of society so that the "oppressed" become "beings for themselves" (Freire 1972: 48), even though some members of staff may be sympathetic to this standpoint at a personal level. As Kingsbury (2004: 227) notes, arguably the largest difference between Freire's revolutionary pedagogy and the role of education in contemporary community development is that "the latter is based upon a more localized and, hence, contained basis, and that it seeks to allow its recipients to participate in wider economic and political spheres, rather than to overthrow them." It is in this more contained, practical form that elements of Freire's pedagogy are applied in Vencer.

Vencer and SSP both use sports activities throughout their programs to motivate and teach young people. They are built on the belief that sport provides a great learning environment because it is an arena where many youth spend time willingly, which is not always true for time spent at school (Danish et al. 2003). The football activities in Vencer are used to facilitate a fluid learning environment for supporting and delivering educational content to young people, that is, sport is used as both a physical and an intellectual background for learning. During the first phase of the program, participants play approximately 50 hours on the field and spend around 50 hours in the classroom. In the classroom, sport is still the language that is used; for example, a lesson on timeliness is built around a sport example, and gender is taught within the sports context. In the remainder of the program, members of staff continue to use sports contexts and provide regular opportunities for games. The Vencer methodology is informed by the theory of experiential learning (Kolb 1984), with the football activities comprising the first stage of a learning cycle (i.e. the concrete experience). This is followed by reflection and analysis of the activity (with the educator as facilitator), conceptualization (assisted by the educator) and the group-based transfer of learning (see Spaaij, in press).

Members of staff acknowledge, of course, that football and other team sports can divide individuals and groups as much as it unites them. Given this, they aim to present sports activities in a safe and suitable learning environment to ensure that all participants—female and male, experienced and inexperienced—can develop skills and enjoy being physically active. Thus, physical education teachers in Vencer change the team compositions on a daily basis to reduce the competitiveness of the football activities. They also modify the rules of the games to foster active, participatory learning and to vary their physical and emotional demands. This modified football is generally appreciated by participants, especially by those who may be less skilled in this particular sport. Juliana, a former participant in her 20s, says that even though she is "terrible at playing football," she "really enjoyed it": "It was fun because it wasn't normal football, it was different. There were always activities that made us respect one another. . . . When you play football in the street this mutual respect doesn't exist, it's much more competitive."

Although most respondents value the less competitive nature of the football activities in Vencer, Sergio, an 18-year-old former participant, argues that the competitive aspect of the game actually has educational value: "It's part of the process. In life there is also a lot of competition: people when they look for employment, interviews, those things." In this view, ritualized competition and conflict in sport allow teachers or coaches to create opportunities for players to resolve these situations in a way that will impact positively (Lambert 2007: 17). Program assistant Renata notes that conflict situations "are inevitable" and that it is therefore "so important to have good facilitators who can take advantage of those moments and turn them into something positive." She stresses that these situations generate valuable teaching and learning moments: "On the sports field, emotions come out and a lot of these youth respond to conflict with aggression or anger, which can be nerve-wracking but also bring out a lot of really great real-life teaching moments." Renata's remarks resonate with recent research which suggests that coaches who maintain good relationships with players reduce anti-social behavior and that exposure to high levels of sociomoral reasoning within the immediate context of sports activities promotes pro-social behavior (Rutten et al. 2007).

SSP staff also demonstrate a deep belief in the value of sport as a tool for motivating young people to participate in educational activities. This view of sport as a motivator or hook is articulated by Kees, SSP's physical education teacher, who also works as a coach at a local sport club:

> At a sports club you are used to attract motivated people, but here [at SSP] it's different. There are a number of people who are really motivated. But there are also several people who are not and you try to get those on board. I think that's the most important thing about sport [in SSP]. They get their classroom activities and are continuously studying. Then including a bit of sport is very good. And you get to know them in a very different way. They can express themselves differently. And you notice that certain people feel more comfortable with that. One person in particular. We hear that he is very quiet in the group, but during football he is very assertive and active. For a young man like him I believe it's very positive that the program has a sport component, which gives him the opportunity to express and prove himself.

However, compared with Vencer, playing sport is a relatively minor aspect of the learning activities in SSP, even though three two-hour sessions per week are devoted to physical activity. While the sports activities are regarded as important opportunities for relationship building and skill development, the emphasis is more on the prospect of working in a sporting environment. As part of their training, SSP participants are given the opportunity to gain practical experience through working as crowd control assistants at major events, including professional football matches. During these traineeships they co-operate with each other, stewards, security staff, venue operators and urban supervisors, allowing them to develop professional and social experience in a different environment. Program director Edwin explains the value of this experience as follows:

> If you look at what goes on with the youth in this neighborhood, it's this kind of thing, major events, that they love. They want to go to concerts and football matches, you name it. That usually costs a lot of money, which they don't have. So you offer them another way to experience part of what happens at an event, and they even get paid for it. . . . And crowd management has an important mirroring effect on them in regard to their attitude towards other people. The moment they become aware of this, like "hey, if I react like this, that's the response I

get, and the moment I react a bit differently I get that response." Practice is the best learning environment you can have. It enables them to become aware of their non-verbal communication and what responses they can elicit from another person. At this type of event they can be part of it and contribute to it as well. That confirms their self-worth and self-respect.

For the vast majority of participants, the sport focus of SSP and the prospect of working at major sporting events are important incentives. For example, 17-year-old male participant Ali reports: "I don't like books or classes. I only like sport. That's why I chose this program. I read that it was a sport-based education. I would love to work in a sporting environment." Slightly different responses are obtained from Vencer participants on this issue. Almost all respondents report that football contributed significantly to the learning process. However, more than 90% of Vencer survey participants view playing football as a means for personal and professional development, not as an end in itself. The interviews corroborate this finding. For example, when asked whether in her view football was an important aspect of the Vencer program, 21-year-old former participant Julieta argued: "It was important because football comprises so many things that people don't know. Teamwork, responsibility. We thought that football was just football and that's it, but that's not the case." Her friend Glória adds:

> It allowed us to develop and talk about our skills. I'm more interested in learning things through football than in just playing football. I actually started playing sport here [at Vencer]. I was never very interested in sport.

As noted in Chapter 2, finding employment and developing new skills and professional attributes are their principal goals. Very few Vencer participants indicate that they actually want to work in a sporting environment in the future. Twenty-two percent of participants also report their aim to meet new people and make new friends, which is indicative of their desire to achieve increased social connectedness and social engagement. It should be noted here that it is difficult to determine whether these were indeed participants' principal motives beforehand, or whether they express these motives because members of staff have been preaching this message to them. For example, a few Vencer respondents note that they did not really have a major reason for entering the program, and that they enrolled in the program primarily because they wanted to do something useful with their time. Overall, however, their concern about their employment prospects closely reflects the social issues facing poor young people in general in urban Brazil, as discussed in the previous chapter.

In contrast, people's main reasons for becoming involved in MG or NCFL are far less focused on career aspirations. As noted earlier, many respondents in the MG and NCFL studies report intrinsic motivations (i.e. playing, fun) as well as a desire to be part of and contribute to community life, for example as a volunteer. For several people who play sport in the NCFL, community sport is very much part of their habitus, being passed on from generation to generation and rarely a subject of conscious reflection. They just practically "feel", rather than reflectively think, that playing sport is "right for me". Patrick, the vice-president of an Australian football club, describes this form of intergenerational transmission as follows:

> Dad's father was the football president when I was only a kid. [Patrick's dad later became club president.] I started playing football when I was only about eight. Then just followed it all the way through and started coaching myself. I put away coaching for a few years, now I've come back and I'm more involved in the administration side of things. Still playing but involved in the vice presidency, so come the full circle.

Intergenerational transmission of this kind is very common in the NCFL and reveals one of the ways in which access to social networks is structured. This issue is further examined in Chapter 4.

THE ART OF RELATIONSHIP BUILDING

Relationship building is a fundamental component of developing social capital. The narratives of MG and NCFL players and volunteers articulated in this chapter suggest that although relationship building is very much at the heart of their experience of sport, their investment in social relationships occurs in the absence of a clearly articulated educational approach. In the MG and NCFL cases, social relationships are not purposely crafted as part of a formal sports program; rather, they occur in a largely spontaneous, organic way. Hockey player Sally argues that relationship building in the NCFL involves "all those sort of unwritten and unspoken things that you sort of just take for general knowledge." Relationships established in the sports context can carry over into other social spheres. Sally asserts that relationship building at the local football and hockey clubs also informs her interactions with children and parents at her local school: "They see you on that human levelat the footy, and sometimes that can sort of help your relationships at school too. And they don't see you as, this, you know, triple-headed school teacher. Well, you're more approachable, I think. It can break down barriers in other areas." These issues are explored further in the discussion of social capital formation in Chapter 4.

In contrast, in SSP and Vencer relationship building is perceived as underpinning the outcomes of the programs and therefore merits greater attention here. Both programs acknowledge that it is the adoption of a personal and social development model which is sacred rather than sport itself (cf. Crabbe et al. 2006: 19; Taylor et al. 1999: 50). In other words, what is significant is not sport as such, but the context in which it occurs. Members of staff of both SSP and Vencer stress the importance of amplifying the horizons and aspirations of young people to help them achieve a sense of personal autonomy. The programs seek to provide a space where participants can meet new people with different backgrounds, enter unfamiliar locations and be encouraged to take personal and mutual responsibility, thus refining their sense of both individual potentials and mutual dependencies (Crabbe et al. 2006: 17).

Within both programs sports activities are instrumental to these processes by providing an environment in which participants can develop a commitment toward each other and display their willingness to work as a team. Educators, who perform the role of facilitator, are believed to play a key role in this. Vencer assistant Renata argues:

> The relationship between the participant and facilitator is really important because it's more of a "coaching" relationship than a traditional teacher-to-student relationship. During the facilitator trainings, we really try to emphasize that the facilitator must be on the same level as the participant in order to gain trust and that the learning experience is mutual, not unilateral.

Put differently, Vencer facilitators seek to avoid what Freire (1972: Ch. 2) dismisses as a "banking concept" of education. Instead, they aim to foster a non-hierarchical, dialogical encounter in which teachers and students "become jointly responsible for a process in which all grow" (Freire 1972: 53).

Members of staff in the Vencer and SSP programs seek to develop respectful forms of social interaction. This involves giving young people the opportunity to make their own choices and to respect and support these choices, rather than to subsume their autonomy (Verweel 2007). They attempt to open up possibilities and share experiences, forming the basis of mutually respectful and trusting relationships through which guidance may be sought (Blackshaw and Crabbe 2004; Van Ginkel et al. 2007). Research participants in the Vencer and SSP programs confirm Crabbe et al.'s (2006) finding that it is important that staff members display certain characteristics, including concern for participants' well-being, familiarity with personality traits and participants' social environments, willingness to invest time and effort into building reciprocal trust and respect and warmth and humor. Although being a good teacher in the more traditional sense is also deemed a valuable characteristic, most members of staff consider this quality to be less vital to the overall effectiveness of the program. Vencer coordinator Ana expresses this as follows:

> We always say to the teachers and mentors that the most important thing is not the subject they are going to learn with you. . . . Sure that's

important too, but you must create relationships with them. Not because you need to become best friends for life. . . . The relationship with a teacher is one of mutual respect. And of authority, of course. Because you must learn to respect someone who has more authority than you. OK, that's how society operates. But it's also someone who you can look to and listen to and think "if I do the right things, someone will respect me as I respect him." So it's a projection of your future, of your own desires.

The social impact of SSP and Vencer is grounded in part in their role as cultural intermediaries, "opening access to social worlds and opportunities which are not currently accessible to the young people with whom they work, in order that those young people are in a stronger position to make positive life choices from a wider range of options" (Crabbe et al. 2006: 15).[7] This role enables the programs to bridge part of the gap between marginalized young people and dominant social groups through their appeal "as somehow legitimate and authentic to individuals, groups and agencies on either side of this discursive divide" (Blackshaw and Crabbe 2004: 171). As Blackshaw and Crabbe (2004: 171–2) note, whilst "from above" such interventions are valued as an innovative and effective approach to tackling the adverse consequences of social exclusion, the constituencies they target appreciate the intervention "because it is perceived and experienced as being of a non-interfering and non-threatening variety." By performing the role of cultural intermediary, it may be possible for such programs to ease some of the aforementioned tensions that may exist between the objectives of sport as social welfare and sport as social control.

There is no single profile as to what constitutes the "right person" for this task. SSP and Vencer both employ a disparate array of staff with distinct skills and backgrounds. It has been argued that members of staff need to have the capacity to connect with the target group relating to their own biographies and social outlook. For example, Crabbe (2005) found that, with significant exceptions, there is a stronger identification among participants with staff members who are "local" rather than with those who are not. Recent studies of the contributions of peer educators and embedded role models to sport-for-development programs echo this finding (Coalter 2007; Nicholls 2009; Meier and Saavedra 2009). The SSP and Vencer programs employ staff whose socio-cultural distance to participants is relatively small, for example local youth who are themselves former program participants, or mentors or coaches whose social backgrounds are broadly similar to those of the target group. However, respondents stress that there is no "one size fits all" approach to relationship building. SSP coordinator Danny, who many local youth consider to be particularly "streetwise", argues:

It depends on the individual young person. One person prefers one type of coach or mentor, the other another. And they can be quite different types of people. John [another SSP coordinator] and I are also partially different characters. It could even be someone in a suit, but also a road cleaner. But they have to be people who have found their place in society and who can tell the young people off if necessary. They have to have certain skills, but I wouldn't put it down to a very rigid format like "it has to be a such and such person."

In the following chapters it is demonstrated how the presence of a disparate array of staff with distinct skills and backgrounds can indeed facilitate the development of multiple forms of capital, not least bridging and linking social capital.

4 Crossing/Creating Boundaries

This chapter examines the operation and possibilities of social capital in and through sport. Building on the conceptualization of social capital in Chapter 1, it presents a detailed analysis of the extent to which, and the ways in which, the sports activities being studied contribute to or inhibit the development of bonding and bridging social capital. Particular attention is given to the role of social markers such as gender, class, race, ethnicity and place of residence in the accumulation, maintenance or diminution of social capital. It is shown that social relationships in the sports context can help cross or break down social boundaries and provide an important source of social support and social leverage. However, social capital is also boundary creating and maintaining, and it has the potential to reproduce or reinforce certain social divisions which may result in perceived social exclusion.

SPORT AS A CONTEXT FOR MEANINGFUL SOCIAL INTERACTION

Sports activities serve as a context for meaningful social interaction, which can be a basis for the development of social capital. The meanings people give to such interaction and the resources that accrue from it vary across space and time, and they are dependent on the particular social context in which the interaction takes place. In a social environment characterized by social marginalization and high levels of violence, sports activities can provide a "safe space" where people can interact with one another in a relatively safe and democratic way. The notion of "safe space" is particularly important for young residents of Rio de Janeiro's favelas, who are at risk of physical violence, prejudice and discrimination throughout their daily lives, as described in Chapter 2. Favelas have historically been characterized by dense social networks and a vibrant community life (Zaluar and Alvito 1998; Valladares 2005), but in recent decades the social marginalization and stigmatization of its residents has increased (Perlman 2006; Wheeler 2005). Despite the return to democracy, favela residents tend to feel more excluded, with less political power than before. The level of sociability, the use of public space for leisure and recreation and membership of voluntary associations (except religious) have all diminished considerably (Perlman 2006). The survey results show low rates (less than 10%) of youth participation in community organizations outside of the Vencer program, with the single exception of religious activities (23%), as Figure 4.1 indicates. The social capital of the communities had been one of the few effective assets in getting out of poverty during earlier periods, but this appears to have been greatly reduced (Perlman 2006: 173).

In many favelas it can be dangerous to be outside, especially at night. Young people are often confined indoors after school, further limiting opportunities to form social relationships outside of their family homes. In such conditions, the formation of supportive peer relationships requires a facilitating institutional context which enables young people to get to know and learn to trust one another (Stanton-Salazar and Spina 2005: 412). The young people in Vencer have a strong interest in services close to their home, thus they look for safe spaces in their community where they can be among peers and engage in sports and other social activities. Vencer provides just such a space where young people can come together and create and maintain friendships. The informal nature of the sports activities and the common focus and teamwork involved allow open and democratic relationships to develop between young people and members of staff. Vencer interviewees argue that team sports such as football are particularly well suited to the creation of this form of social support because on-field activities make easier the interaction and approximation among participants and because co-operation is essential (even though, as Chapter 3 shows, sport can also generate interpersonal conflict). This view reflects the argument

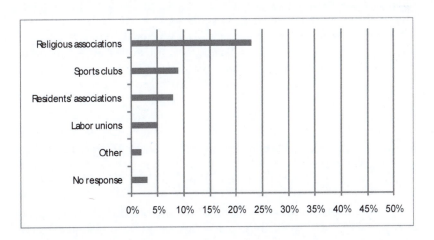

Figure 4.1   Youth participation in community organizations in seven Rio de Janeiro communities.

that a sports team's success is often dependent on a strong norm of generalized reciprocity, that is, on players' ability to co-operate (Walseth 2008).

The focus on collectivity and shared experience is recognized as an important aspect of the Vencer program generally and of the sports activities in particular. For example, 17-year-old Thiago describes his experience of Vencer as follows: "We constructed a kind of family. We studied, made mistakes, had various experiences with various teachers. Each of us developed in a certain way, helping each other." Thiago's comment is indicative of the development of bonding social capital: the formation of close ties and peer networks among participants. These ties facilitate a context for mutual social and emotional support. They also provide an opportunity for greater social connectedness. Former participant Helena, aged 18, claims that her social life was very "closed" prior to entering Vencer. She only had three girlfriends whom she knew from school, and they were virtually the only people she socialized with outside of her home. Vencer was different, she argues, because it allowed her to "chat to the largest number of people possible" and to "get to know different people." Helena describes how she "lost a bit of my shyness, I went to talk to them, and I had to present myself and my work in class, which was important." Helena's experience is quite typical of the young people's accounts of the significance of building and maintaining close ties with peers, which includes the bonding of already-established friendships. Key to this process is the development of supportive, longer-term trusting relationships that transcend the duration of the program. Many participants continue to meet with each other outside of the program activities; they form groups to study together and, in several cases, become friends.

There is also evidence of how the bonding aspect of the program affects young people's personal lives in terms of self-confidence and social skills. Flavia, a former participant in her early 20s, reports: "In the beginning it was quite difficult for me because I was very shy. I was quiet and didn't really talk to anyone . . . but as time went on I came to see that one cannot live without others. It was a very close group, like a family, it was very nice." Paula gives a similar account of the relationship building process in Vencer:

> [Socially] a lot has changed. . . . In the past I stayed indoors. . . . I was only thinking about my husband and myself. . . . I thought that the world was just me and my husband, nothing else. . . . Now I have great friendships. We know new people, people whose friendships will last. We always see people who participated in the program, different people.

The young people's narratives highlight the importance of the sports and classroom activities provided by Vencer as a means of developing bonding social capital. Their desire to create and maintain friendships with other young people in the local community indicates their appreciation of the social support that peers can offer. Many of the young people in the study argue that their local communities have valuable social support networks which consist of extended family, close friends and neighbors. Despite the aforementioned process of social marginalization, they view their immediate social environment as being uniquely placed to offer such support. For example, when Helena was asked whether she would move to another, more affluent neighborhood if she had the opportunity, she replied:

Helena: I'd prefer to stay here. I think that in the community there is more human warmth. You learn to live with the people. I believe that if you live in an apartment [outside the favela] all by yourself, you wouldn't have that physical contact with people. The community has a lot of that. It has friends.

RS: Is there a strong social network in the community?

Helena: Very much so. So much in fact that it's difficult to see people who want to move to another neighborhood.

Helena's comments indicate that even though many young people and other community residents regard violence as a serious problem affecting their communities (Castro and Abramovay 2002), they very much feel "at home" in their local communities because this is the social environment where they grew up and have social support networks at their disposal. Furthermore, some of the young people interviewed express their commitment to "make a difference" in their local community, for instance through providing health or social services. For example, Ana, a former participant in her mid 20s, argues: "Personally, I would like to leave the community but also leave a part of me there. Try to help the community in some way or another, pull children away from drug trafficking." She currently works as a community worker at a local NGO.

The above shows that sport-for-development programs can act as a facilitating institutional context which enables the development of bonding social capital. The SSP program lends further weight to this argument. Some former SSP participants indicate that they have become close friends with other participants who they did not know before entering the program, while others argue that the program has enabled them to bond already-established relationships. These relationships can provide access to valuable resources, for instance social support in times of hardship. During the fieldwork, a female participant who was evicted from her home was given shelter by another female participant, and they morally and financially supported each other throughout the program. Fellow participants at times also seek to assist each other in studying, finding employment or accessing services. Fatima, a female participant in her 20s, regularly collected job advertisements and shared them with the group and with staff. Tutors were very supportive of these efforts and routinely followed up on these ads, especially when participants were enthusiastic about them. Social relationships established during the program can thus provide and facilitate information for the individuals involved, including useful information about opportunities and choices otherwise not available to them.

In some cases the established peer relationships transcend the duration of the program. For others, however, the bonding social capital facilitated by the program can become redundant once they complete the program, especially for those who already enjoy strong and supportive friendships outside of the program. Sylvia, a former SSP participant in her 20s, says that she occasionally runs into other former program participants in her new job as a steward at football club Feyenoord but that she doesn't really socialize with them anymore: "You run into each other once in a while and you have a chat, like, 'how are you and what are you doing now?' But real contact, no, not anymore. But of course I talk about [SSP] with my girlfriends outside of the program." In a similar vein, Fatima explains that although she keeps in contact with a few people from the program, she "didn't really have much time" to maintain these relationships due to her demanding job which includes regular night shifts. However, Sylvia and Fatima both value the contribution of bridging networks in SSP to their knowledge of and encounters with people with different backgrounds, even though these encounters do not necessarily transcend the duration of the program. Sylvia notes:

> I already had a lot of knowledge about other cultures before I came [to SSP]. I live among many Antillean, Moroccan and Turkish youth. But here it's different . . . you really live with each other at that moment. So you come to respect each other more and you start asking each other questions. Definitely. I mean, we're all people from the street really. So you ask them "how did you get here?" You create more time for each other. By knowing how they ended up on the street, you can help your friends to prevent that they end up on the street in the same way. So you can help others [within and outside of SSP] to keep going to school or to continue their education.

Sylvia's experience indicates how SSP contributes to the objective of enhancing social interaction among youths with different backgrounds.

Fatima's experience also highlights some of the exclusionary mechanisms at work in the development of bonding social capital. She describes how there was a young male in her group who had a tendency to "force his opinion on to other people." After a while people became fed up with him, especially because he was seen to "demand respect without giving it to others." Fatima and other participants refused to interact with the young man any further, which led to his informal exclusion from the group. Similar minor interpersonal conflicts are reported in the Vencer study. Such conflicts are recognized by some Vencer and SSP staff as being part of life and potentially providing valuable learning moments, as noted in Chapter 3.

Bonding Social Capital in and through Football: The Somali Refugee Experience

Organized sport has been identified by policymakers as a key sphere for social "mixing" between different ethnic groups due to its relatively low threshold for entry and participation (Krouwel et al. 2006; Gasparini and Vieille-Marchiset 2008). This argument tends to be premised on the belief that ethnically diverse sports clubs stimulate the social integration of minority ethnic groups in ways that ethno-specific sport associations do not. Pooley (1976), for example, argues that in general the policies and practices of ethnic football clubs inhibit the assimilation of their members. What is absent in this view is the strong preference among several people with a refugee background to be among those with whom social interaction is uncomplicated, symmetrical and meaningful. Bonding relationships with one's own ethnic community are important for a sense of belonging, for learning from others "like me" and for accessing the social and material resources shared among extended family and ethnic networks (Loizos 2000). Former MG coach Mohamed expresses the significance of this as follows:

> People don't ask the question why some Somalis prefer to play in their own soccer clubs. They think it's a sign of arrogance, of deliberate exclusion. But it's not. There are many reasons. The mother doesn't speak much English so she prefers to talk to other Somali women at soccer. Easier interaction. High level of trust as well: they don't really know what happens to their kids when they drop them off at another club, whereas here they know other people will look after them. Also more flexible: they adapt playing and training times to school times, mosque, Ramadan, et cetera. Normal clubs don't do that. Playing fees are also an issue. They cannot afford to pay $400 per child. [Melbourne Giants] is much cheaper, and has easy access as they live near.

Participation in MG allows Somali refugees to temporarily escape social spheres with tense relations (e.g. the neighborhood, school and workplace) and to be among members with similar cultural backgrounds (Krouwel et al. 2006; CMY 2007). Many young people in the study express their desire to create a safe and relaxed environment to come together to play football, to socialize with other Somalis or to just "hang out" (see also Amara et al. 2004). They also use the club as an arena to strengthen already-established friendships. Many of them have good friends or sometimes even best friends among their teammates, and in many cases they entered MG as a result of information provided by friends who were already involved in the club (cf. Walseth 2008). In other words, bonding social capital is not merely a potential *outcome* of sports activities; it is also put to work to negotiate *access* to sports clubs.

Participation in MG is seen to contribute to the rebuilding of strong social relationships that have been eroded or disrupted by displacement. Abdi, a club official in his 20s, observes:

> The club gives players and their families an environment where they can come together and develop friendships. Even though many of them live in the same area, they don't always know each other. It gives them a socializing environment where they can chitchat and come out of their houses and into the public area. Some of them are really good friends now, not only those who play but also those who just come and watch. So it can provide that environment where they make a stronger bond of friendship. It also contributes to a general sense of respect, where people respect each other more. I have gotten to know many families through my involvement in the club. I feel that families are friendlier with me than in the past, even though I knew some of them already. When I walk past them they smile and give me a handshake, and we talk about the game as well. So it gives us something to talk about outside the game as well. It develops trust. They know me and I know them. And they trust me more, because before I was a kind of stranger to them. It develops trust also between the parents, coaches and managers, and other members. And between the kids at school.

Abdi is one of the young males who spend significant time at the club. For them, the club has an important function that transcends the role of a traditional sports club. Social encounters in sport are important to them, arguably even more important that the sports activity itself. They frequently consult one another on work and family issues. Members also regularly help each other out, for instance in completing or translating official forms, driving their children to and from matches or to and from school, moving items or providing information regarding jobs or courses (cf. Verweel et al. 2005). Abdifatih, an engineer in his 30s, explains that "soccer is quite unique" in this regard because "outside of the Friday prayer or a wedding, you hardly see anyone, only your closest friends and family." Abdifatih further indicates that the type of leadership role he fulfils in MG is not available to him at the football clubs where he and his best friend used to play:

> [Ahmed] and I used to play for [Club B]. . . . We left two years ago because we have our own club [MG] which is a role model to us and we wanted to coach the junior teams. To me, playing for [the previous club] they needed me as a player, but to actually develop the club or promote the club they didn't need me. But [MG] actually needs me because we are the same people and together we're trying to promote the club and our own culture. We want to be able to say that we own the club, that we own our own club. But there we were just participants.

It's also harder to get into leadership roles at other clubs. Compared to even [Club C] where I used to play, these clubs are owned by a family. If you're not one of them and you are a good player, they may want you to play for them. But they will do nothing for you administratively. At the end of the day when I won trophies at [Club B] and [Club C] I didn't really feel that I won something. But last year with [MG] I actually felt that I won something, because it's my own club.

This comment reveals not only Abdifatih's pride in his Somali heritage and his desire to invest time and effort into building MG, but also the subtle processes of social exclusion that can occur in mixed sports clubs (Verweel et al. 2005), in this case in relation to access to high-status positions within the club. His experience indicates that social mixing in the sports context does not automatically lead to full acceptance or integration into club life. Abdifatih feels that he did not fully fit into the club environment of the other clubs he played for. In contrast, sport participation among those with similar cultural backgrounds requires the establishment and maintenance of their own organizational structures, which tends to provide greater opportunities for motivated individuals like Abdifatih to assume a leadership role in the club.

Another important element in the development of bonding social capital at MG is social interaction across clan lines. Clanship acts as an identity marker for many Somali refugees in Melbourne (McMichael and Ahmed 2003; Omar 2009; cf. Bjork 2007). Although many areas are now mixed in clan terms, the fractured nature of the Somali communal identity is indicated by phrases such as "there is not one Somali community, but at least eight," and "the Somali community of that clan." For many Somalis, especially the older generations, the crisis in Somalia has been experienced in terms of clan conflict and division, and the crisis "at home" continues to affect the social identities of Somalis in the diaspora (Griffiths 2002: 107). Clan divisions have been particularly salient at the level of community organizations that compete for power and funding, fuelling the fragmentation of the Somali associational landscape (Hopkins 2006). Several interviewees note, however, that bonding in the sports context has overcome some of the clan-based cleavages which were endemic in Somalia. Thus, involvement in sport is seen by many as playing a significant part in enhancing the internal cohesion of the Somali community in Melbourne. Abdisalam, a community organizer in his 40s, argues that:

Sport, especially soccer, has no clan borders. In that sense it can strengthen the community bonds, the community relationships. It can, in a way, minimize clan tension. Most other activities are linked in one way or another to clan divisions and clan lines, but when it comes to sport, sport is actually above clan lines. It helps to integrate the community itself among its members.

MG player Abu Hassan observes that his club "has moved on from the clan politics of the 1990s, and other people see this. It is a model for community integration. It brings different clans and to some extent different Muslim communities together." However, clan politics do appear to have affected MG in its early days, as Abdifatih recalls: "One person came with the ideology that one club should only represent one people. But if you run a club like that it won't exist for long." His friend Ahmed confirms that, today, people's motive for participating in the club "has nothing to do with clans or tribes." He asserts:

> We are all different clans, different tribes. But for us, at the end of the day, we're there for the club and to look after the kids. That's the main reason behind it. And they realize that even though there are so many different communities, we have them on the right track. And hopefully for the future we can set the right example for the Somali community: to be only one.

Sport, Social Networks and Community Engagement in Northwest Victoria

The aim of bringing local residents closer together through sport also features prominently in the NCFL despite its fundamentally different social setting from MG. Participation in sports clubs in rural Victoria, as a player and/or volunteer, is predominantly motivated by the fun, friendship and social aspects associated with sports activities and club membership. Research participants describe sports clubs as important hubs for social interaction, providing a shared focus and outlet and a collective identity (see also Tonts 2005a; Atherley 2006). Football club president Steve expresses this sentiment as follows:

> It brings everyone together. It's a meeting place I suppose for the weekend and other than that you've really gotta come up with an excuse to get together with your mates or whatever. If you get down to the footy, well everyone's there: the parents, the grandparents. All ages go down so you've got the whole community involved pretty much.

Sports clubs in the NCFL play a vital role in maintaining and improving community facilities, such as leisure centers and social club rooms. For many residents, the significance of sport as a site for social interaction has increased in recent decades as a result of mostly negatively perceived structural changes. Several residents observe that some of the historically dominant forms of associational engagement, such as church groups, have diminished and that few major forums for social interaction remain, with sports clubs occupying a prominent place in the towns' social and cultural landscape.

Given the relatively small population sizes of the rural towns in the NCFL, it is perhaps unsurprising that many residents indicate that they already knew most club members prior to joining a sports club, for example through family, school or work. Involvement in sports clubs allows them to get to know others better and to bond already-established relationships. This social aspect of sport, of course, does not interest everyone to the same degree. Several residents spend a large amount of their leisure time at local sports clubs, but others are more pragmatic in their sport participation. For example, new resident Peter reports: "My two sons play junior football. They enjoy football and have made new friends through their involvement. I take them to the games, but I do not stay around all day. I usually go home straight after the game to do things around the house."

For farmers who live in relatively remote areas, Saturday afternoon sport is quite literally one of the few forms of face-to-face interaction available to them. Farmer Robert comments:

> I live on a farm 12 kilometres from the town, quite isolated. If it wasn't for sport, I would probably stay on the farm to fix a fence or something. At footy I talk to other farmers about sport and farming issues, for example new methods, machinery and funding options. It is also a great way to meet other types of people, like teachers and doctors.

In times of drought and economic hardship, involvement in sport is believed to contribute to a sense of belonging. Alicia, a tennis player in her 20s, argues that sport "gives the opportunity for people to share their thoughts and find out what other people are thinking and feeling and experiencing which then helps them think, 'okay, I'm not experiencing this on my own'." This view is shared by Trevor, a local farmer who states: "For me it is a switch-off cue, to get away from the farm and a sort of outlet, fun, to release tensions and stress. To share experiences or just to crack jokes. It gets you out of your isolation." Comments of this kind are fairly common and underline the belief of many local residents that "sport gets people out of their homes," and that it allows them to "meet people you wouldn't meet in a social context otherwise."

The creation and maintenance of social relationships in and through sport can have tangible benefits. Local sports clubs serve as an arena for social support and information exchange. Hockey player Alison argues that social interaction in this arena constitutes a major source of information, for example "farmers sharing information about what herbicide they are using or what might be problems on their farms." She asserts that "any social networking opportunity provides those opportunities for information exchange, so the more varied activities that people are involved in, whether it be sport or other things, they'll be mixing with different people and accessing different information." Geoff, who is the father of two netball players and a health care professional, also regards information exchange as a key aspect of participation in sport:

> The commonality of experience is the important thing I think. Just knowing that in all sorts of areas whether it's to do with your health you know you'll meet people within your footy club setting who've done this, done that, might have had prostate exam or those sorts of things. You learn that from other blokes. So it's just that central function of a club, yeah.

Other types of tangible outcomes include financial and emotional support for struggling residents. Local football clubs regularly organize fundraising campaigns, the proceeds of which may benefit individual residents who experience, for example, house fires or expensive surgeries. Some residents stress that it is "good for business" to be involved with a football club. Alex, a tradesman in his 30s who is a volunteer at an Australian football club, argues that some of his football-related contacts have resulted in new business opportunities, such as being contracted to work at the farm of another club member. The owner of a local hotel notes that many of his customers visit his hotel because of his status as a football league representative. Access to job opportunities, however, is not restricted to individual towns based on bonding social capital but extends to other towns in the region as a consequence of loose sport-based ties among people in different towns. For example, Alex claims to have acquired several short-term plumbing and trading jobs in other towns in northwest Victoria by virtue of the bridging social capital accumulated through his involvement in the NCFL. In other words, on such occasions he has successfully converted his social capital and cultural capital (i.e. his reputation as a qualified tradesman) into economic capital. It is to the creation and conversion of bridging social capital that I will now turn.

BUILDING BRIDGES

The literature on social capital has documented how bridging ties tend to be more important for social leverage than bonding ties to kin and close friends, which are generally more suited to get by (Briggs 1998; Putnam 2000). The above analysis shows that bonding social capital also constitutes a valuable resource that operates through the four social mechanisms identified by Lin (2001): information, influence, social credentials and reinforcement. As Alex's experience with the NCFL indicates, these social mechanisms can also lie at the basis of the accumulation and conversion of bridging social capital. In his case, the most relevant bridging networks created and accessed in and through sport are those that bring residents of different rural towns into increased contact with each other. Alex's experience is quite typical in this regard.

The development of inter-community relations in the NCFL is particularly relevant in the context of the local government amalgamations in northwest Victoria during the mid 1990s. Alexander (2008: 10) argues that these reforms have generally failed to establish inter-communal bonds of trust and reciprocity based on the new administrative boundaries, which points to "the continuing difficulties posed by small-town parochialism and inter-community competition over scarce resources in the post-amalgamation era." Despite the persistence of generally good-natured rivalries among sports clubs representing different towns, however, the NCFL is seen by virtually all research participants to enhance inter-community bonds of trust and reciprocity, indicative of which is the close and constructive collaboration among NCFL officials representing different towns and clubs. For example, Grant, a former Australian football club president in his 60s, argues: "At the political level there is a lot of competition and jealousy over who gets what but in sport people work together more. Sport is different in that sense. People co-operate to get things done collectively but can still go off and do their own thing as well."

The significance of sporting competitions in the creation of bridging social capital in northwest Victoria is enhanced by the particularities of the local sports landscape. The NCFL incorporates three sports, and match days feature a large number of matches involving people in different age groups (from juniors to seniors) in male and female sports teams. This set-up stimulates interaction between different generations and between men and women, diverging to some extent from the more traditional view of rural sport as heavily male-dominated (Dempsey 1990, 1992). For example, Australian football coach Jim argues:

> One of the great strengths of the [NCFL] is that it is a three-sport league. It is hockey, netball and football. That provides a family environment. Tomorrow morning at eight my family will leave and we will go up to [Town B] because we are playing at [Town B] and the whole family will be involved in that. My wife will be the time keeper. I will run around as the secretary. [My son] will play football and then hockey and then later on in the day we will come home. So it is a family day.

The particular configuration of the league is principally a consequence of adaptive strategies of sports clubs to cope with wider social changes, notably population decline, with some sports teams struggling to field the required number of players, especially in the lower-level teams. Teams from different towns may therefore borrow each other's players, thereby generating more multiplex sporting relations. Consider the following observation by Claire, a hockey volunteer in her 50s:

One team has too many junior players, so they are on a roster system and each week some players have to play for the opposing team, but not just the worse players. They see this as a fair play system, and it brings kids into contact with each other and as a consequence their parents as well.

Claire's remark suggests that the bridging social capital that is facilitated by the particular configuration of the NCFL is a welcome by-product, rather than an outcome that is explicitly sought by members of the sports clubs. Nevertheless, the social ties created in this context are seen by many research participants as an opportunity to break down social boundaries. Simone's experience might be seen as typical of this sentiment. Simone, a netball player in her 20s, feels that "the league is important in that sense because you're not limited to your own town anymore. Actually it physically gives you a reason to go to other towns to see what things are like and what other people are like." Simone further describes how she and her team mates use away matches as an opportunity to make it a night out with players of the opposing team, as well as pointing out that:

It's a pretty important part of that social networking of different towns in the same locality. . . . Sport is one of the only . . . well pretty much the only avenue for exploring relations in other towns. I've still got friends I used to play against and coming down to Melbourne for uni[versity] I recognized some people I used to see playing footy and you'd say "You must be from [town A], and I'm from [town B], I recognize you from seeing you playing footy." And that immediately gives you something to work with. I've met loads of people that way too.

The belief that sports clubs in northwest Victoria facilitate social connections among people from different walks of life is also voiced in relation to social class. Many interviewees note the increased blurring of class boundaries in the small towns being studied due in part to the changed demographics of the region (see Chapter 2). In addition, local residents place considerable emphasis on the way in which sport is able to transcend class divisions, as reflected in phrases like "at the footy social barriers don't exist." Research participants claim that social networks created in the NCFL can connect different social groups that might otherwise remain disconnected from one another (cf. Tonts 2005a; Townsend et al. 2002). Joseph, the vice-president of a football club in the NCFL, argues that in everyday life:

Some people wouldn't have anything to do with them [people with a different social background] at all. They wouldn't talk to them. They would probably never see them. But ah, at the football club there's no avoiding them, there's no avoiding the different group. So when clubs form, they are a melting pot, there's really no way around it. Which is a great thing.

According to Joseph, there is "still a class difference but when you go to the footy everyone's a person. There's no room for real egos because you get brought down really quickly." In a similar vein, local journalist Anthony states that "when you get to the football it doesn't matter whether you're a doctor, a lawyer, a newspaper owner, or an apprentice. You're all in there together, you're just . . . you can relax and just enjoy the day." The fact that sports activities in the NCFL are relatively inexpensive is seen by several residents as a contributing factor to cross-class interactions in the sports context. For example, netball player Renee argues: "There are other people from completely different backgrounds and financial situations that can participate in sport very, very cheaply. That's one thing in the country [compared to the city]: sport is so cheap to participate in."

The extent of cross-class bridging networks in sport and their transferability to non-sports contexts should, however, not be overestimated. Even though the NCFL is generally thought of as egalitarian and inclusive (see Chapter 3), there appear to be social divisions along class, gender and status lines, as well as in relation to the length of residence (cf. Dempsey 1990; Tonts 2005a). Some residents note that people in certain occupations, such as teachers, pharmacists, doctors or bank managers, are relatively likely to hold high-status positions in local sports clubs, reportedly owing to their adequate skills (i.e. cultural capital). Simone's experience is instructive in this regard. She explains that although sport certainly plays a major role in fostering cross-class relationships, "it's not always based on explicitly positive reasons." At her own football/netball club, she experiences this as follows:

> You get people together from different socio-economic situations because someone is very talented rather than going out to include people. You're not saying "Come on everyone, come down to the club and have a kick and we'll put you in the team because you tried really hard." It's "If you're talented and poor we'll put you in the team." . . . So it does get lots of different people from different walks of life together and from different social circles but you might find that the same people are always in positions of power in the club.

She adds that social status in sports clubs is often associated with traditional family and friend relationships: "You find that the same families are friends across generations and generations . . . and that permeates everywhere. So sometimes it's hard to break down barriers and be involved. But once you're involved and you make a positive contribution you're generally recognized for it."

Football, Social Mixing and Inter-ethnic Relations

Simone's comments regarding the relatively closed nature of certain sports clubs resonate with the sporting experiences of Abdifatih (an MG interviewee) discussed earlier in this chapter. Both point to the existence of insider–outsider dynamics in their sports clubs. These dynamics are reminiscent of the established-outsider figurations described by Elias and Scotson (1965), with members of the established group being more highly integrated and in that sense more powerful than outsiders in demarcating in-group boundaries. For Somali refugees like Abdifatih, the nature and the significance of bridging networks within and outside of sport are nevertheless qualitatively different than for white, Anglo-Australian females like Simone.

The narratives of Abdifatih and other young males associated with MG illustrate how being part of the club can contribute to the development of bridging social capital. The young men bridge networks across various ethnic groups, which gives them the opportunity to learn more about the cultural traditions of other minority ethnic groups (Walseth 2008: 11). Although members of MG and the related clubs included in the multi-sided ethnography are predominantly first- or second-generation immigrants from Somalia, the clubs also have a small number of members with other backgrounds, notably from other African countries such as Eritrea, Kenya, Sierra Leone and Ghana. Abdullahi, who plays for one of the other clubs in the MG study, argues that social interaction with members from other African communities is "not a problem" because "they feel comfortable here." He recalls that when he was a student he recruited other African players for his team "because it used to make me more comfortable, because we're the same color and everything. Most clubs can call you any name they like, like 'chocolate'. You want another person to say, like, 'I'm chocolate too'."

Abdullahi's remarks point to the role of race and skin color as an identity marker in structuring the social relationships between young Australian Somalis and other social groups. For some interviewees, shared religious identity and attendant values are also significant identity markers that inform their bridging efforts. In this context, Abdifatih argues that a shared Muslim identity binds most people at the club, including the handful of Saudis, Lebanese, Iranian and Afghani immigrants who visit the club at times: "Where else do you see Muslims from different backgrounds get together? Only at the mosque and at soccer. Soccer is a very prominent activity for this type of interaction." Thus, a focus on similarities can be an important aspect of bridging, just as it is of bonding. Bridging networks are also created with Muslim players on opposing teams. For example, MG player Yusuf notes: "I find a lot of times when we play against, say, Turkish teams, we have a lot more in common . . . Islamic way and all that, different ways of greeting, like 'G'day how are you.' That makes it easier [to socialize with them] because you have something in common." In most cases, however, these social connections are relatively weak and confined to match days.

A recurrent theme in MG members' understanding of bridging and bonding opportunities in sport is the historical association between migrant communities and the game of football (soccer) in Australia. Football in Australia has long been distinguished by its popularity among sections of migrant minorities. Many football clubs were founded and organized along non-Anglo lines, and they remain a vital power base for the game (Mosely 1997; Hallinan et al. 2007). Football clubs and teams preceded formal community organizations for at least some migrant groups (Hay 2009: 824). This historical association is readily observable in the league in which MG competes, where most clubs are closely aligned with a particular ethnic group, notably the Greek, Italian, Turkish, Iraqi, Macedonian, Polish and Croatian communities. Ethnic divisions of this kind do not preclude the development of bridging social capital; indeed, some young Somalis have actually played for clubs associated with other ethnic groups and invested in social relationships at these clubs. Nevertheless, most of the inter-ethnic ties created in such instances are restricted to the sports activity itself (cf. Elling 2004). For example, a young woman associated with MG argues: "There aren't many opportunities created between the players. It is very much limited to when they play. It would be good to have more interaction with other teams."

In the MG case, few bridges are created across the boundaries of immigrants/non-immigrants. The club does not have any players without an immigrant background due in part to the particular demographics of the neighborhood, which has a strong concentration of new migrant groups, mainly from Africa. Although the club is officially "open to everyone," including non-immigrants, in practice club representatives are primarily concerned with the day-to-day running of the club and to ensure its role as a community hub for Somali families. However, some research participants express their desire to create bridges across the boundaries of immigrants/non-immigrants in order to learn more about each other's cultures and customs and to tap into their knowledge. Mohamed, a former player and coach in his mid 20s, argues: "It's very important to have Anglo Saxon people here. They would not only come on board as members, they already probably have . . . they know how to run a club, or they've already been part of a club." Mohamed uses other ethnically-based football clubs in Melbourne as an example: "But obviously I think even if you go back to other generations that were before us, the Greeks and people with different identities, they would have had clubs that were just based on Italians and Greeks. We are just going through that phase now, but down the track I don't see the reason why it shouldn't open up, and it will open up." A similar sentiment is voiced by Samatar, who serves as club secretary:

> I'd like to see a mixed club in the future, a club which consists not only of Somalis or Eritreans or Ethiopians, for example, but also other ethnicities such as Indigenous people if any of them live around here. Indigenous Australians, European Australians, and other people as well. So we get a diversity; a multicultural team. At the moment the players

are mainly Somali, which is due to the structure of the team because it hasn't been well structured in the past. It's kind of hard to see a fully mixed team due to the demographics of the area we live in. It's mainly African background in this area. But the club is not restricted to any particular group and we would really like to get everyone on board and be part of the team. But at the moment it's mainly Somali and Eritrean demographically in this area.

The accounts of Samatar and Mohamed are indicative of the resettlement experiences of the younger generation of Somalia-born residents in Melbourne. Many of them regard older community members as being "out of touch" and too concerned with maintaining traditional norms and values. Indeed, several Somali parents and community leaders worry that the youth are forgetting their culture, religion and language (cf. Bigelow 2008; Omar 2009). Mohamed articulates this debate as follows:

The reality is that the parents need to know where they're at, and Australia is a different identity, you know. You need to create a different identity, but that doesn't mean you have to leave your old identity behind. There is a generational gap you know, our parents are very conservative. . . . I respect my parent's culture, I take some aspects out of it, I go into the Australian aspects, I take the best out of that, and I create my own culture, my own identity, you know, African-Australian. And that's what's going to help me to understand both sides. A lot of people say "why do Africans take a long time to integrate?" Well the reason is because of language barrier. Not understanding the culture itself. But the younger generation, we are integrating. Most of us are actually assimilating because we understand both sides . . . It will take time, but when I have kids, when I have my own kids hopefully in the future, I think the gap will close.

Mohamed continues:

For our parents to say that we and the kids who are born in Australia [have] to have the same cultural background, the same understanding as the parents who came from Mogadishu, that's a no-go zone. . . . I support the young person yes to be on the right path, to be a good citizen of this country, but also to pick up the goodness. There's a lot of good aspects of Australian culture, and why not pick up that and move forward, because we need to move forward, not stay static. Status quo is not something that's going to work for the younger generation.

Some of the older Somalis interviewed actually support this standpoint. Saeed, a teacher in his 40s, expresses his concern that the Somali community in Melbourne is inward-looking. He worries that this might affect the opportunities and world views of young Somalis growing up in Melbourne. In his view, the youth tend to socialize in a rather closed environment, which limits their opportunities to get to know the "outside world": "We need to interact more with other groups because this will increase our integration and increase our and our children's knowledge of the world outside our community. That's what settlement means, not just to stick to your own little world."

Although several participants in the MG study indicate that opportunities for bonding and bridging in the football context play a role in the process of cultural negotiation, the data show that bridging encounters in sport are not always peaceful exchanges. Sporting encounters between Somalis and other ethnic groups can magnify inter-group differences and tensions. Miscommunication, distrust, verbal abuse and discrimination can even lead to aggressive or violent behavior in a context of direct sporting confrontation (Krouwel et al. 2006; Veldboer et al. 2007b; Verweel et al. 2005). Fadumo, a local resident in her 20s, gives several examples of how verbal abuse and discrimination have the potential to escalate into inter-group conflict on the football pitch. She says that although she has witnessed some fights, she is actually surprised that the Somalis, "as the hot-headed people that they are," are generally "very respectful of the rules":

> There have been some very, very horrible examples [of racism]. For example there was one time when the staff of the opposing team accused our players of . . . [she starts to laugh] . . . they said that our children and women were in fear and in danger. Just because there were all these black boys. Imagine that, what an exaggeration. It sounds like something out of the 1800s or something. And the police came, they were called. The boys just sat on the ground because the referee told them too. Yeah, incidents like that have occurred.

On one occasion, verbal abuse did degenerate into a major brawl between players and spectators of MG and the opposing team, which consisted predominantly of Polish immigrants. The fight followed a controversial refereeing decision, to which a few supporters reacted by running on to the ground. The incident received significant coverage in the local media, and the team was suspended for the rest of the season. Those implicated in the incident reject the media's attribution of blame, which portrays the Somalis as the sole culprits. Abdi, who was a coach at MG at the time of the incident, says: "We know some kids have got bad temper and we were trying to work around them, but there are also other clubs who are throwing racism comments and sometimes kids just can't handle that."

Abdi further suggests that discrimination can have a significant impact on well-being, and he is not alone in this regard. Some players report that they are regularly subjected to racial abuse or discriminatory remarks relating to their skin color or their cultural or religious background. The focus group with MG coaches also addresses the issue of racism. The question "Have you ever personally experienced discrimination or racism in football?" elicited the following volley of responses:

Roble: It's common.
Yusuf: Yes, absolutely!
Asad: That's normal, very common. . . . They would call you all names during the game. On one occasion after the game he said sorry, and he said that he tried to put me off my game.
Roble: But it's hard to tell, you know.
Asad: Absolutely, it's hard to tell whether they mean it or not.
Yusuf: We were playing with [our previous team] against an Italian team. They had a very good player, a striker, and our coach asked me to man-mark him the whole game. So I did. The whole crowd turned against me, calling me a monkey and shouting 'uh, uh.' [Laughter erupts among the group]

However, other Somalis who have played for MG argue that, in their personal experience, overt biological racism is relatively uncommon. Direct observations at matches of MG indicate that subtle forms of discrimination occur more frequently than overt racism, notably through reference to the perceived insurmountability of cultural differences. This type of discrimination, which has been termed "cultural racism" (Balibar and Wallerstein 1991), does not postulate the superiority of certain groups of people in relation to others but rather the incompatibility of lifestyles and traditions. For example, during a home match of one of MG's junior teams, a female supporter of the visiting team accused the players of rough conduct and the referee of bias (in the absence of an official referee, the MG coach acted as referee). She commented that rough conduct and referee bias were "un-Australian" and added: "We're not in Africa here, but in Australia. Get used to it." Cultural racism of this type has its ideological basis in xenophobia (Balibar and Wallerstein 1991) and involves processes of social inclusion and exclusion based on perceived cultural differences.

Participants in the MG study generally acknowledge the existence of cultural racism. However, they seem to deal with it in very different ways. While some try to ignore it or "laugh it off", others advocate a more proactive approach. Mohamed is typical of the latter category in taking a strong sense against victimhood:

And, you know, there's some sort of discrimination. But then discrimination exists within the wider community, you know? People kind of take it lightly to discriminate against anyone. But then if you sit back and say "I am discriminated against, I can't do nothing about it," then that's when people discriminate against you because you're just too lazy to do something about it. If people discriminate against you, go up to them, invite them, you know. I said to them "why don't we just hold one day called African day, you know we put posters around the whole of [the neighborhood], everywhere, everyone is invited, you're all welcome, and we showcase our culture, we showcase who we are to the Australian population."

Exploring the City: Bridging Social Boundaries in Vencer

As discussed in Chapter 2, stigmatization and perceived cultural difference are also prominent themes in favela residents' experiences of social and economic disadvantage. The Vencer program seeks to make a modest contribution to breaking down social boundaries by investing in bridging networks that facilitate meaningful interaction between young favelados and residents of other neighborhoods in Rio de Janeiro. The aim of this investment is to give participants the opportunity to broaden their horizons and to familiarize themselves with life outside of their own immediate surroundings. ICT teacher Rafael argues:

> When a young person leaves the community they broaden their horizon. The age group of the Vencer program is very much a prisoner of their communities, their group is their community. . . . They don't explore the city a lot. When they have access to the labor market they succeed in seeing other possibilities; when they leave to do a course they have to position themselves in a different manner so they are in a different space.

Isabel, a mentor in her 30s, emphasizes the impact of this on young people's habitus and self-image:

> Because they do everything here in the community, they don't know how to behave themselves outside of it. They have fear of the outside and feel that they are different. So the issue of taking them to those other spaces is very important because it enables them to see that the world is not just inside their own communities.

In other words, many young people seem to feel "out of place" outside of their own local communities. These comments resonate with the literature on social exclusion in Rio de Janeiro's favelas, which shows that young people tend to "circulate in a restricted area, segregated in their neighborhoods, not necessarily exercising their social citizenship rights such as the benefit of using the city in which they live" (Castro and Abramovay 2002: 157).

Vencer stimulates participants to engage more fully in urban social life, for example though volunteering, internships, community work and leisure activities. According to several participants, these activities play an important role in building bridging social capital. Former participant Lucia reports that she discovered many new aspects of city life during the program:

> We went to the main street [*pista*], we went to the museum in the city center, the cinema, theatre. We visited a farm. I used to look differently at the people in the city, and with these trips we became equalized. The difference between the world inside the community and the main street disappeared. You get to know new places. You know, we live here and we don't know . . . we remain prisoners in our little world. It's great to know places and people on the outside, to go to the *rua* [street].

Lucia's reference to the perceived difference between her own community (the favela) and the *rua* (or *pista*) is more commonly expressed in terms of the distinction between the *morro* (literally hill, i.e. hillside favela) and the *asfalto* (asphalt), a slang term often used to indicate the "legitimate" city, that is, the non-favela areas that surround favelas. This phrase has persisted despite the almost universal paving of favela entrances and main passageways through the Favela Bairro upgrading program (Perlman 2005: 185). For example, João, a former Vencer participant in his late teens, argues:

> Many people who live here on the *asfalto* don't know our community very well. Sometimes they have the wrong impression of what goes on. They think it's only gunfire, violence and drugs. But people on the *morro* have dreams and are thinking about how to realize those dreams. They want friendships and the same opportunities.

The term *asfalto* (or *rua*) is used not only in the sense of public life but also assumes the significance of a "complementary opposition" to the *morro* (Piccolo 2006: 134). It denotes a relationship between "home" (*a casa*) and "the street" (*a rua*). The latter is the site of the unknown, of danger, of adventures. The former, on the other hand, is a space of protection, of personal relationships, and of known hierarchies (e.g. DaMatta 1985). The significance of this construction of "home" was noted earlier in the discussion of Vencer's contribution to the development of bonding social capital. It is also reflected in comments such as "living in the *rua* wouldn't be that great, there is nobody to talk with" and "it's great because here [in the favela] you don't pay for water, you don't pay for electricity." Former participant Maria describes her mother's perception of *a rua* as follows:

> My mother was always very careful: "My daughter cannot go out, there is violence there." And she raised me that way. She talked about how dangerous it was. . . . When I obtained the internship she called me all the time "Hey, did you arrive safely?" I've only started to go places on my own since I began my job there [outside of the favela]. Before it was

only from school to home, and from home to school. Even going to my grandmother's house she would accompany me.

Like Lucia, Maria and João, Fernanda (aged 26) regards the interaction with people with different social backgrounds as a very positive experience that is instrumental in broadening her social networks. After she graduated from Vencer, members of staff encouraged Fernanda to enrol in a Spanish language course and to apply for a scholarship. She admits that when she first entered the course she felt very much "out of place." However, having persisted, she now values the bridging social capital that her enrolment in the language school facilitates:

> In the school everyone is from the upper class, so when you go and mingle with people from there you have fear. The first time I was dying of fear! When I saw them all with car keys in their hands I said to myself "what am I doing here?" One girl is a journalist, another studies law. They are studying Spanish because they want to travel, or because they already speak English or Italian and now want to learn Spanish. They have been to places like Florida, to the US, whereas I have never been anywhere. But I do well with my group. I love them and I am not embarrassed to say that I am a scholarship student. . . . You have to go out there, not just sit in the corner and not speak because you are a scholarship student. I have my difficulties, they help me. They have their difficulties too. . . . They send me text messages. I only see them on Saturdays but I am already a friend to them. So that's really enjoyable. It's not class-based, like, because I live here and they live in [an upper-class area] I cannot be in contact with them. But if you enter with the belief that they are not going to accept you, that's exactly what will happen.

The stories of young people like Fernanda indicate that Vencer contributes to the development of bridging social capital for individual participants, especially for those who are motivated and confident to explore public spaces outside of their local community, that is, to explore *a rua*. At a deeper level, this bridging social capital has the potential to make a modest contribution to the longer-term process of transforming the relationship between favela and *asfalto*, that is, to the renewed appropriation of the urban space on the part of those who have been socially excluded from this space. This finding constitutes an important corrective to the view that the information exchanged in urban sports associations is "generally irrelevant to the population's adaptation to the city" (Berlinck and Hogan 1979: 178). The Vencer data show that if such information exchanges take place within the context of a well-designed sport-for-development program that facilitates the creation and maintenance of bridging networks, they can make a significant contribution to the bridging social capital of disadvantaged young people and to their social inclusion and sense of belonging more generally. This finding is explored further in Chapter 5 in relation to the linking potential of the Vencer program.

GENDER INEQUALITIES IN SPORT

Although social capital can cross social boundaries, it is also boundary creating and maintaining and therefore exclusionary and laden with power. Social capital as a basis for social exclusion manifests itself in multiple ways. The above analysis, then, provides insight into the processes of boundary formation and maintenance in relation to social markers such as race, ethnicity, class, social status and place of residence. Chapter 3 also gives evidence of the experience of exclusion that may emanate from competition and talent/ability barriers in sport.

The data from the NCFL and MG case studies highlight another dimension of social capital as boundary creating and maintaining: gender inequalities in sport. Organized sport in rural (and urban) Australia has long been identified as a site of "masculine power and privilege" (Alston 2005a: 142). Dempsey (1992) notes the significance of rural sports clubs as a forum for male bonding and the construction and reproduction of masculinities, with sport arguably providing the strongest marker of masculinity in rural towns. Gender relations permeate sports clubs in northwest Victoria in several ways. Some of the interviewees comment on the pressures associated with the cultural perceptions of different sports, with Australian football being regarded as a "man's game" compared with games such as hockey. Netball, on the other hand, is traditionally viewed as the most prestigious and culturally appropriate game for women, with talented players often having substantially more social status than female hockey players. However, although these cultural images persist to some degree, they have been subject to considerable change in recent decades. There are now more men who play hockey in all-male or mixed hockey teams in the NCFL, with hockey providing new participation opportunities for men who dislike Australian football and/or its culture. Indeed, some parents discourage their sons from playing football due to fear of injuries. A number of reserve football players also play hockey, which at times has concerned football teams for fear of decreased interest in their game.

Gender relations in the NCFL can also be analyzed in terms of the division of labor in sports clubs, which may lead some female club members to feel (partially) excluded. Women are often responsible for activities such as preparing food, cooking and cleaning. They tend to run the catering, bar and kitchen, with very few men taking on these tasks. As netball player Claire notes: "Women are really involved in football but in traditional ways. It wouldn't work without women because who is going to run the canteen and who would do the catering and who would clean up after?"

This division of labor can contribute to a spatial division within clubs, with women and men regularly occupying different parts of a sports venue, which in turn may limit their interaction with players and spectators of opposing teams (Tonts 2005a). However, also in this respect gender relations are subject to a variable degree of change. Gender roles in the sports clubs are no longer as traditional as they once were; at most sports clubs all members are on the roster to cook and clean, not just the women. Football club vice-president Patrick articulates these changes as follows:

> I've started working in the canteen because [my wife], she's in the netball team, and young kids, so I'd go and work in the canteen. Things like that have really broken down [gender inequalities]. We've got a roster system where every player works in the kitchen at least two to three times a year, and every player does their duty around the ground. They have to clean the leaves, mark the ground. I think it's a really inclusive club. I know what you're saying; it used to be a real boy's club. It used to be . . . I think that was society, I think that was country society in general. The men used to do the work, the women used to stay home. Now it's changed completely.

Patrick and other research participants explain these changes in terms of evolving cultural norms, the shortage of volunteers (resulting in increased opportunities for women to take up leadership roles in sports clubs) and the fact that more women in small towns work nowadays. Jules, who is the secretary of a hockey club and a local teacher, asks: "Why would we have to do all the work at the club when we also work during the week?"

Australian football may still be a man's game in most respects, but women are now more centrally involved. A number of women occupy leadership positions in Australian football clubs in the NCFL as trainers or administrators. It should be noted here that in mixed sports such as hockey and netball, women are far more prominent in management positions, both historically and at present. Claire argues that although in most football clubs women have long been relegated to traditional roles as cooks, caterers and cleaners, the incorporation of hockey and netball clubs in the NCFL enables women "to be involved in a different sense," including at the management level. She believes that women are now "actually more in the forefront in the way things are run," and she gives the example of a female president of a junior football club. Although Claire is skeptical of women's access to management positions in senior football ("I would say that [a female president] would never happen in the senior football club"), she experiences that, overall, "they are important and it's recognized now." Tennis player Sally, who regularly attends local football matches, is also somewhat ambivalent about the improvements made: "In terms of women's involvement in, say, in the footy club, yeah, like, a lot of the trainers and people involved in sort of the fundraising activities are certainly women. But, yeah, we could probably improve in that area and be a little more inclusive."

The issue of gender inequalities in access to social capital is highly relevant also to the MG case. The club does not provide game-playing activities for girls and young women, even though there is a demand for sports activities among young Somali women in Melbourne. Many of their brothers, cousins and other male relatives play football at MG or other clubs, and several young women indicate that they would like a similar opportunity to take part in team sports or other physical activities (cf. Palmer 2009).

The narratives of research participants reveal the great diversity in the ways Somali Muslims interpret Islam and how these interpretations influence cultural norms and expectations as they relate to gender. Overall, they express both approval and constraint. The vast majority of respondents refer to the fact that sport participation conforms to Islam (i.e. to take care of the body through exercise; Amara 2008) and support participation for this reason. However, those who express support for participation in sport also stress that this is only acceptable if it is done in religiously and culturally prescribed ways. Hence, constraints arise from the circumstances in which women can participate (Kay 2006; Walseth and Fasting 2004). The most commonly expressed constraint on female participation in sport is the requirement for a gender-segregated provision, which according to most respondents cannot be accommodated within MG. For example, Abdi, a player in his late teens, argues: "A soccer team for girls; that's very hard for us because it's against Islamic values in a way. It's not something I would promote." Several of the parents in the study are happy for their daughters to play sport in a female-only environment, but the religious requirement of concealing women's bodies from male view dictates their reluctance to let their daughters compete in an environment where men would be watching (cf. Palmer 2009). This attitude towards gender-segregated sport "has its origin in Islam with the view that women should not perform exciting (sexually arousing) movements in front of men, because this can lead to sexual attraction between men and women" (Walseth and Fasting 2004: 122).

There exist among Australian Somalis young women who subscribe to this view and who therefore do not want to participate in sport if there are men present. However, those who hold a modernist position may be more critical of what they perceive as the conservative beliefs held by many older community members. Ayan has been an advocate for female sport participation in MG, but her efforts have thus far not had the desired effect. She explains:

> There are no girls' teams. There should be a girls' team. They have a great team going but with organization and so on we wanted to start with girls. One of the committee members has several sons and one daughter. I am sure that he would love to have his daughter play, even

though she wears a headscarf. It's like he really wants it but no one would have backed him. I am not sure what it is.

Ayan notes that there is no agreement within the Somali community on the extent to which women should play sport. "But," she argues, "as long as some women feel that it is inappropriate for them to play outdoors we will need to offer sporting activities that are acceptable for them too. You need to provide opportunities for everyone." Her view on female sport participation resonates with that of a Somali women's health worker, who asserts: "We need to provide sports activities for the women too, because many of them are stuck at home and don't go out."

To fill this void, community workers and NGOs have initiated a number of projects which offer low-threshold sports activities to culturally diverse women, including Somali women. These projects are independent from MG and other organized sports clubs in the area and usually take place indoors. By providing gender-segregated activities, these agencies give Somali women an opportunity to take part in sport that has rarely been available to them. For Ayan and other young women, gender-segregated opportunities for sport allow them to exercise in comfort and to mix with women from other cultures (see Cortis 2009). Multicultural youth worker Faizal describes the rationale for these activities:

> The idea is that we've seen a lot of girls who are isolated. Mothers who have kept their girls at home. Then we thought, OK, so how are we going to do this? How are we going to get the trust to take the girls away. Slowly, slowly you get into this community, introduce yourself. We tell them "we're going to play soccer," and you involve one of the parents. Yeah slowly, slowly get in to this. And then the girls they play basketball now, soccer, and things are changing. It's not like five years ago [when there were no organized sports activities available to young Muslim women].

This comment illustrates the point made earlier that potential constraints on young Somali women's participation in sport are mediated in large part by family influences. Families need to be assured that appropriate provision is being made and that female participation does not transgress religious or cultural requirements (Kay 2006). If parents are uncertain about the suitability of the occasion and facilities, they could prevent their daughters from attending. NGO worker John expresses this challenge as follows:

> The biggest challenge we see for young women's sport is getting the fathers to buy in. And that's one of the things we're working on: how can we engage them? Because if we can engage them, we'll get their support. Whether it's getting them to coach or referee, or to be involved at some level. But that's the issue that we're seeing.

The vast majority of MG players and representatives appreciate these activities as part of their general support for gender-segregated sports activities for young Muslim women, but they also indicate that these activities cannot be accommodated within MG, at least not at present.

Although there are no game-playing opportunities for women at MG, the degree to which Somali women are socially excluded from MG should not be over-estimated. A more complex picture emerges when we take into consideration other forms of participation in the club, notably non-playing roles. Some Somali mothers spend significant time at the club and fulfil important support roles, such as driving children to matches, laundering uniforms, cleaning the premises, running the canteen and organizing social activities. Furthermore, some Somali girls under the age of 12 regularly attend home matches of MG with their parents in order to watch their brothers or cousins play. On match days these girls often play games (e.g. kick a football) on the sidelines of the football pitch with their parents or siblings. This form of involvement is widely accepted and encouraged by club members as part of their perception of MG as a family-orientated football club.

The focus of this chapter has been on the contribution of sport participation to the development of bonding and bridging social capital. In the next chapter, the attention shifts toward a third type of social capital: linking social capital.

5   Scaling Up? Sport and Linking Social Capital

Most sports researchers consider the main source of social capital to reside in voluntary associations rather than in state institutions (Long 2008: 209). Nevertheless, fostering durable linkages with institutional agents is potentially critical to reduce social and economic disadvantage (Woolcock 2001; Stanton-Salazar 1997). Chapters 2 and 3 show that the social impacts of the sports activities being studied need to be understood within the context of, *inter alia*, the role of public institutions in the lives of local residents. In some cases this role can be described as what Wacquant (1998) calls "the erosion of state social capital," that is, the decline and/or withdrawal of formal organizations presumed to provide civic goods and services. The social control perspective discussed in Chapter 3 highlights how public institutions may stigmatize, control or exclude disadvantaged young people in ways that reflect a lack of "bureaucratic respect" (Sennett 2003). For Wacquant (1998: 35), state structures and policies play "a decisive role" in the formation and distribution of social capital. The state, through supportive and creative action at various levels, may be able to nurture an environment which fosters vibrant community social capital. As Evans (1996: 1122) contends, social capital inheres "not just in civil society, but in an enduring set of relationships that span the public-private divide" (cf. Putnam 1993; Field 2008).

In this chapter, these issues are explored in relation to the notion of linking social capital, which refers not only to the resources that accrue from social relationships between individuals and groups in different social strata but also their capacity to leverage resources from formal institutions beyond the immediate community (Woolcock 2001). This notion is discussed by outlining the ways in which Vencer, SSP and RSVL manifest linking social capital and achieve durable links with institutional agents, as well as the types of resources that accrue from such linkages. In relation to MG, however, this is discussed in terms of cultural negotiation and social capital, with particular reference to a reflexive exploration of my research endeavor as a source of data. As Edwards (2004b) notes, analyzing one's own activities and experiences in the field can progress the understanding of the social capital processes at work. There are two sides to this: on the one hand, how I, as a researcher, utilize social capital in research relations and, on the other, the ways in which my presence influences and becomes part of the social relationships that are being built and maintained in the field. Finally, this chapter will open up some of the manifestations of social capital by examining the issue of family-level effects of social capital as it relates to MG and Vencer, as well as the perverse social capital challenge that Vencer faces. The latter issue is informed by, and informs, the idea of social capital as a basis for exclusion.

DEVELOPING LINKAGES WITH INSTITUTIONAL AGENTS

In Chapter 4 it is shown that the provision of a facilitating institutional context which enables people to get to know one another and broaden their social horizons is a key aspect of the contribution of non-professional forms of sport to the development of social capital. In sport-for-development programs, this impact is also closely associated with their ability to develop linkages with institutional agents. Institutional agents can be defined as those individuals who have both the capacity and commitment to either directly provide or negotiate the provision of institutional resources and opportunities (Stanton-Salazar et al. 2000: 215). Stanton-Salazar's (1997) work on institutional agents complements Woolcock's notion of linking social capital and Bourdieu's approach to social capital. He argues that the development of social ties to institutional agents is crucial for the social development and empowerment of disadvantaged youth because these ties represent consistent and reliable sources from which they can obtain key forms of institutional support. Institutional agents, Stanton-Salazar (1997: 15) contends, take on great importance "precisely because such agents can choose, and do often choose, to transmit institutional support as part of an *explicit* and *strategic agenda*," and because, when they do so, the impact on disadvantaged youth "is considerable, if not life-altering."

Stanton-Salazar (1997) primarily uses the notion of institutional support in relation to the school system, but, as we will see in Chapter 6, it can also be applied to informal learning activities including those that take place in the sports context. In this context, institutional agents can include sports coaches and volunteers, club or league officials, program coordinators, teachers, mentors, social service workers, government officials, private business representatives, community leaders and researchers. Through relationships with these institutional agents, young people who participate in sport can gain resources and support "necessary to advance and maintain their economic and political position in society" (Stanton-Salazar 1997: 6).

As will become clear in this chapter, the Vencer and SSP programs explicitly and strategically invest in the creation and maintenance of linkages with individuals who can offer information and resources not currently available to the participating youth and their families. Furthermore, participants' relationships with members of staff themselves represent valuable sources of institutional support, with both programs employing a disparate array of staff with distinct skills and backgrounds, with ties to a variety of public, private and non-profit organizations.

Institutional Agents and Linking Social Capital in the Vencer Program

The significance of these institutional linkages for Vencer participants should be understood within the context of the absence of supportive state provision. This issue is addressed in the Vencer stakeholder surveys. Stakeholders are asked whether they believe that state institutions have a positive and active presence in the local community. As Figure 5.1 shows, 90% of survey respondents report that this is not the case. This is reflected in statements such as "the state cares very little about poor communities," "the state is absent in numerous segments" and "there is a complete absence of the state in Rio." Survey respondents emphasize the lack of resources and services offered by state institutions and the poor quality of public education as key obstacles to social development. This is exacerbated, they argue, by the often negative presence of police and security forces in the favelas, which, instead of generating public safety, tends to contribute to the high level of violence and mortality rates (Leeds 2007).

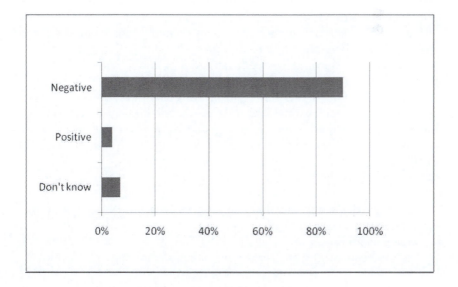

Figure 5.1 The presence of the state in Vencer communities.

Most respondents in the Vencer study believe that NGOs and social programs feature prominently in the favelas precisely because of a paucity of positive involvement of the state in the favelas. For example, one of the mentors argues: "The state leaves much to be desired and it is for this reason that we have the actions of many NGOs in our country. If it wasn't for the initiative of the actual citizens, our country would be in an even worse condition." Although they recognize the potential synergies between state and civil society, respondents assert that these are only momentarily achieved and never sustainable (cf. Ireland 2005). Akin to Wacquant's (1998) notion of negative social capital, the political exclusion of residents in poor communities in Rio de Janeiro and their unequal treatment on the part of public bureaucracies has affected their capacity for collective action (Gacitúa Marió and Woolcock 2008; Perlman 2006; Wheeler 2005). Given this, programs such as Vencer seek to develop more positive synergies among public, voluntary and private institutions in order to contribute to the transformation of this social reality.

In essence, Vencer aims to link participants to a range of educational, employment and leisure opportunities that were previously unavailable to them. Teachers and mentors offer several of the key forms of institutional support identified by Stanton-Salazar (1997). First and foremost, they provide various funds of knowledge associated with ascension in the labor market and education system, including task-specific knowledge (i.e. subject-area knowledge), technical funds of knowledge (e.g. computer literacy, study skills, time-management skills), knowledge of labor and educational markets, problem-solving knowledge and network development. These funds of knowledge are examined in detail in the discussion of cultural capital in Chapter 6. Other forms of institutional support offered by Vencer staff are advocacy and related forms of personalized intervention, role modeling and "the provision of regular, personalized, and soundly based evaluative feedback, advice, and guidance" (Stanton-Salazar 1997: 11).

One way in which the Vencer program contributes to the development of linking social capital is through the student–mentor relationship. Mentors are recruited from business, education, government and other professions with the aim to transmit to participants their knowledge of working in private or public institutions. According to physical education teacher Mauricio:

> They [participants] really like the mentors. When they talk with directors of major companies or [employees] with important functions, they create aspirations as to what they could be one day too. Mentors also end up being mental advisers, which creates a link between them.

The interview data support this observation. Former participant Paula describes her interaction with her mentor as follows: "He [the mentor] shares his experience and vision with us. Because he works at a major company here in Brazil, so he knows how people view employers, how it is inside the company. I believe that's important." Her friend Fabiana gives a similar account:

> My mentor worked in a hotel. I believe he was the manager of a hotel. He gave many tips, he stimulated people to go to university. He talked about different areas of hotel management. . . . He explained what every sector did, what the function of each employee was.

As these comments indicate, the relationship between mentor and participant in the Vencer program is focused primarily on professional development.

There is great diversity in the perceived quality of student–mentor interactions. Whereas overall the self-reported quality of the experience is moderately positive, some Vencer participants argue that they would have liked the interaction with their mentors to have been more personal and more intensive.[8] For instance, former participant Paula says that she communicated with her mentor principally by email and only once met him in person during the program. On other occasions, however, a very personal relationship between participant and mentor develops which transcends the duration of the program. For example, 18-year-old former participant Gabriela claims that she maintains contact with her mentor via email and face-to-face. They catch up three or four times per year, and Gabriela sometimes contacts her mentor to discuss career opportunities or personal dilemmas. Gabriela describes this experience as follows:

> He is a kind of father figure. He is also a great teacher. . . . He took me to visit his office [and the Rio office of national oil company Petrobras]. That was really interesting. A reality that's very different from the one we live in. Even today he asks me how I'm doing, how my internship is going. We still keep in touch.

Gabriela's mentor, Beto, is the manager of a medium-size company in the city center. Beto is one of the more active and experienced mentors in the Vencer program and invests considerable time and effort in his relationship with Vencer participants. In Beto's view, it is of great import to develop mutually respectful relationships through which guidance may be sought. Beto believes that the role of mentor complements that of the teacher in that the former is a person with whom the young people can engage more freely outside of the classroom. The mentor "is also a mirror for them, in the sense that they know that we are not here to earn money, but to collaborate, to give a living example of the type of work they are interested in." Beto recognizes the potential contributions that a positive role model can make to the careers of young people, but he is also cognizant of the dangers and limitations of role modeling:

I think that [mentors] can and should be a mirror for [the participant], but we need to be very cautious that he doesn't end up envying my position. I have to show him that I began barefoot, on a plantation. I studied and went and went, and had relative success. But from there on I cannot talk too much because that would create a very high expectation which he will find difficult to achieve. So I have to pass on a realistic message.

Beto's experience allows us to reflect on the process of relationship building in sport-for-development programs, as discussed in Chapter 3. He displays certain characteristics which his students find important, such as genuine concern for their well-being, warmth and willingness to invest time and effort into developing mutual trust and guidance. In many respects, Beto operates as a cultural intermediary through providing access to social worlds and opportunities which are not currently accessible to the young people with whom he works (Crabbe et al. 2006: 15). Beto's experience also reiterates the point made in Chapter 3 that while sport-for-development programs may find that educators who have many affinities to the target population will be the most effective, there is no single profile as to what constitutes the "right" type of cultural intermediary. Although Beto describes himself as coming from a "humble background," he did not grow up in a favela and is already in his 40s, unlike some of the young peer educators who work with the program. However, his personalized approach and the experiences and resources he is willing to share with participants form a rich basis for the development of supportive, longer-term trusting relationships with participants that transcend the duration of the program.

Beto's acknowledgment of the dangers of acting as a "mirror" is of great import in this regard. His concern about the disjunction of expectations and achievements, and the potential failure to achieve positively valued goals, points to the need to create realistic expectations and avoid invidious comparison. The discrepancy between expectations and achievements can trigger multiple modes of adaptation, of which conformity is the most common mode (Merton 1968). Conformists will accept, though not always achieve, the goals of society and the means approved for achieving them. Others, however, may desire societal goals but have few legitimate means to achieve those goals, and thus they adopt other means to get ahead. Beto recognizes that the young people's social milieu may offer powerful alternative messages as to which path will maximize individual desires (see also Meier and Saavedra 2009: 1172). For instance, for many young males growing up in the favelas of Rio de Janeiro, drug factions and traffickers may serve as attractive role models, offering a sense of identity, social status and access to desired consumer goods (e.g. Castro and Abramovay 2002). In this context, Dowdney (2003: 223) recommends that:

Children must be offered the chance to be part of something else that will give them a sense of identity and pride. An important part of this is the creation of youth leaders that provide positive role models that children can respect. Drug factions and traffickers have been idolised by children in many favelas. Children need other idols, and just as importantly, ways to become like their idols.

Dowdney's reference to the need for "ways to become like their idols" re-emphasizes Beto's challenge: he must not present his life story as an example of great meritocratic success, or as the only pathway to follow, but rather communicate a "realistic message" and a wider range of achievable outcomes in order to avoid invidious comparison and damage to young people's self-respect (cf. Sennett 2003).

The Development of Linking Social Capital in the Sport Steward Program

The role of institutional linkages is equally vital in the SSP. This program provides an extensive social network which contains valuable resources, including the funds of knowledge discussed earlier. Like Vencer, SSP employs a disparate array of staff with distinct skills and backgrounds. Members of staff combine their work with the program with part-time or full-time jobs in a range of environments, such as government, education, youth work, police and correctional facilities, physical education and sport. Danny, the SSP coordinator quoted at length in Chapter 3, serves as an example of how members of staff can operate as institutional agents. Danny holds a senior position in the municipal government, where he is responsible for the development of urban social policy. In this capacity, Danny maintains resourceful relationships with government agencies, social services, schools, businesses, community leaders and key sports organizations in Rotterdam and beyond. In his role as SSP coordinator, Danny is committed to either directly providing or negotiating the provision of institutional resources and opportunities for SSP participants, for example access to job and educational opportunities. Danny performs the role of cultural intermediary through a personalized approach to fostering mutually respectful relationships with participants and advocacy on their behalf. While "from above" his involvement in SSP is valued because of its contribution to tackling the criminogenic consequences of social exclusion, participants appreciate the respect, guidance and support he is able to offer. For example, former participant Sylvia expresses her appreciation for the way in which Danny and other staff members treat her:

> I have had a lot of contact with [Danny]. I was really struggling with myself, and he was like "OK, we'll meet up so you can talk about what's bothering you." And then things would be fine again. But if there is an issue, you can call him straight away. That's very useful. By now they know your personality and circumstances, and we know how

they work. If something is wrong, they just know what is going on with you. So when you suddenly disappear for a day, they say "it's OK, just leave her for now." That's helpful.

Sylvia's sentiment is typical in this regard. Michael, a former participant in his 20s, also developed a close personal relationship with Danny. Danny has been able to arrange several temporary jobs for Michael despite his criminal record. Michael expresses admiration and gratitude not only for the way in which Danny advocates his case with police and prospective employers but also for the sense of responsibility he has helped him to develop. Michael has graduated from the SSP program, but due to his criminal record he has struggled to find employment in event security management, which is the environment he would like to work in. Michael describes how Danny has lodged an appeal for him and uses his social credentials to try to convince prospective employers to hire Michael. Michael agrees with Danny that prospective employers "should be slightly more lenient," but he also stresses that "people need to question their own behavior": "You need to take responsibility for your actions. I will have to carry the consequences for what I did." Michael and other participants also emphasize the importance of mutual respect in their relationships with SSP staff. Julio, a former participant in his 20s, argues: "The way in which you interact is important. I respect you, you respect me. If you don't respect me then who are you? But [Danny and John] also set boundaries. . . . That's fair." Danny describes his approach to fostering mutual respect as follows:

> I don't have the illusion that they tell me everything, or that they always tell the truth. . . . But I do think that because of the way [John] and I approach them they tell us more than the ordinary high-school teacher. We don't use the Dutch pedantic finger. We work in a different way. I don't tell you that you cannot smoke pot or drink, but I will say "think about when you can and cannot smoke pot, and when you can and cannot drink." . . . I'm pretty sure that they know that I understand how they think and feel and how things work on the street. . . . I think that I am quite able to tell them things just as clearly but without giving them the feeling that they are being pushed into a corner or humiliated. If you develop a bond with them in that way, they will become more open towards you. They know they can come to see me, and even though I may disagree with them, I will tell them in a way that's normal to them. A way of communicating which people in my other job [in government] may find very strange, but for these youth it works. . . . I think participants experience our relationship that way: that I know a fair bit about their lifestyles but that I also know how it is to have a serious job and that I can explain well what is expected of them in the big people's world and how they can do certain things just a little differently.

It is because of cultural intermediaries like Danny and his investments in relationship building with participants that SSP is able to link young people to a range of educational, employment and leisure opportunities that were previously unavailable to them. The linkages created and maintained by members of staff can generate the four mechanisms of social capital effects described by Lin (2001)—information, influence, social credentials and reinforcement—as shown in Chapter 4. Program staff facilitate the flow of information, providing participants with useful information about opportunities and choices. They also exert influence on recruiters or supervisors of an organization who play a critical role in hiring participants. Further, members of staff reinforce identity and recognition, providing not only moral support but also public acknowledgment of participants' claim to certain resources. Finally, the program facilitates certifications of participants' social credentials. The result of this is that SSP is increasingly recognized by the major events industry as a reliable partner with a vast base of motivated and well-trained stewards. The CEO of an event security company describes this as follows:

> Our perception of SSP has changed profoundly over time. At first we were like "do we really believe in this?" . . . We nevertheless decided to give it a go, mainly because of our previous experiences with the program director [who used to be a senior police officer]. But what we have seen is that through their involvement in the program some of these youths have obtained certain competencies. Some of them are really great workers. . . . We currently employ around twelve former participants.

These experiences reinforce the feedback loop created by these participants' personal success stories. For example, Sylvia, who works for the above company, still visits SSP on occasions to share her experiences with participants, which helps them to gain a better sense of the profession. She also supervises some participants during their internships at major sporting events and provides social credentials for those who apply for a job at her company, which in turn enhances her own sense of identity and recognition. Sylvia expresses this recognition as follows:

> I think that people look at me differently now. I sort of started from zero. I now have my own home and continuing employment. . . . I feel that people [at SSP] look up to me a little bit. When I tell them something they listen carefully. I like that. They may not know me that well, but they would have heard from [Danny] that I now work in the security business, that I completed this program, and perhaps for them that's sort of inspiring. I talk with them and explain a few things. That's great.

Institutional Structures and Linking Social Capital in the North Central Football League

The SSP and Vencer programs illustrate Stanton-Salazar's (1997) argument that the significance of institutional agents lies principally in their ability to transmit institutional support as part of an explicit and strategic agenda. However, Stanton-Salazar (1997: 17) also notes that "opportunities for the successful development of supportive relationships with institutional agents," that is, for the creation of linking social capital, "are systematically undermined by institutional structures that are deeply alienating and exclusionary." The NCFL is a case in point. Chapter 2 describes how many public and private agencies that formerly provided services to residents in small rural towns in northwest Victoria have relocated or disappeared, which has decreased the ability of community residents to access resources from formal (state) institutions. Hence, these emerging gaps in public service provision in northwest Victoria have been increasingly filled by community development initiatives and local volunteers. Talbot and Walker (2007: 489) point out that although deficits in state social welfare generate compensatory norms of reciprocity in order to meet local needs, these deficits "also leave some people increasingly poor and isolated, less able to withstand the demands made upon them." They conclude that "when the links between community, agencies and bureaucracy become weaker, strained and more distant, the networks of association of linking social capital are undermined" (Talbot and Walker 2007: 489).

The erosion of state social capital in northwest Victoria also affects the realm of sport, as described in Chapter 2. The data from the NCFL study show that, compared with bonding and bridging social capital, opportunities for linking social capital in and through sport are relatively limited in the NCFL. This is not to say, however, that participation in NCFL sports clubs cannot contribute to the development of linking social capital. Some league and club representatives report that they leverage resources and information from institutions beyond the immediate community, for example from regional sports organizations, health services, NGOs and the Victorian government. These resources, they argue, contribute to their stocks of linking social capital and cultural capital. Geoff, a local health care professional, argues that sport participation contributes to linking social capital in the sense that "lots of new links are put in the web," for example to employment, health and social services. Some of the sports coaches in the NCFL also stress the importance of synergies between sport and other social fields, notably politics, health, education and the labor market. For example, Andrew, an Australian football coach in his 20s, believes that, at the community level, "they're all linked, integrated":

> If you don't have your sport as [Jim] was saying, he wouldn't move to a town without a football club. However, a football club wouldn't be able

to operate if there were no jobs for young people. Without one you're not going to have the other so . . . and the same with health. If the services aren't there then the populations are not going to be there.

Andrew also gives the example of league representatives' involvement in recent Victorian government projects and parliamentary committees, which he feels renders these individuals considerable political power within and outside of the sports context. However, for the vast majority of sport participants in the NCFL, who do not occupy leadership roles within their clubs or league, linking opportunities are far more limited due in part to the withdrawal of public and private services from the area.

CULTURAL NEGOTIATION, SOCIAL CAPITAL AND RESEARCHER'S STATUS

Thus far I have explored social capital primarily as a distinct product of people's social relationships in the sports context. Shifting the analysis to exploring social capital as an integral part of the researcher's socialization into the communities being studied allows me to illuminate the ways in which my presence in the field may have influenced these social relationships and, more generally, to assess the degree to which social networks contain bridging and linking ties. My encounters with the Somali community in Melbourne serve as an example. Issues of trust were paramount in the early stages of the Melbourne Giants fieldwork and continued to be an issue throughout the research. Early in the research process it became important to have one or more individuals associated with the club and the community who could grant initial research access and vouch for my presence. I was able to leverage symbolic capital as an academic based at La Trobe University (which has approximately 30 Somalia-born students) as well as my connections with a respected community organizer and a local youth worker, both of whom were Somali refugees. Both men were central to the early stages of the research, providing guidance, support, insight, interpretation and access to prospective participants. Their positive recommendation enabled me to gradually expand and strengthen my social connections at MG and in the Somali community.

Much of the research was accomplished by spending time with Somali men and women, listening to their stories and to issues they deemed as important and understanding that they "are not simply refugees but people with diverse histories and lives" (McMichael 2003: 197). Attending or participating in sports and related activities was one of the commitment acts that helped foster rapport, effectively showing my willingness to spend time and share space with the people being studied. It also normalized my presence in the field. Listening attentively and respectfully, and demonstrating genuine concern for research participants and their interests, appear to have contributed to me being seen as a trustworthy person, and in return community residents came to talk more openly about their public and private lives.

The normalization process does not, however, eradicate certain barriers between the researcher and the researched, which are present even when a relatively high degree of mutual trust and respect has been established. Race and ethnicity were meaningful markers in defining my initial research identity. Being a white non-Somali male not only marked my status as an "outsider" but at times also generated confusion as to the nature of my presence in the field, that is, which particular outsider role I performed: was I a researcher, a coach, a scout looking for new talent, a government official, someone's friend or colleague? First encounters with new individuals in the field were regularly met with questions such as "Are you with the football federation?" or "You are [X]'s friend, aren't you?"

My experience is that although racial and ethnic differences may play a role in a potential respondent's initial reaction to the researcher, once an encounter between the two takes hold, these differences have little effect on the quality of the research relationship (see Weiss 1994: 139). The ideal-typical distinction between outsider and insider is problematic also for another reason. The relationship between researcher and respondent cannot be determined *a priori* such that the researcher can be categorically and unidimensionally designated as either an outsider or an insider. Rather, research status is something that the participants and the researcher continuously negotiate and locally determine through a "collaborative process of meaning-making" (Kusow 2004: 598). My Dutch nationality distanced me from Anglo-Australian residents and enabled me to build rapport with Somali refugees as a fellow immigrant who had recently migrated to Australia. For example, it facilitated casual conversations regarding their and my own migration experiences as well as life in the Netherlands, where some of them have family members or lived themselves prior to migrating to Australia.

My Dutch background also invited informal conversations about football which formed a basis for building co-receptive trust. When Ali Hassan, a young male in his early 20s, found out that I was from the Netherlands, he enthusiastically started to talk about Dutch football: "That's a great football country. So many good players, but their defense is a bit weak." He mentioned some of the Dutch football players he admired, and the conversation then shifted to the upcoming 2010 World Cup and the English Premier League. Our shared enthusiasm for football appeared to be more relevant as a basis for social interaction than perceived racial or cultural differences. This experience is typical of my encounters with players and volunteers of MG, especially with the several young males with a strong interest in and knowledge of football, as the Dutch anthropologist Cindy Horst (2006) also found in her research with Somalis in a refugee camp.

There is another element to my presence in the field and its influence on social relationships. During the fieldwork MG club officials asked me to perform certain tasks in the club due to the perceived shortage of volunteers with appropriate skills. The performed tasks include match officiating, refereeing, coaching and administrative assistance. I viewed this request as a fair research bargain and an opportunity to give something back to those who were generous enough to talk to me about their public and private lives. Furthermore, performing these tasks was thought to be beneficial to data collection, providing an opportunity to intensify my rapport with research participants and to gain a deeper insight into their lived experience of sport.

MG officials' request for me to perform several tasks in the club appears to have been informed by their recognition of my status as a resourceful institutional agent. They seemed to regard me as someone who was familiar with and sympathetic to their needs and concerns, while also possessing useful social and cultural resources that could benefit the club as a whole, as well as individual members. Earlier in this chapter I show how sport-for-development programs can serve as cultural intermediaries, opening access to social worlds and opportunities which were not previously accessible to the people with whom they work. My research with MG leads me to conclude that researchers can also perform the role of cultural intermediary. In doing so, they can facilitate the creation of bridging or linking social capital, for example by providing social credentials or information about available grants, courses or job opportunities. In addition to passing on information about small grants, courses and scholarships available to the club or to individual club members, I also engaged in a number of media and social activities as requested by club officials, such as media releases and contributions to local newspapers aimed at enhancing the public image of the club and speeches at public functions in the community.

My ability to provide opportunities for the creation of bridging and linking networks was affected by my ambiguous status as a white non-Somali male who was well integrated into the club. On multiple occasions, coaches, administrators and spectators associated with opposing teams singled me out as a point of contact instead of other MG officials, all of whom were Somalis. For example, at a time when MG was undergoing major changes to its club leadership and structure, the coach of an opposing team offered to help the club improve its organizational structure by sharing his knowledge and skills with MG officials. Both parties requested that I operate as an intermediary in this process by assessing the club's needs and communicating these to the coach, and by setting up a meeting in which the issues could be discussed in greater detail.

It is important to note, however, that I was not the only person at MG who sought to create and tap opportunities for diversified social capital. Samatar, the club secretary who is in his 20s, emerged as a proactive social agent in the process. He recently completed a Bachelor's Degree and a prestigious leadership program, where he was mentored by the director of a consultancy firm. His cultural capital, social confidence, English proficiency and commitment to enhancing the well-being of the Somali community co-shape his proactive attitude toward developing linkages with institutional agents. Like some other young men and women in Melbourne's Somali community, Samatar has developed what Stanton-Salazar (1997) calls a "bicultural network orientation." This orientation involves "a conscious-ness that facilitates the crossing of cultural borders and the overcoming of institutional barriers, and thereby facilitates entrée into multiple commu-nity and institutional settings where diversified social capital can be gener-ated and converted by way of instrumental action" (Stanton-Salazar 1997: 25). This is what Samatar means when he refers to his "knowledge of the system," a form of knowledge which he feels many older Somali refugees lack. He expresses this as follows in relation to MG:

> The club is in a situation where it cannot support itself. So it's good to see that it gets outside support where needed. There is this support but the management of the club don't really know where the support is. They don't have the experience to know how to get support, how to fill in forms and applications. We need people who know the system and who know the language.

The bicultural network orientation of English-proficient immigrant stu-dents like Samatar arguably makes them the most likely candidates for the accumulation and conversion of social capital within and outside of the education system (Stanton-Salazar 1997: 33). Samatar feels that his involvement in MG as a player and volunteer has contributed to the devel-opment of his bicultural network orientation. For example, he reports that besides providing "great satisfaction," working with the club "increases my awareness of the community and their relation to other communities. . . . I learn different cultures from these different people [at other clubs], how their clubs are organized, and all sorts of things." He has also been able to leverage resources through his sport-based interactions with formal institu-tions, including local government and NGOs. However, other social fields have clearly been more central to the development of this orientation, most notably education (i.e. tertiary education, language training) and the labor market, as discussed in Chapter 6.

FAMILY-LEVEL EFFECTS OF SOCIAL CAPITAL

Samatar's experience raises the issue of the transmission of social capital beyond the level of the individual, particularly the ways in which young people can generate social capital for their parents, siblings and other fam-ily members (Edwards 2004a). Samatar actively seeks to share the acquired resources and opportunities with his family members and other community residents. He plays an important role in assisting his mother and older sister with negotiating the school system and state institutions, for example by translating or completing forms and applications, and by attending parent–teacher meetings. He also acts as a tutor for his siblings, nephews and nieces. Further, Samatar is the co-founder of a local community organization that provides cultural activities for young Somali immigrants. In sport, Samatar seeks to transmit part of the social and cultural resources accessed through his bridging and linking networks to other volunteers associated with MG. He assists them in their administrative tasks, grant applications, media engagement and negotiation with sports organizations and public institutions.

Samatar's orientation toward his extended family and other community residents reflects the collectivist nature of Somali culture. Several participants in the MG study find it hard to describe their own lives without referring to their family, clan and group relationships (cf. Williams 2006). For example, former MG secretary Bashir sees his involvement in MG and other community activities as an integral part of the vast social support network that exists in the local Somali community. He says that he can always count on the support of his family and clan, which allows him to garner family or clan-based social capital (cf. Bjork 2007). In return, he supports relatives and clan members as much as possible. Bashir regularly takes his friends' children to school or to sports activities, and he and his wife are renowned for providing goods such as food and clothes to those in need. He also contributes to and takes part in the community insurance system, which means that he and his family can count on financial support from the community in times of need (cf. Roble and Rutledge 2008: 101). In relation to MG, Bashir observes:

> When we've got away games mothers ask me "can you take my kids, can you take him in the car?" I do it with pleasure. When it comes to club members gathering for an occasion they are always doing things together. It becomes like a family thing, you know, even when they are not related in terms of blood, they see each other as united.

Bashir's family and clan networks are profoundly transnational. He has strong transnational ties to relatives in Somalia, Kenya, Malaysia and the United States. Bashir is one of many Somali refugees who send remittances "home" or to relatives in refugee camps. He does so not only because of feeling a moral obligation but also because of being pressurized by his relatives. Having been in Australia for 15 years, Bashir feels that the social pressure tends to increase with time. As Horst (2007: 278) notes, "the longer someone is abroad, the greater the expectations of remittances, sponsorship for resettlement, or relevant information." Bashir explains that he sends his relatives hundreds of dollars per month, which significantly affects his own financial situation: "There's a huge responsibility to send that money home. Each family sends back home one way or another every single month. It gets really hard." In the same vein, former MG president Mohamed says:

It's a burden to the people who have left the country and gone overseas. You know it doesn't matter if in Australia or Europe, you help these people. . . . Once they hear that Mr. X is living in Australia or he's living in the States or Europe they will definitely think that [you have] plenty of money. If you send them $100 or $150 they will be very appreciative. If they heard that this person came from abroad, Australia, they say "What did it cost you to come here?" . . . They say "why did you spend all that money to come here, why didn't you send us that money?" They will become angry automatically. "We would settle all of our problems, instead of you coming down here." They don't see the lifestyle or situation in the western countries.

Tess Kay and I (in press) argue that by addressing the family context, researchers can take a significant step toward locating young people's sports involvement within a broader understanding of their social and cultural environment. We consider, for example, how family practices and ideologies might differ between the individualized cultures of the western world and the predominantly collectivist societies in the non-western world. This argument is pertinent not only to the MG case but also to the Vencer program.

Vencer contributes to the accumulation of social capital beyond the level of the individual, most notably at the family level and, to a lesser degree, at the level of local communities. Family effects are recognized in the literature on Brazilian favelas. For example, Pino (1997: 4) notes that, in Brazil, "the participation of the poor in community life takes place through the family." Vencer participants' development of social and cultural capital can contribute indirectly to the social connectedness and skills of their relatives. Some Vencer participants describe how they contribute to the family income and assist in the education of family members, for example by paying for a course or university entry exam. One girl's mother is illiterate, and the girl reportedly encourages her to learn to read. Carolina, a former Vencer participant in her 20s, now holds the rank of sergeant in the Brazilian army and earns approximately six times the minimum wage. She lives in São Paulo where she rents an apartment in a middle-class neighborhood. She uses part of her wage to pay for her sister's tertiary education. Carolina claims that when she first arrived home dressed in her new uniform, the entire neighborhood came to visit her to learn more about her new life. She adds that some local youth want to pursue a similar career and regularly ask her for information and advice. According to her mentor, Carolina serves as "an example for other young people in her community" to follow.

Thus, Vencer staff recognize the significance of family-level impacts of social capital and actively seek to engender these by involving participants' family members in the process as much as possible. However, the program's ability to foster the meaningful involvement of family members is affected by factors such as resource constraints and the logistical difficulties of accessing family members. Engaging families in sport-for-development programs appears to be a universal challenge (Kay and Spaaij, in press).

The experiences of SSP staff are very similar in terms of the family-level effects of social capital. SSP coordinators John and Danny are cognizant of the mediating effects of family on young people's responses to the program. Hence, they aim to get to know the participants' parents and involve them throughout the program. Whenever possible they conduct the intake interviews at the young people's homes in order to meet their parents and/ or other family members. John is nevertheless critical of the extent to which SSP presently engages family members:

> We don't have enough contact with family members. It usually happens coincidentally. It has a lot to do with capacity constraints. But I would love to do it more often. The question is also to what extent family members are open to this. What really struck me is that at the official opening of the project [in the Sparta stadium], not one parent showed up, despite the fact that many participants live in Spangen [the local neighborhood]. That was a real eye opener for me. It says a lot about the involvement of parents in their children's education. Also, I have never seen a single parent at the diploma presentation. Not once. I find that remarkable because for these youth it's quite something. Sure, it's only a diploma for a short program, but in most cases they have very few or no diplomas, and it's an achievement. I learn from that experience that they cannot always rely on their home environment, to put it euphemistically.

John's remarks raise the important point that the impact of family on young people's participation in sport is not necessarily positive. Families may resist young people's participation in programs like SSP, for instance opposing long-term strategies (e.g. the education of their children) because short-term needs are more pressing (e.g. income generation, caring duties). For a few participants in the SSP program, the prospect of social advancement through sport is strongly influenced by their caring duties within their families. For example, two former SSP participants look after family members with long-term illnesses, which profoundly affects their career choices. John describes the family situation of one of these participants as follows:

> She has a difficult home situation. She has to do a lot for her family. One family member is seriously ill, another died recently. The moment something happens in the family, they all turn to her. We've talked with her about how she deals with this. How far do you want to go in this? And to what extent are you going to choose your own life for once? Because you need to move on too. That's the type of problem where you [as a mentor] exert too little influence from a distance. [Danny] has arranged certain things for her, but she always ends up saying "Thanks but I need to do this and that for my family."

Similar sentiments are voiced by some of the Vencer staff, who note that the survival strategies of poor Brazilian families tend to be focused on short-term economic needs rather than long-term returns (cf. Silva 2003). A female NGO worker associated with Vencer argues:

> Often these children, when they are 10, 11 or 12 years old, they have already superseded the educational attainment of their parents. Many of these parents live entirely in the present. The idea of going to university for four years and to only start a career afterwards doesn't make sense to them, like "how do people live until then?"

In such a context, sport-based educational activities may be regarded as a luxury that many families cannot afford, and parents may therefore discourage their children from taking part in such activities. This is a clear example of how in certain circumstances close social bonds can hinder the development of cultural capital, which supports Wacquant's (1998: 27) argument that although affiliative ties and bonds of obligation with family and friends constitute a resource for survival, they can create impediments and obstacles when attempting to move up and into the formal labor market. Indeed, family relationships may exert downward leveling pressures on younger family members who want to get ahead. In these instances, close family relationships do not increase cultural capital but prevent its acquisition. Vencer coordinator and NGO director Julieta illustrates the relevance of such pressures in the sports context:

> Once we had a boy [in the Vencer program] who was upset because his father told him that he was their worst son because he didn't help him and only wanted to study. [The boy] was upset because he wanted to study to change the cycle. He wanted to have more salary and take [his family] from the favela and change their lives. Two of his brothers are in jail because of involvement in drugs. He wants to be different, but his father says that he is the worst, that he is useless.

This comment reveals some of the complexities and ambiguities in the operation of social capital in the favelas. This issue is discussed in detail below.

PRODUCTIVE AND PERVERSE SOCIAL CAPITAL: THE VENCER CHALLENGE

Chapters 1 and 4 argue that the view of social capital as being inherently good and wholesome is very naïve and that social capital is inherently laden with power inequalities. Reflexive exploration of my research endeavor in Rio de Janeiro allows me to explore this important criticism further. Early on in the Vencer fieldwork, it became clear that my outsider position was problematic in some of the communities being studied, particularly those that were *de facto* controlled by drug factions. In one community characterized by regular violent conflict between rival drug factions and the police, Rosa, an NGO worker in her 40s, habitually accompanied me from the Vencer program site to the main road (*a rua*) for safety reasons. During one of our first walks, Rosa explains: "In the evening you cannot walk by yourself as a visitor because they [drug traffickers] will hassle you and ask you questions. It's too dangerous. In the daytime it's less of a problem, especially if they know your face because you've visited the program before." Arias (2006: xi) notes that "if we exclude people visiting to buy products available in favelas, be it drugs or more legitimate forms of entertainment, virtually all other outsiders who spend any time in a favela have a direct personal connection in the community." My personal connections with respected NGO workers, who could vouch for and explain my presence, turned out to be key in obtaining research access in such settings. They identified me to traffickers and other community leaders as either "one of us" or "a foreign visitor," effectively downplaying any suspicions regarding my presence.

The dominance of drug factions in the favelas and its effects on local social institutions can be usefully conceptualized by distinguishing between "productive" and "perverse" social capital (McIlwaine and Moser 2001; Rubio 1997). This distinction is directly relevant to the discussion of the role of institutional agents in the creation of linking social capital. Productive social organizations can be defined as "those that generate favourable outcomes both for its members and for the community at large" (McIlwaine and Moser 2001: 968). In contrast, perverse social capital or social organizations are those that have positive benefits for their members but include negative outcomes for the wider community. Perverse social capital is often based on the threatened or actual use of violence and/or other illegal activities.

At first glance, drug factions in the favelas can be seen to exploit their social capital for purposes that are socially and economically perverse, the benefits of which accrue only to their members. The perverse social capital accumulated by drug factions operates through a system of "forced reciprocity" maintained by the double tactic of supportive coercion and repressive violence (Dowdney 2003: 52). The Vencer survey results support this interpretation. Vencer staff and participants name violence related to drug trafficking (including police violence) as the second largest problem in their communities (25%), just behind lack of education (26%) and ahead of unemployment (21%). Several young people in the Vencer study express fear and sadness in relation to the death of family members and friends as a result of the *tiroteos* (shootouts) between opposing drug factions and between drug traffickers and the police (cf. Piccolo 2006). However, this interpretation conceals the ambiguities in the operation of perverse social capital, not only because social and economic "perversity" exists in part in the eye of the beholder (Field 2008: 92), but also because it conflates differ-ent units of analysis, notably the individual and the community levels.

Young favela residents have an ambivalent relationship with the drug trade (Piccolo 2008). On the one hand, drug factions frequently generate high levels of fear and contribute to crime and violence that can damage communities. On the other hand, they provide important survival mecha-nisms for the people involved, including economic livelihoods and social support (McIlwaine and Moser 2001: 981). For many young men, *o tráfico* offers a sense of identity and the prospect of social advancement and status in the face of social marginalization (Castro and Abramovay 2002; Dowd-ney 2003) and "invisibility" (Soares et al. 2005). Rafaela, a Vencer mentor in her 40s, describes the seductions of the drug trade as follows:

> It's not just because of the lack of alternatives that a young male enters the drug trade. The trade has a fascination of power. It enables him to become visible. With a gun in your hand the world will see you. It's a form of having status within his community. The young people are very short-term focused, so they don't think about the future. He is going to have this status, but generally these youths die young or go to prison. They have no future. We try to give them an alternative but we have to compete with the glamour that surrounds the trade.

Rafaela suggests that the seductions of the drug trade should be under-stood within the wider context of social exclusion (see Machado da Silva 2006; Leeds 2007). In such circumstances, perverse social organizations may provide more viable or attractive alternatives than legitimate or pro-ductive activities, particularly for young males who are excluded from the labor market (Rubio 1997). Local resident Elisa gives a similar explana-tion, arguing that many young males enter the drug trade "to gain visibil-ity" and "to be someone": "He is nobody for this society but when he is a trafficker he is." She adds:

> The gun makes him feel that he has power over other people; that he rules. He is an important face in the local context so he has the best looking girlfriends, his own money which gives him access to goods that other young people don't have, like designer clothes. But this is offset by the fact that he will never leave the favela. He will waste away here.

As Rafaela and Elisa point out, a young man's bonding social capital vis-à-vis drug factions is likely to come at a high price: death, imprisonment or, at the very least, life-long commitment. What is commonly perceived by poor young males as *dinheiro facil* (easy money) is in reality *dinheiro dificil* (difficult money): social advancement through drug trafficking is usually short-lived.

The Vencer program is tolerated by drug traffickers and their allies for the services it provides to at-risk youth. For example, Rafaela reports that some traffickers do not want their own children to end up in the drug trade, and that they themselves got involved in the drug trade out of rebellion or because they did not encounter viable alternatives. Vencer's ability to attract young traffickers to the program is nevertheless very limited in cases where a strong bond already exists between the young male and the drug faction. Vencer coordinator Bianca argues that this largely depends on the young person's status within the drug faction. Many recruits commence at a very young age (e.g. 12 or 13) carrying out basic jobs, such as transporting drugs from one location to another, and from there they can gradually rise through the ranks (Dowdney 2003). Bianca argues that "if you take this boy, who is just in the beginning, it doesn't matter to the leaders whether he dies or goes to Vencer. But we never take someone who is 19 or 20 and who is really at the top. This guy can never get out."

At the community level, drug factions have become a recognized sociopolitical force in the favelas being studied. Their power has been accepted by favela populations due to fear and a lack of alternatives (Dowdney 2003; Arias and Rodrigues 2006). Drug faction dominance has been built upon pre-existing local structures of social control and protection which were developed into a system of forced reciprocity (Dowdney 2003: 52).[9] Drug faction leaders use a control system based on violence or the threat of violence whereby traffickers receive community "protection" and anonymity in exchange for providing an array of services that the state generally fails to provide. These services include internal security (e.g. preventing and punishing theft and rape, resolving disputes, minimizing violence against those who are respected), minimum social services (e.g. transport to and from hospitals), financial assistance (e.g. for medicines or funerals) and the provision of leisure activities (Dowdney 2003; Arias and Rodrigues 2006; Leeds 1996). Although only a small percentage of the community may receive direct monetary benefits, the community as a whole may benefit from the internal security system and social services provided by the drug faction (Leeds 1996: 61). Some of the Vencer participants feel that they are actually relatively safe thanks in no small part to the efforts of the traffickers, even though they live in a highly violent environment. They comment on how drug traffickers make some positive contributions to community life. Heloisa, an NGO worker in her 70s, voices this sentiment as follows:

> The people here are happy. There is a pool now; the traffickers paid for it. Every weekend there is a party, with food, paid for by the traffickers. And many residents are indirectly employed by the trade. The number of soldiers [actual traffickers] is limited, but there are many friendship and family ties between residents and traffickers.

Heloisa's comments suggest that perverse and productive social networks are not mutually exclusive. Drug factions are an integral part of community life and are firmly embedded in the social fabric of the tightly knit favelas. The social and cultural services drug traffickers provide may be seen to counter-balance (or deepen depending upon one's point of view) the lack of state social capital in the favelas being studied. Another source of social and cultural resources is the numerous NGOs and social projects that operate in and around the favelas, which arguably offer more productive social capital. These are particularly valuable for "scaling up", that is, for creating and strengthening bridging and linking networks that connect the favela, surrounding neighborhoods and other parts of city, as shown earlier in this chapter for the Vencer program.

The social resources provided by drug factions, however, are not beneficial to all residents. Rather, access to these resources is characterized by selective marginalization. For example, the right to personal security is not evenly distributed, and the way to secure this right is to demarcate one's membership of a group deserving rights relative to the excluded. Traffickers allow certain favela residents, through personal relationships and local respect, to escape being marginal (Arias and Rodrigues 2006: 78). In other words, the right to personal security is dependent on residents' social capital and attendant social status. Well-connected favela residents, or those whom respected residents will vouch for, are less likely to be on the receiving end of traffickers' use of force. In general, those most likely to suffer punishment are those residents who are least connected to the community and those who individually have the least respect (Arias and Rodrigues 2006). This highlights the tangible benefits that can accrue from favela residents' localized social capital in their quest for personal security and (limited) social advancement in a situation of forced reciprocity and selective marginalization. At the same time, the social capital that may enable respected residents to secure the right to personal security is not only unlikely to be fungible outside of the local community, but it is also based in the exclusion of others, notably marginal, undeserving residents. This reiterates the point made in Chapter 1 that social capital for some implies social exclusion for others.

This chapter has explored the role sports activities can play in the creation and maintenance of linking social capital, particularly in relation to the development of linkages with institutional agents. In the next chapter, the attention shifts toward another aspect of institutional support and leverage, namely the educational outcomes of sports activities. The chapter focuses on the accumulation of cultural capital in and through sport which, as we will see, is strongly influenced by the particular social settings in which the sports activities operate.

6 Sport and Cultural Capital
Opportunities and Constraints

Educational attainment is a fundamental basis for upward social mobility in capitalist societies. The importance of education, however, is not limited to formal schooling but also includes lifelong informal learning (e.g. Field 2005). Indeed, as Esping-Andersen (2007: 27) observes, "the foundations of learning . . . lie buried in the pre-school phase of childhood," and "schools are generally ill-equipped to remedy a bad start." The concept of cultural capital sensitizes us to the fact that such "foundations of learning" are unequally distributed. Further, Bourdieu and Passeron (1977) argue that schools are not institutions of equal opportunity but mechanisms for perpetuating social inequalities, which suggests that the education system might provide few genuine opportunities for social advancement on the part of disadvantaged groups. In this context, Goldstein (2003: 95) contends that "the liberal solution that proposes education alone as a realistic route to social mobility is deeply flawed." However, I also argue in Chapter 1 that the analysis of cultural capital should uphold the idea of agency and change. This argument resonates with contemporary education research, which has in large part set aside concern with social reproduction as a conceptual focus in favor of approaches that emphasize individual or group initiative over structural constraints (Collins 2009).

This chapter examines the cultural capital effects of the sports activities being studied and highlights that the quality and benefits of education are experienced very differently across the four settings. What aligns these diverse cases, however, is that the sports activities in each of these communities are perceived to contribute to people's cultural capital in a number of ways, and that the development of cultural capital through sport can work to alleviate disadvantage rather than reproduce it. Furthermore, it is demonstrated that in all four settings the extent, impact and longevity of these cultural capital gains are mediated by exogenous factors and institutional structures outside of the realm of sport. This is illustrated through an analysis of the influences of family and school environments on the development of cultural capital.

THE DEVELOPMENT OF SOCIAL AND
EMPLOYABILITY SKILLS IN VENCER

Brazilian youth with low-income backgrounds are generally poorly prepared for the evolving knowledge economy and face a major skills challenge
(Esping-Andersen 2007; Abramovay et al. 2002; Gacitúa Marió and Woolcock 2008). To enhance participants' preparation for the labor market, the
Vencer program teaches basic employability skills, which are defined as "a
set of skills common to most kinds of employment, including discipline,
teamwork, respect, communication and results orientation, which assist
in the condition of successful employment" (Inter-American Development
Bank 2003: 2). Vencer coordinators see young people's lack of employability skills as stemming from four interrelated issues: limited technical and
task-specific skills; few opportunities to put skills into practice (i.e. work
experience); few partnerships among business, education and government
agencies to create practical opportunities; and limited resources available
to address the problem.

Recent research into the employability skills of Brazilian youth confirms these issues. Abramovay et al. (2002) note the growing incapacity of
the labor market to absorb poorly qualified and/or inexperienced youth.
They argue that young people suffer the effects of the gap between the
educational system and the new demands of the labor market, often experiencing great difficulty in obtaining their first employment. In their study
of disadvantaged youth in Rio de Janeiro, Castro and Abramovay (2002)
identify several perceived obstacles to employment, including: lack of work
experience, insufficient educational attainment, discrimination and *analfa-
betismo digital* (computer illiteracy). Many young people abandon school
in search of employment but lack the qualifications and skills necessary to
obtain steady jobs (Sansone 2003; Hasenbalg 2003b). These young people
commonly end up working in precarious jobs in the informal sector from
an early age, where they tend to earn less than the minimum wage and
receive far fewer benefits than those in the formal sector (e.g. no social
security or paid vacations).

Chapter 5 shows how Vencer educators provide various funds of knowledge associated with the development of employability skills. These include
task-specific knowledge (i.e. subject-area knowledge), technical funds of
knowledge (e.g. computer literacy, study skills, time-management skills),
knowledge of labor and educational markets, problem-solving knowledge and network development. To examine whether participants actually
acquire these funds of knowledge and/or other types of employability skill,
Vencer respondents are asked whether they feel they have learned any new
skill during the program. Ninety-two percent of survey respondents answer
this question affirmatively, reporting a range of personal, social and professional skills which they deem important. Reported outcomes include communication skills, improved self-expression and self-confidence, teamwork

skills, enhanced attitudes toward professional employment, administrative and technical skills and increased knowledge of the labor market and citizenship rights. Vencer staff observe similar changes in participants' personal and skill development. A former participant in her late teens reports that she acquired the following skills during the program: "To behave correctly during a job interview, speak in public, work in a team, and basic notions of ICT, among other things." Another young woman adds that she "learned to interact with people who are different, to communicate better." Several Vencer survey respondents emphasize teamwork as a valuable acquired skill and note how, at a personal level, they have become more open and sociable. For example, a 21-year-old female participant writes: "To work in a team and lose my shyness, and to express myself better." In a similar vein, a male participant aged 18 says: "To work in a group, my shyness diminished and I improved my knowledge about the labor market."

Nathalie, a former participant in her late teens, argues that participation in Vencer "turned out to be the best thing I have ever done. Because today I am working, I know new people, my composure has changed a lot. I was very closed in terms of communication, shyness. I learned to speak in public." Her classmate Ariana adds:

> [I]t's a very good opportunity for everyone. Many people think that it's just another course, but when you start to attend the classes you see that it's really different from what normally happens. You learn innumerable things, how to interact with other people, independent of prejudices. . . . You learn to respect one another's space, learn to have respect, have a goal.

Improved self-expression and self-confidence are frequently mentioned as positive outcomes in the interviews, for example by 19-year-old Thaís. When asked what aspect of Vencer has improved her self-confidence, Thaís responds: "The incentive that you know that you have the capacity to talk about any topic. And that you know how to express yourself in a conversation. . . . Because before I was ashamed, I was shy."

The issues of "interacting with other people" and "respecting others" are also raised in the interviews, indicating the meaning Vencer participants give to improved communication skills and social relationships. Twenty-six-year-old Fernanda reports: "I learned to deal with those around me, something which I wasn't very good at before. To respect others." Fernanda also comments that she has developed "more discipline, a goal orientation." She adds:

> Today I try to obtain a goal orientation in everything I do. So for me [Vencer] was really important because I learned skills on the sports field which today I use in the outside world. I have achieved better communication skills and mutual respect with those around me.

Like several other interviewees, Fernanda argues that the football games at Vencer provide a particularly valuable vehicle for developing skills relating to teamwork, communication and a focus on results due to the shared experience and collective identity that they can create (cf. Kay 2010). However, she also recognizes that although football (and team sport more generally) is central to this process, "the other aspects of the program are needed as well. It's all about the combination of these different aspects."

Fernanda further explains how her aspirations in life have changed as a consequence of her participation in Vencer. She used to be quite pessimistic about her future and lacked the self-belief and skills to pursue higher education and a professional career. In particular, she felt that "because I was black I wouldn't get a job in other places [outside of the favela]." But, she argues, Vencer educators "showed me that I can achieve things, that I do have capabilities, that I am communicative," an encounter which she feels "changed my life completely." At present she is enrolled in a Spanish language course, has completed an accountancy course, and wants to go to university: "I've changed completely. I am not the old [Fernanda] anymore; today I have a different world view. I am a different person now." Other former participants voice similar sentiments, albeit often in more practical and confined terms. They stress, for example, how their participation in Vencer increases their awareness and goal orientation, as well as their ability to plan their future. For instance, 18-year-old Gabriela, who now works for an NGO, asserts: "I think [it has given me] more confidence, a greater sense of responsibility and aim in terms of what I want. . . . It's an important step that you take and it opens your eyes more. You become more motivated to do things."

Fernanda's reference to the use of acquired skills "in the outside world" also points to another key process: cultural capital developed in Vencer can be transferred to other contexts. Thus, participation in Vencer can be viewed as a means of acquiring new skills and knowledge which transcend the specific program context and serve young people in a very real and practical way in other facets of life (see also Sandford et al. 2006). The transferred skills that are most commonly reported by Vencer participants include: improved communication and relationship skills which help participants assert themselves in interactions in family and other settings; decision-making skills of use at home, in school and at work; and enhanced self-confidence which transfers as a life skill (cf. Kay et al. 2008). Fernanda gives specific examples of how this affects her own life:

> I had problems with my family, with my dad, and thanks to the project I managed to deal with this. Nowadays I kiss my dad, whereas before I didn't even want to see him. It helped me because in the classroom we sometimes talked about parent-child relationships, and I heard other people's histories. I came to see that our problem is small and that there are people with much greater problems. So I saw that my dissension

with my dad . . . that I had to be more kind and talk [to him] even though I didn't want to. It's helped me quite a lot, there is peace at home now . . . something that I hadn't achieved before. So it's something you internalize as well. To treat him with respect of some sort . . . whether he is wrong or right I have to respect him.

Whereas Fernanda stresses the primacy of family relationships in this regard, other former Vencer participants point to the transfer of task-specific knowledge and technical funds of knowledge. Paulo, who now works as an ICT assistant, notes that he previously had very poor computer skills. At Vencer and the implementing NGO he was able to improve his computer skills, and he subsequently completed other ICT courses to further enhance his computer literacy. He not only applies these skills in his current job but also seeks to transmit his computer skills to other young favela residents. Paulo and one of his friends are enrolled in a computer science degree at university, where they seek to leverage resources for their local community: "We explained our financial situation and our social work here in the community to the guarantors [of the university], and they are considering to offer scholarships [for local youth]. At the moment the ICT course [at the local NGO] faces extinction, but I'm sure it will be back in 2011, and that they are going to have a guaranteed scholarship." Knowledge transfer of the kind Paulo experiences is particularly relevant in the context of the computer illiteracy many poor youth in Brazil are confronted with, which impedes their full participation in education and the labor market (Castro and Abramovay 2002). As one of the program mentors argues, participation in Vencer enables young people to "leave behind their computer illiteracy" and thereby "better prepare themselves for the labor market."

As noted in Chapter 2, an important component of Vencer is the practical application of the taught workforce and employability skills. Participants are expected to complete at least 180 hours of on-the-job experience through internships in areas such as telemarketing, administration, ICT, sales or community services. The significance of this component lies partly in the novelty of this experience for participants, with many of the young people being unemployed or working in precarious jobs. The work experience component of the Vencer program contributes to the development of task-specific and technical knowledge, as well as to enhanced knowledge of the functioning of the labor market. Vencer educator Reinaldo expresses the value of this experience as follows:

They get at least one month of practical experience to know how the labor market is, because some have never had any such experience. To know how to deal with the labor market, to know its function, to know the company, the employees, how to behave within a company; I think that's important.

Several former Vencer participants express similar views, indicative of which is the following comment: "[The work experience] is very important. . . . When you are doing a course to train for a profession, there is nothing better than to go out there and apply what you have learned." Ana, aged 22, argues: "[W]e learn things in class, but when we go there for work experience, we see how the labor market is, how things really work." Twenty-four-year-old Marta has completed an internship at a telemarketing company. Whereas several of her fellow Vencer participants have subsequently obtained a contract at this company, Marta left after her internship and enrolled in another course. She now has a full-time job as a call center operator. Marta describes her internship experience as follows:

> I came there [the telemarketing company] with this goal [of personal and professional development] in mind. At first I didn't think I would stay there long but I did because of all the learning I could do. . . . We had an ICT class there. I didn't know how to operate a computer and I learned a lot. For any other job anywhere else I will need ICT skills. So I wasn't thinking about [the company] because for me it was a small space. I wanted something bigger for my future. So I didn't stay there.

CULTURAL CAPITAL FORMATION IN THE SPORT STEWARD PROGRAM

There are striking resemblances between Vencer and the Sport Steward Program on the theme of cultural capital despite the fundamentally different social settings in which these programs operate. As noted in Chapter 2, SSP recognizes that many unemployed youth in Rotterdam want to work but lack the educational qualifications and experience to obtain secure and rewarding employment. The vast majority of SSP participants left school without completing secondary education and are either unemployed or hold temporary jobs with high levels of job insecurity. In the Netherlands, low educational attainment strongly correlates with ethnic minority background. In a country where class-based and gender-based inequalities in educational attainment have decreased over time, ethnic-based educational inequality remains very apparent (Tolsma et al. 2007), affecting many SSP participants. Recent research in the Netherlands shows that low educational attainment and early school drop-out are associated with fewer employment opportunities, lower income and poverty, and that unemployment rates among young people with low levels of schooling are particularly high in times of economic downturn (ROA 2009; WRR 2009). Former SSP participant Mustapha, who is a first-generation immigrant from the Middle East, describes this experience as follows:

I wanted to build a future, a better life. I had enough of being welfare dependent. I wanted to start something new because no one would hire me because I don't have a diploma. I have had many temporary jobs, but I wanted a long-term perspective. It was always six months or a year, and then they would tell me they weren't going to renew my contract, that the economy was bad, blah, blah. That's why I decided to join the program. I really had the feeling that without a diploma I would never have job security, because I was always the first one to be laid off. I knew that was my problem.

In this context, SSP aims to improve participants' socio-economic status through a focus on teaching workforce and employability skills which are relevant to the profession of sport (and city) steward. SSP teachers are primarily concerned with the development of subject-area knowledge specific to the sport steward training, as well as more general funds of technical knowledge, including computer, language and study skills. Mustapha acknowledges the value of these skills, which he feels help him to take "a really positive step" in life. He claims that although he "already knew a lot of stuff," SSP enables him to improve certain skills, for example how to prepare for and do a job interview. Mustapha argues that "I needed a push in the back. Without SSP I would probably still be in the same situation [of being unemployed]. SSP gave me that push, and that helped because eventually I enrolled in education. I really like it." He now has a job as a security guard for 32 hours per week and studies one day a week in order to become fully qualified in his profession. Mustapha also works as a steward at football clubs Sparta Rotterdam and Feyenoord on a part-time basis. Former participant Mario also notes that he "learned many things that I didn't know," such as computer skills, first aid and other subject-area knowledge.

SSP coordinators emphasize the importance of personal development alongside professional development, notably the development of social skills. For coordinator Danny, the development of social skills constitutes a vital outcome of SSP participation which underlies the more task-specific competencies:

The subject teachers mostly think it's great when [participants] are good at the Basic Instructions Steward or the Frisk Training or the ICT. Personally, I find the actual content less important than the total package . . . I find social skills most important, and related to that self-confidence, world view, you name it. And the skills and knowledge they learn in the task-specific subjects will bring them a step higher because it gives them tools to work with, to go into the security industry or elsewhere. So in that sense it's also important that they learn task-specific skills. But the most important thing for me personally is that you can see that they have grown a little as a human being.

In the same vein, former participant Sylvia argues that her communication skills have improved markedly as a result of her participation in SSP. She describes how she used to be "very angry" and easily agitated. During her participation in SSP, she learned to reflect on and manage her temper, which also helps her in other aspects of her life:

> That's something I've really learned [at SSP]. I notice that I've become more and more relaxed, and people react to me differently now. A lot of my colleagues say "You are really becoming more relaxed." . . . It has helped me to get ahead in my work in the security business. And it's also useful outside of my work. You need to be able to understand other people. During the education [at SSP and subsequently in her training as event security officer] you learn to look at people's body language. If you don't pay attention to that, you can easily get in trouble. They really focus on that. . . . That's useful, both at work and in my private life.

Sylvia, who now works as a steward at major sporting events, also appreciates the formal qualifications which can be obtained through participation in SSP. She believes that these qualifications in the form of a number of diplomas and certificates give her competitive advantage in the labor market:

> I'm glad I've got those certificates. It puts you a step ahead of others who haven't done the program, and of course the vast knowledge you acquire in those six months [of participation in SSP]. Many stewards lack that knowledge . . . the quality of stewards is often poor. They only get two evenings of training. The program has given me a lot of confidence in how to do my job. You work in a more self-confident manner. I notice that my boss also observes this. When he needs to leave he asks me whether I can keep an eye on things.

Sylvia's appreciation of her formal qualifications in areas such as stewarding, first aid, traffic control, crowd management and social hygiene resonates with SSP's aim to endow participants with modest stocks of institutionalized cultural capital, which is based on the belief that the cultural capital bound up in a degree or certificate is increasingly mandatory for obtaining challenging employment. She also stresses the value of the practical work experience at major sporting events in Rotterdam, which in her case initially continued on a casual basis after she graduated from the program. Sylvia's view reflects that of Mustapha, as described earlier. Both believe that opportunities to improve their socio-economic position are constrained, if not blocked, by their limited educational attainment and work experience. Their lack of institutionalized cultural capital, they argue, translates into a shortage of career opportunities. Mustapha has previously participated in other government-led social programs. However, he is rather critical of most of these programs due to their sole focus on finding a job regardless of the nature and longevity of the job: "With those other programs you were looking for jobs on a daily basis, but that was all it was. It gave you a temporary job, but after a couple of months you were out on the streets again. It didn't give you any lasting improvements, no diploma or certificate." The narratives of Mustapha and Sylvia resonate with those of the Vencer participants discussed earlier in their emphasis on the importance of educational qualifications and relevant work experience in order to get ahead, albeit that the latter often face a far greater distance to the formal labor market, as opposed to the informal economy.

SKILL DEVELOPMENT AND CULTURAL CAPITAL IN THE NORTH CENTRAL FOOTBALL LEAGUE

Compared with the SSP and Vencer programs, the prospect of cultural capital formation is generally less pronounced in the NCFL and MG. Whereas the SSP and Vencer programs can be termed "sport-for-development" programs which strategically invest in personal and professional development through sport-based education, the NCFL and MG provide sporting opportunities without the incorporation of formal educational activities. This does not mean, however, that skill and knowledge development is not a relevant aspect of people's lived experience of sport in the NCFL and MG. In addition to claims of increased social connectedness, as discussed in Chapters 4 and 5, NCFL and MG participants report a range of skills which they develop through participation in sport.

The most widely reported acquired skills in the NCFL are sport-specific skills: mastering technical skills associated with a particular game and becoming a better player or coach. For example, Dan, a former cricket player in the NCFL, argues that participants "can learn their hand-eye coordination and ball handling skills." However, several NCFL participants also point to the development of key aspects of cultural capital as defined in Chapter 1, notably social and professional skills. Alan, the secretary of an Australian football club in the NCFL, notes that "diplomacy is something you develop. You have to sort out all these issues . . . diplomacy didn't come easy to me as I was more of a black and white person. People skills are the most important skills." Others stress how they themselves and/or the people around them develop social skills and social confidence and acquire new knowledge through their involvement in the NCFL: "[Our club president] used to be paranoid about needing to speak in front of a public audience and he's quite an accomplished speaker now and feels as though he can get up and speak. He was hopeless he really was, but now he's getting far better."

Alicia, the president of a local tennis club who is in her 20s, is a case in point. When asked whether she develops any skills through her involvement in the club, Alicia comments:

> Definitely. Before coming to [this town] I hadn't held any sort of position within a sporting club . . . I think you learn skills about obviously communication and problem solving, conflict resolution. . . . When you have a leadership role, even [in] a small club, you kind of have to take on some sort of level of responsibility and leadership and ownership to try to resolve some of those things.

She also describes how finance skills and problem-solving skills developed in the sports context have been useful to her in other spheres of life. Alicia acknowledges that people who already have relevant skills or high social status may be more likely to acquire leadership positions in sports clubs in the NCFL, as discussed in Chapter 4. However, from her own experience she argues that this is not always the case:

> Sometimes in small communities you don't have the luxury of someone having a finance background in order to take over the books. So you're relying on people's endeavor to learn themselves and that's the instance where it's good because people do have to . . . it's sort of forced on them to learn a new skill and to take it up. So there's a mixture [of previously skilled people and those who can learn new skills by doing].

Other NCFL participants display a similar ambivalence toward the accessibility of cultural capital in and through sport. NCFL president Paul argues that "if you're going to take on league positions, to take on those positions you've got to have those skills anyway or you wouldn't take the position on, but I think it broadens them a bit . . . it makes you a little bit more savvy about how it all works."

The sporting experience of Grant, a former mayor of one of the towns in the NCFL, illustrates how involvement in sport can facilitate the kind of "broadening" of skills that Paul refers to. Grant has held various positions in his local football club over the years, such as president, treasurer and coach. He became club president at a relatively young age, which he experienced as being thrown into the deep end:

> I was 33 and that was really considered very young then because they were all older blokes. But I remember the first week, the first match when I was president . . . something drastic happened and they come to see me. . . . That was the first day it really hit me you had to start making decisions yourself.

Grant believes that his positions as club president and treasurer have been valuable for enhancing his cultural and social capital. He argues that "you learn heaps" and that this experience has been of major significance to his subsequent positions in the community: "There's an old saying if you can be president of the football club you can do any job in [town]; you can be a councillor. After you've been president of the football club you can do any job in [town] because that's about the toughest job going around. [The skills required] were always the same." Grant has since held several high-status positions including president of a farmers' association and the school council, which in his view illustrates the transferability of cultural and social capital acquired in the sports context.

Grant's experience is exceptional but not unique. Some of the other NCFL respondents similarly note the life skills which are facilitated by sports volunteering. For instance, Robin, who is in his 40s, reports that he became a secretary of his local football club at the age of 21, which in retrospect he sees as a major life experience that has helped him set up his own business and carry out its financial management. Football club president Shane, who is a farmer in his 60s, describes a range of professional and social skills he has developed through his long-standing involvement with the football club, including public speaking, finance, administration, conflict resolution and "people management." He says that he has been able to use these skills in his job and to develop new business opportunities. Based on his personal experience, Shane argues that young people with little or no previous experience should be given the opportunity to take on leadership roles in their sports clubs under the guidance of older, more experienced persons.

The narratives of NCFL participants like Shane, Robin and Grant show that cultural capital does not necessarily arise because people make a calculated choice to invest in it by means of formal education but also as a by-product of activities engaged in for other purposes, in this case sport. Their stories reveal that sport participation involves an informal learning process which can span large parts of one's life. In other words, sport is an area of life in which people can create and acquire new skills and knowledge throughout their life, hence providing a context for lifelong learning. The findings from the MG study lend further weight to this argument.

THE USES AND LIMITS OF INFORMAL
LEARNING AT MELBOURNE GIANTS

Football coaches at MG highlight the importance of developing game-specific skills. Ali Osman's observation that playing football helps children and young people to increase their ability and self-confidence as players is typical in this regard: "When you start to play, you have some ability, you get the confidence. That's why now most of them have confidence [in their football skills]. However, several MG respondents also describe how they develop transferable social and professional skills through their involvement in the club. Former club president Abdirahman, who now works at a major bank, argues that although he "used the skills I had before" to perform the role of president, such as his computer and finance skills, he also acquired new skills "like how to look for funds" and liaising with public institutions and sport organizations. His involvement in MG also enables him to increase his knowledge of other cultures through his interaction with representatives of other clubs, which he sees as being particularly important: "You have to have that sort of link. If you don't have any link with the outside communities, you miss out. You definitely need to be having contact with different people from different community backgrounds." In his view, outside of football, "there is no other thing where that happens with the [Somali] community." Those who work closely with Abdirahman at MG confirm his experience. For example, when asked whether he acquires any new skills through his involvement in the club, MG coach Roble comments: "Yeah definitely. Like talking to, for example, soccer federation, submitting letters, getting network, knowing the rules like how soccer functions in Australia; financing, regulation. Yeah, definitely . . . I learn a lot every day." He also reflects on the transferability of the acquired skills, using Abdirahman as an example:

> Yes, yes [they are transferable]. You know, [Abdirahman] as a member of the Somali community now has a lot of respect cause he's running the club. Everybody goes to him "I want my kids to join the club." They see the club in stable hands so it's become like a community club where everybody just goes there, you know. And they go to him for advice outside of the club.

Roble is critical, however, of the extent to which MG has been successful in encouraging young people and their parents to develop their skills in the football context. His complaint that "it always comes down to one or two people" reflects the argument made in Chapter 2 that the pool of motivated volunteers is small at MG. Roble explains: "It's always one or two people who take it on for a few years, but then they leave because they have too many other things going on in their lives. But there's no one to take over the job." He also notes that the persons who end up in leadership positions in the club are usually the ones who already have relevant skills and experience mainly because they are put forward by others who feel that they are themselves incapable of leading the club. Again, Abdirahman is a case in point here. After leading the club for five years, he and another Somali male publicly vent their frustration about the reluctance of other club members to relieve them of some of their duties, including finance, administration and travel to and from away matches. Their desire is to focus more on their professional careers, and they therefore urge other fathers to take on certain tasks in the club. Abdirahman offers to "help them learn [the relevant skills] this season so that next season they can take over."

The stories of other MG participants provide further insight into the process of cultural capital formation in and through football. Local youth worker and former MG volunteer Ayan argues that she has "learned so much" during her time at the club: "I have learned personally . . . that I cannot be everywhere and [that] there have to be other people who have to take over. For me at a personal level that is what I have learned. The other thing that I have learned is the Somali community, how they work." Ayan testifies to the skill development of young MG players:

> I was there for two years and although two years may not be long in an adult's life, it is a very long time in a teenager's life because a lot of things change over that time. And I remember observing those boys and observing the ways in which they reacted to directions from a referee or a player, or to an incident, and then how that changed a year later. They have become a lot more strategic, you know. They choose their words carefully; they are a lot more diplomatic. So it definitely teaches them skills that are useful in the outside world.

However, Ayan also observes that at MG the development of skills and knowledge is mostly informal and unorganized and therefore underestimated by at least some people. To this end, Ayan has sought to add a more formal educational component to the football activities: "When I was working with the club I organized a few workshops around communication and networking and all this sort of thing, as well as study skills and workshops, got speakers to come in and talk to the players." In a similar vein, a local NGO offers a homework program to children and young people with African backgrounds. Some MG players attend this program on a regular basis, often encouraged by their parents. In this context, Ayan notes that "there are a few good parents, fathers who even though they drive taxis value good education, so they encourage these workshops and study skills development."

It should be noted here that these educational activities are offered independently from the club and its football activities, and in this sense they differ markedly from the way in which they are organized in the SSP and Vencer programs. MG secretary Samatar recognizes the need for personal and professional development courses for young people with Somali backgrounds in order to "invest in their capabilities plus link them to opportunities." Nonetheless, he argues that in his local community, including MG, "this is lacking" and that small courses like the aforementioned homework program "are not very visible" and "not that proactive." On the other hand, some of the parents in the MG study use football as a way to discipline their children in relation to their schooling. There have been several instances where parents threaten their sons that if they fail to get good results at school, they will not be allowed to play football on the weekend. According to Roble, this is an effective parenting strategy because "the kids love soccer and hate missing the game." This comment points to the importance of the family environment as an influence on the development of cultural capital. This issue will be explored further below.

FAMILY ENVIRONMENT AND CULTURAL CAPITAL

Thus far the analysis has focused primarily on individual and endogenous factors that influence the accumulation of cultural capital through participation in non-professional forms of sport, showing how individual abilities such as skills, drive and persistence are affected by the formal and informal learning activities that take place in the sports context. In doing so, it presents the people being studied as proactive social agents with a considerable degree of autonomy and subjectivity. However, as articulated at the beginning of this chapter, contextual factors which influence educational attainment should also be taken into account. While sport is a relatively autonomous field (Bourdieu 1978, 1984), it cannot be viewed in isolation from other social fields such as the family, education, labor market and politics. In the remainder of the chapter I will focus on two major spheres of influence: the family environment and the education system. These themes feature prominently in three of the four cases (MG, SSP and Vencer), and specific findings from two of these case studies (MG and Vencer) are used to illustrate the ways in which family and school environments affect the operation of and possibilities for cultural capital in the sports context.[10]

Family environments have a significant impact on young people's educational aspirations and achievement (Brassett-Grundy 2004; Israel et al. 2001; Buchmann and Hannum 2001; Duncan and Brooks-Gunn 1997). Coleman (1990) argues that parental investments of time and effort (e.g. in shared activities or helping with homework), the affective bonds parents create and maintain, and the pro-social guidance they offer, positively affect well-supported youth's educational performance. However, the degree to which parents and other family members are able to make such investments depends in part on their own cultural, social and economic capital (see Chapter 5).

As shown in the previous section, respondents in the MG study are somewhat ambivalent about whether Somali families provide a fruitful and encouraging learning environment. This ambivalence is reflected in the literature on the educational attainment of Somali youth in western societies. Scholars such as Omar (2005, 2009) and Panferov (2002) note the negative impact of interrupted schooling on young people's study skills. Many Somalis who migrated to countries such as Australia have experienced years of interrupted education in Somalia and/or in refugee camps, which hinders their integration into the Australian educational system. These authors also highlight the fact that some Somalis (especially older women) experience gaps in their English language comprehension, which may constitute an obstacle to enhancing their knowledge of the education system and their ability to actively contribute to the education of their children. They stress that there tends to be "little support for English literacy in the home environment" and that the support at school is often inadequate (Panferov 2002: 306). More generally, Omar (2009) and Panferov (2002) contend that in many cases the home environment is not conducive to vigorous learning activities due to overcrowding, lack of space and a quiet environment to study, lack of privacy and shortage of learning and reading materials.

These findings resonate with my own fieldwork experiences. Some of those interviewed argue that the shortage of educational support at home and in the community, as well as gaps in English language proficiency, hinder their own and/or their children's achievement of educational aspirations. MG player Yusuf explains how parents are often unable to help their children with homework, do not have a computer at home and have very few books. Yusuf argues that "these parents need to understand that children cannot do without these things in the 21st century." Halima, a former MG volunteer in her 20s, asserts that many fathers are absent in their children's education, while mothers may not have enough education to help the children:

> Fathers are really, really absent. I have some really bad examples for you of fathers who would not want to pay for kids to have a workshop, like one of the workshops we ran. They don't want to pay the fee. . . . Some don't see the benefits of investing small amounts of money like $20, which is really unfortunate because they drive the taxi 12 hours per day so they don't really get to see their kids. If they were to see the opportunity it presents for their kids, a good opportunity to be around examples, mentors, good role models, I am sure that they would invest the $20 or even $100 to have some sort of a personal improvement experience.

Mohamed, a community organizer in his 40s, is particularly critical of what he regards as the shortcomings of the home environment:

> Many Somali parents highly value education, but to actually live it is another thing . . . it's abstract but not practical [like] learning the language, knowing the system. Most of them are not putting their children in the right learning environment. The educational background is a very important factor. Honestly speaking, they have no learning culture in the family or in the community at large. When you go to their houses you rarely see books. It's an oral society. That's another factor. So there are many factors. Australia has a very different learning culture, so Somalis are in a transitional stage in which they have to change their learning culture, including technology. That will take a long time; it's not easy. But the younger generation is always different from the older ones. They are in the mainstream, they go to schools; they read and write in English.

With regard to what he refers to as the lack of a "learning culture" in many Somali families, Mohamed gives examples of households that do not invest in books or study space at home. Instead, he argues, "they go out and buy big

TVs and stuff, all shallow things." However, Mohamed recognizes that the significance of this varies across families and "depends on the family, where they come from, and on the individual," and that we therefore "cannot generalize too much." These observations allude to the fact that there is broad variation in the level of education attained by the Somalis interviewed, with educational attainment ranging from none to the tertiary postgraduate level, as well as in their attitudes to education (cf. Omar 2009).

Notwithstanding the aforementioned obstacles to educational attainment, the vast majority of MG participants believe that education is paramount, offering a key pathway to social advancement. This belief informs their decisions about how to allocate their time and resources to their own and/or their children's education. Some families invest considerable amounts of money in education, including private schools, tutoring programs, religious classes and weekend schools. For example, some young MG players attend the community-driven Sunday school straight after their football game. The Sunday school offers low-cost English, Somali and Arabic language tuition as well as Islamic classes. For MG coach Abukar, tuition in these subjects is "important for religion and identity, but also useful for children's intellectual and cognitive development." Abukar, who is a business student in his late 20s, acknowledges that the ability to master English and any other language constitutes an important form of cultural capital (Trueba 2002) which enables people to develop the kind of bicultural network orientation discussed in Chapter 5.

Abukar is not alone in his attitude toward allocation of time and resources to educational activities. MG secretary Samatar describes how his own stance on the importance of education is informed by the Somali saying *aqoon la'aan waa iftiin la'aan*, which translates as "lack of knowledge is lack of light." Samatar's family is large, and they all work together to help each other succeed. They pool their skills and resources and show that they value success at school in tangible ways (cf. Bigelow 2007). Samatar is a valuable source of cultural capital for his family members. As noted in Chapter 5, he assists his mother and older sister with negotiating the school system and sits with his siblings, nephews and nieces to complete homework assignments. Samatar spent four years in a refugee camp in Kenya where he learned to speak "very basic English." He says that many refugees did this because of their dream to migrate to a western country and most likely an English-speaking country. His family then moved to New Zealand, where he enrolled in secondary education. He recalls that at first he "really struggled with language," which he says is "easier for the next generation because they grow up with English in Australia." However, Samatar is now fluent in English, Somali and Arabic and thus holds considerable linguistic capital.

In relation to education, Samatar notes that his family invests considerable resources in the education of the children, for example by sending them to extra-curricular courses and bilingual weekend schools. Samatar's sister is a single mother with nine children. She lives on social security entitlements, but despite this she pays for extra-curricular computer courses for her children. Samatar states that "even though she cannot help in practical ways with homework [due in part to her low educational attainment and gaps in English language comprehension] and doesn't know the system that well," she invests significant time and resources in her children's education so that they can "have a future she never had." Samatar stresses that this "lack of knowledge of the education system" is rather typical and obstructs parental ability to help children plan and realize their educational aspirations: "Most of them [the parents] haven't been to school here; language difficulties, etc. So it's important to have role models and mentors to educate parents and young people about these things." By taking education and learning very seriously, Samatar offers a good "learner" role model for his younger family members (see Brassett-Grundy 2004: 87). Put differently, he is a key source of social capital for his family members, which is being converted into educational achievement, "a valuable piece of cultural capital" (Bigelow 2007: 16).

Having role models in education is considered important by several MG respondents. Although these respondents value sport in general and its role in their local community in particular, some of them also problematize the notion of role modeling through sport. Community organizer Mohamed is particularly outspoken on this issue. He recognizes that some young Somali males have a major interest in football (and to a lesser extent basketball and Australian football) and are focused on furthering their professional sporting careers as a means of social advancement, with sporting celebrities forming their main role models. Mohamed argues that this may lead not only to unrealistic expectations but also to the neglect of investment in education, which he sees as having greater achievement returns than sport (cf. Eitle and Eitle 2002; Covey 1998: 221). Mohamed's sentiment resonates strongly with that of the critics of the myth of social mobility through professional sport discussed in the Introduction. He explains this as follows:

> If we talk about young Somalis, I believe that there are also some negative aspects of sport. The way they think is that it's good to have fun, but many of them also think that it will help them to become millionaires. They look up to those who have built a better life through sport and say "I want to become a millionaire like them." But very few of them can make it. They are not in a proper situation to live that position. They don't have good services and facilities and education for that. It's a lie. It's a false expression. But many of them talk that way, also about African American basketball players. It's good to have ambition but for that whole generation to have that same ambition is not good because they focus less on other ambitions and opportunities. For some young men, it's a way of justifying their failure in education.

Hence, Mohamed argues, it is important to stimulate role modeling in relation to education and learning.

The Vencer program raises similar issues in regard to the influence (both positive and negative) of the home environment on learning. In the previous chapter, family-level effects of social and cultural capital are discussed in relation to the issues of valuing and supporting education in general and participation in Vencer in particular. Here we should add the theme of role modeling, that is, of parents or other (extended) family members serving as model learners for young people (Brasset-Grundy 2004). Some Vencer participants report that family members act as good learning role models and provide significant moral and/or practical support for their education. For example, Consuela, a former Vencer participant in her late teens, describes her aunt as a major influence on her educational aspirations:

> Only my aunt studied at a university and she is always saying "let's go do university" and "are you studying a lot?" She studied law, that's how I learned about it. . . . I ask her many questions out of curiosity. . . . I love it when she talks about these things, but only because of her. I find it interesting to have a person close to you who has already done what you want to do. You get more motivated to really go out and do it.

A few Vencer participants refer to older brothers or sisters who have been enrolled in tertiary education and encourage their younger siblings to follow their footsteps. Paulo, whose educational experiences are described earlier in this chapter, notes that his family "is always focused on studying, always gives priority [to] do university," particularly his older brothers and sisters, some of whom have a university degree. However, Paulo recognizes that his situation is quite different from that of most families in his local community, which "do not have this stepping stone." In families where medium or long-term investments in schooling are not valued as principal strategies for social advancement, young people are far more likely to abandon the education system at a young age (Silva 2003), which may well result in the reproduction of their socio-economic disadvantage.

It is important to understand the wider social and economic contexts in which families make educational decisions for their children (Buchmann and Hannum 2001; Kay and Spaaij, in press). Thus, the process described by Paulo needs to be understood within the context of, *inter alia*, the poor quality of public education in the favelas. This issue is more pertinent to the Vencer program than to the other cases being studied, and for this reason I will focus on this program here.

SCHOOL ENVIRONMENTS AND CULTURAL CAPITAL: THE VENCER CHALLENGE

Brazil's highly class-segregated school system is viewed by many Vencer respondents as a major obstacle to social mobility of disadvantaged youth.

The Brazilian education system, Goldstein (2003: 94) rightly argues, "is 'classed' from the very start, with a public school system that functions (rather poorly) for the masses and differing levels of private school education that cater exclusively to the middle and upper classes." Drawing upon Bourdieu's (1984, 1986) work on cultural capital, scholars such as Goldstein (2003) and Souza e Silva (2003) show that the urban poor in Rio de Janeiro do not always know how to act "appropriately" in many of the social spaces belonging almost exclusively to the middle and upper classes, including private and tertiary education. Thus, they may feel "out of place" in such spaces, as discussed at length in Chapter 4. In Jailson Souza e Silva's (2003: 128) words, favela residents often lack an "institutional orientation," that is, a high degree of understanding of the "rules of the game" in the field of education and how to "play" by these rules.

Access to and length of schooling has increased significantly in Brazil over the past few decades (UNICEF 2009). However, the quality and resources of Rio's public schools remain poor particularly in disadvantaged communities (Abramovay et al. 2002; Leeds 2007; Perlman 2010). Vencer educator Catarina asserts: "Education is the main obstacle to get a good job. In Brazil at the moment about 96% of children are enrolled in school, but that does not mean they actually frequent school and that the schools are good. We need to make sure that people stay in school and actually learn." Vencer teacher Edu adds:

> The problem is the quality of public education and this is a national problem. With the universalization of primary education . . . we have solved the problem of children who are not in school, but we haven't resolved the question of the quality of schooling. The classrooms are overcrowded, not enough teachers are hired, nor do we train those who are teaching. That's why those students arrive at secondary schools with terrible formation. In secondary education we see the same problems: classes are packed, teachers are poorly paid and trained, lack of teachers in some disciplines, and teachers teaching in disciplines in which they are not trained.

To the shortage of qualified teachers and their low wages we should add the negative impact of violence on learning. Education is particularly difficult in neighborhoods characterized by high levels of violence due to a lack of stability and community safety. Violence leads many teachers to feel insecure and de-motivated, leaving them less inclined or unable to invest time and energy to teaching in trying circumstances (UNICEF 2009: 108; Leeds 2007). In some of the communities in which Vencer operates, several examples exist of drug traffickers ordering children to stay away from school if there is to be a threat from a rival faction. Some schools are closed for prolonged periods of time as a consequence of the intervention of drug traffickers. Violence can also affect the implementation of the

Vencer program, as program coordinator Bianca notes: "Often the violence in the community ends up affecting the day-to-day running of the project. We know that the majority of absentees are related to this." In contrast, Pedro, a local teacher in the militia-dominated community with low levels of public violence, argues that safety is key not only to fostering a vibrant community life but also to the quality of education:

> Many communities in Rio have problems with violence and traffickers, but we don't have those issues here. . . . That makes it more attractive to teach and do community work. There is little fear here. People can go outside and participate in public life. Sure, [our school's] resources are always limited, but if you press hard enough you can get some. And you have to be creative and do some unpaid work, and arrange [teaching and learning] materials yourself with the support of the community.

Vencer staff use the term "education" in a broad sense to include extra-curricular and informal learning activities. In particular, they point to other aspects of cultural capital which are pertinent to the educational attainment of young favela residents. For example, Catarina contends:

> Students in public education are disadvantaged compared to private education students. Not only in terms of the quality of the schooling they receive, but also in terms of their restricted access to various other forms of informal education such as quality books, magazines, Internet, theatre, cinema, cultural events.

To stimulate informal learning, members of staff in the Vencer program encourage participants to read. The implementing NGOs have small libraries and study rooms to compensate for the lack of study space in overcrowded dwellings. A few former Vencer participants now work as librarians or assistants in these libraries. One of the NGOs runs a reading project in which young people can borrow books free of charge and request book titles which they would like the NGO to purchase. Several Vencer participants are enrolled in this reading project and read up to 20 books per year. The NGO also organizes relevant leisure activities such as visits to museums, cultural events and cinemas. Vencer staff's efforts to stimulate learning through acts such as reading are informed in part by Paulo Freire's view of reading as a key means for developing critical consciousness (Freire and Macedo 1987: Chapter 1).

In addition to stimulating informal learning, Vencer staff also seek to enable participants to familiarize themselves with tertiary and private education in order to enhance their institutional orientation. Vencer coordinator Márcia recognizes that the Vencer program cannot make up for the poor quality of public education. However, she notes that "we do focus on things that regular education does not cover. To get a job they need to talk well, read well, understand what they read. That's what we try to work on here." According to Márcia, developing a "feel for the game" includes a need to

> improve the way they talk because otherwise people will say "you talk like someone from the favela." They learn at school that they must talk like this, but they live most of their lives in the favela where everybody talks a certain way. And you try to work on this, we correct them and so they start to correct themselves. Not to put them down but as a learning process.

As noted in Chapter 5, Vencer staff act as institutional agents, for example by assisting participants to identify and apply for scholarships or courses, and to prepare for the university entry exam (*vestibular*). One of the implementing NGOs has established a partnership with a university, one of whose campuses is located on *a rua* in the vicinity of the favelas being studied. Through this partnership, the NGO is able to offer most of its classes at the university campus free of charge. Márcia, who is the director of this NGO, describes the impact of this approach as follows:

> Here we are inside a university. Many of the people in the community would never even think about entering a space like that. So the first time they come here they don't feel very comfortable in that space. But as they progress through the program they feel more comfortable in this space. There is a common space where they mix with people from the university. There was a time when the students said "look at these favelados here." And the youth came back here and asked "what did we do that made them think that we are from the favela? What did we do wrong? What happened?" We said "no, nothing happened, it's just that some people say favelados but not really meaning people from the favela but rather that people are talking too much. It has nothing to do with you, you have a good presentation." But, you see, they try to change the way they dress and the way they talk.

The above analysis raises a number of important questions: can the cultural capital facilitated by the sports activities being studied really make a difference in the face of structural inequalities? Are there other social fields that affect the impact of these activities beyond those discussed here (education system, family and labor market)? How and to what extent are the cultural capital gains described in this chapter convertible into economic capital and hence into social mobility? These questions are addressed in the final chapters of this book.

7   Social Mobility and Economic Life

In the preceding chapters the focus has been on the accumulation and operation of social and cultural capital, with particular reference to the contextual factors that affect these forms of capital. The analysis proffered in these chapters enhances our understanding of the relationship between non-professional forms of sport and social mobility. However, any examination of social mobility through sport, at least in its objective dimension as outlined in Chapter 1, needs to address the issue of economic capital. Even though other types of capital are not reducible to economic capital because they have their own specificity, economic capital may be viewed to be, in the final analysis, at the root of their effects (Bourdieu 1986). In this context, Loizos (2000: 141) rightly argues that while the concept of social capital is "a useful reminder that there is more to life than market or Marxist economics," it was never part of Bourdieu's thinking "that we should forget the priorities of economic life, and allow social relations to pretend to replace a more comprehensive social theory" (see also Fine 2001).

In this chapter, the theme of economic capital is addressed in regard to the four settings being studied. This is dealt with by exploring the direct relationship between sport participation and economic capital as well as its indirect links through the conversion of social and cultural capital, hence touching upon the dynamics of conversion between different types of capital. I will then identify the main contextual and individual obstacles to the accumulation of economic capital through non-professional forms of sport, which are illustrated with examples from MG, Vencer and SSP. The chapter will then proceed to examine the prospects and possibilities for social mobility in both its objective and subjective dimensions. Finally, I will reflect on the extent and nature of social mobility across the four settings.

RECREATIONAL SPORT AND THE
ACCUMULATION OF ECONOMIC CAPITAL

The stories of research participants presented in previous chapters reveal some of the ways in which participation in sports activities or sport-for-development programs may generate economic capital for individuals and their families.[11] One of the more obvious processes through which this occurs is the availability of job opportunities in or related to sport. The coaches at MG are a case in point. In the past the coaches used to work at the club on a voluntary basis, often grounded in their status and experience as former players. Although this form of voluntarism still exists, at present MG financially compensates coaches for their efforts, at $150 per week. MG secretary Samatar argues that "this is an important incentive [because] otherwise it would be very difficult to retain and motivate coaches." Besides skill development opportunities that may enhance their cultural capital, financial compensation offers the coaches "real financial benefits." Former MG coach Yusuf adds:

> We employ coaches now. So every hour they spend at the club is paid. Many people at the club used to say "why are we paying them, it's for the community." But we thought, you know, to get quality and commitment . . . sure, volunteering, but volunteering doesn't exist in our culture. You only do volunteer work when it comes to the mosque and the religious and spiritual sphere, but not for normal things. There isn't that mindset. So the coaches get paid. And they can use that in part to send to their family [in refugee camps or in Somalia].

Yusuf also gives examples of how the social support networks at MG can facilitate mutual economic capital. He describes how some of the Somali mothers at the club work in child care or run their own informal childcare service. Yusuf regularly leaves his children with one of the mothers who care for several children whose parents work: "If you work till five o'clock [she] will pick your child up from school and look after it till 5. You pay [her], but it's much cheaper than commercial child care." Social support of this kind can be financially beneficial for both parties: it provides a source of income for the mothers in question, while allowing Yusuf and other parents to work full-time and access cheap child care.

NCFL participants voice similar sentiments concerning the theme of economic capital. Economic opportunities accrue to individuals as part of the social networks they create and maintain in the sports context. Social connections made in the NCFL can contain significant business opportunities, as in the case of tradesman Alex who argues that some of his football-related contacts have resulted in new employment opportunities (see Chapter 4). In a similar vein, Michael, the owner of a hotel in a small town in northwest Victoria, notes that many of his customers visit his hotel because of his status as a key NCFL representative. Furthermore, sports clubs in the NCFL regularly organize fundraising campaigns, the proceeds of which may benefit local residents who experience economic hardship. In this context, netball player Simone argues: "If you were in need a sporting club is always a good place to go. So if you're playing and you say 'I'm really short of cash has anyone got any work going on the farm?' It's a really good social network in that sense."

More generally, NCFL respondents point to the economic impact of sporting competitions in northwest Victoria, with the viability of NCFL clubs and small town economies linked to a considerable degree. A Parliamentary Inquiry into Australian football in regional Victoria found that "the economic significance of football/netball clubs is particularly pronounced in small rural towns." This economic significance "is not only a product of direct expenditure, such as gate and bar takings, but also of a significant multiplier effect—a 'chain reaction' of additional income and purchases resulting from football and netball activity" (Rural and Regional Services and Development Committee 2004: 45). This argument is consistent with the narratives of NCFL participants and other local residents. Recreation officer James describes the economic impact of NCFL football clubs as follows:

> If there's a home game the businesses are busy. And if there's [another team] going to [an away game] on the way through we often generate business from that so there's huge economic benefit from that, to have a football side in the town. . . . The football club generates about $6,000 on a home game. Other funds come out of sponsorship and memberships. So if you've got a club with a $200,000 turnover that's $4,000 a week, all year round so it's bigger than some of the businesses in the main street. It's an economic business in its own right.

From his own experience, Jim, a cricket player in his 40s, confirms that "the money does circulate" and that "there's a spin-off there for fuel companies to get [visiting teams] up there, and when they're up there they buy food and that at the ground or in the main street, they pay an entrance fee which goes to the local community." In a similar vein, NCFL secretary Barrie asserts:

> The more people we get [to local sports matches] the more the shop people are gonna benefit through what we sell, and whether it be from food, drink or whatever. Same for people that are employed in the town. So the benefits go all over the place in that they help in a lot of areas. So, yeah, there's no doubt [that sports clubs] benefit the towns and if you talk to the towns that do lose their sporting club, those towns slip back massively. So, yeah it would be scary if we ever thought that would happen.

Indeed, on match days relevant local businesses have a higher turnover. The local bakery, butcher, hotel and supermarket sell their products to spectators and support the sports clubs by supplying ingredients (Townsend et al. 2002). Janet, a local baker, argues that "the economic impact of sport is significant for small business like ours. About 50% of the population attend Saturday games and many come to the bakery for pies." However, Janet also suggests that the economic impact of sports clubs in the NCFL is partly dependent on the clubs' on-field successes: "When the club goes well we sell more pies. You get larger crowds and that's good for our business." Further, the following comment by tennis club president Alicia shows that economic spin-offs vary greatly across different sports, with Australian football clubs having the most significant economic impact:

> Football's economic impact is much more than perhaps tennis. With tennis . . . people might stop at the shop on their way home and buy some things as they head out of town, if they're from another town and that sort of thing. I guess that economic impact adds up . . . but [at least in tennis] it's more of a social and a health thing [which] perhaps is the number one driver, and I would see economic as secondary but still important.

Another aspect of the economic and social impact of sports clubs in the NCFL relates to the challenges faced by the rural communities to retain young people. As noted in Chapter 2, the small towns in northwest Victoria have witnessed an accelerated "flight of youth" to seek education, training and employment in regional and metropolitan cities. As a consequence, several football and netball clubs in the NCFL struggle to retain young players. They encourage young people, especially talented players, to return home on weekends to play football or netball by paying their petrol costs and/or offering playing fees. Financial incentives, place identity and community pride go hand in hand in such cases, as netball player Alicia notes:

> Young men in particular who leave town to pursue tertiary education will often retain their connections with the town through sports. Your first four years out of high school and you go to university the club will often pay you to come home and play on the weekends. So there's an economic incentive there but being part of your community in that way is really important for a lot of guys who are valued for their talent, so in that sense it does . . . create an identity.

While this strategy appears to have been fairly successful in maintaining young people's connection with sports clubs in the NCFL, individuals rarely continue to do this for more than a few years. According to a former NCFL football player, "young players only travel back for two or three years normally, then you lose them because they settle down and have family or job obligations."

The Creation of Economic Capital in the Sport Steward Program

Compared with the possibilities for the accumulation of economic capital in the NCFL and MG, individual socio-economic advancement is sought more deliberately and explicitly in the SSP and Vencer programs. Both programs seek to enhance participants' employability prospects and, ultimately, their occupational and educational attainment. One would therefore expect the accumulation of individualized economic capital to be more pronounced in these programs than in the NCFL and MG. This raises the question of to what extent and under which conditions participants in the SSP and Vencer programs are able to generate economic capital, notably through occupational attainment.

The SSP study provides detailed data on the occupational attainment of SSP participants. In the preceding chapters we have seen how former participants such as Sylvia, Mustapha and Fatima interpret the development of their economic capital. All three of them now work as a security guard and sport steward, and they credit the SSP program for equipping them with the cultural and social resources required to obtain these occupations. Mustapha also pursues further education in order to become fully qualified in his profession, having experienced years of interrupted schooling and unemployment. He argues that his participation in SSP has given him "a really positive step" forward in his life, viewing this as "the beginning of my future, a way to build my future." Among other things, it has taught him to become more proactive and responsible in his pursuit of a professional career:

> I speak to many street kids now that I work in the security business. I tell them "you know, you have to work on your future. Just hanging around and doing nothing, that won't get you anywhere." But they say "but we have no choice, it's the society." I think that's rubbish. Opportunities don't just come your way. You also need to take initiative, look for opportunities yourself and take them when they are being handed to you.

Mustapha notes that SSP has given him the "push" and the tools he needed to leave behind his welfare dependency and obtain challenging and rewarding employment: "Without their support it would have been much more difficult for me, to do everything myself. They helped me a lot and that means a lot to me." In the past he had repeatedly failed to get a continuing job due in part to his lack of educational qualifications. His SSP diploma and certificates give him "the extra step I needed," as do the social credentials provided by SSP coordinators: "They really supported me by saying 'this guy is highly motivated and skilled, so give him a chance.' That's how I got my job." Mustapha is confident that the positive impact will be durable: "I'm almost certain that I will not fall back into a social security situation. This year I really need to push through and finish my degree. When I have my degree I can really get a permanent job." SSP coordinator Danny agrees: "[Mustapha] was highly motivated and very serious. He was on social security and ashamed of that; he wanted to be independent. It's great to have people like him in the group because their enthusiasm and commitment reflect on the entire group. He has done really well for himself."

In a similar vein, Fatima, who is in her late 20s, now holds a full-time job as an airport security officer. Like Mustapha, Fatima had been unemployed for several years before she enrolled in SSP. She ended up in this situation as a consequence of family and relationship problems which caused her to drop out of school at a young age. She describes how she "was going through a very rough time" and desperately seeking an opportunity to change her fortunes. Thus, she notes: "I commenced here [at SSP] for a foundation, as a new beginning. And it has paid off . . . I have a little house in Rotterdam and I work at the airport." SSP coordinators stress that Fatima and Mustapha are both examples of disadvantaged young people with great potential. Danny argues:

> I strongly believe that these young people have a lot of capital at their level . . . but that you need to do much more with them at a personal level. They often need more hands and feet, literally, to guide them in that process. They don't have the capability or mentality, for whatever reason, to make use of existing opportunities. As a society you need to invest much more in people like [Mustapha] and [Fatima] because they are gold. They are excellent persons and as a society we are going to reap the benefits. And within their own circle they are a kind of role model. And that's where I believe SSP is worth its weight in gold, because these were two young people who had a lot of potential and qualities but just needed a little help with rebuilding their lives, people and places they can rely on. In their case it had nothing to do with motivation. . . . And what's interesting is that it's not always those with the largest problems who are the most difficult to help with this type of project. [Fatima] had been going through serious problems, but she did very well. And [Mustapha] has also been through a lot. But they are among the most motivated and successful of all participants.

The above "success stories", however, conceal the fact that the volume and the longevity of the economic capital generated by SSP participants vary greatly. Former SSP participant Jennifer is in a broadly similar financial situation to Fatima and Mustapha. She was unemployed for several years but has recently obtained a job with a major events security company. She mainly works at sporting events and concerts, and she studies one day per week to finish her education and become a fully qualified event security officer. She now earns approximately $1,500 per month, which gives her "more security" and the opportunity to rent her own house and pay off her debt. At the moment, however, Jennifer has a temporary contract, and her longer-term financial future therefore remains uncertain. Jennifer's situation is quite typical in this regard. The economic capital formation of SSP participants is characterized by a high degree of temporality and fluidity.

SSP staff recognize that the employment situation of many participants is fragile and in constant flux. For example, SSP coordinator John notes: "The employment situation of participants is a momentary snapshot. For some of them, this situation changes continuously. For others, who are doing well, it's more constant." In this context, Gallie and Paugam (2002) argue that those with an experience of unemployment, even where they enter work, are likely to enter poor quality, temporary work with fewer opportunities for self-control, where they have higher levels of perceived insecurity and where there are fewer chances for self-development and progress. John's comment also points to the limitations of orthodox approaches to social mobility, which tend to assess intragenerational mobility in terms of changes in people's occupational position at a couple of fixed points in their adult life (see Chapter 1). In reality, SSP participants' social trajectories are often fractured and inconsistent progression stories, as discussed in a later part of this chapter.

The above "success stories" thus raise the question of whether they are representative of a broader pattern of systematic accumulation of economic capital through successful occupational attainment. To address this question, Table 7.1 provides an overview of the employment and education situations of former SSP participants at the time of the study in 2008.

Table 7.1 shows that at the time of the study, 38% of former SSP participants are in some form of stable employment. The most common areas of employment are the service sector and manual labor. Most of the youth in this category have been able to considerably improve their financial situation since their participation in SSP. Members of staff have helped a number of these participants to set up a payment plan to pay off their debts and create more structure in their financial situation. A further 18% of former SSP participants have gone back to school or pursue further education in

Table 7.1   Employment and Education Situation of Former SSP Participants

Employment and education situation	No. of people	Percentage of total
Stable employment (minimum one-year contract)	23	38%
Full-time education (inc. paid apprenticeships)	11	18%
Temporary employment	7	11%
Unemployments/welfare dependent	10	16%
Unknown	10	16%
Total	61	100%

Reprinted from Spaaij (2009a: 259).

sport and human movement, youth work, security and event management or specialized manual labor. Although the young people in this category can increase their cultural capital which may, in time, translate into economic returns, thus far they have not been able to make significant financial progress following their participation in SSP. Five former participants have an apprentice-level income that is roughly comparable to the social security benefits they previously received. Seven former SSP participants are in temporary employment with relatively low levels of job and income security. Ten persons remain unemployed.

From this brief overview we can conclude that a sizeable minority of former SSP participants have been able to significantly increase their economic capital. However, it is difficult to assess with any certainty the degree to which (and what aspect of) participation in SSP has been a key factor in this process beyond the compelling personal narratives presented earlier. Moreover, it should be reiterated that the picture portrayed in Table 7.1 is a snapshot at one particular point in time and does not capture the temporality and fluidity of participants' occupational attainment.

Economic Capital and Occupational Attainment in the Vencer Program

How does this snapshot compare, then, to the economic capital and occupational attainment of participants in the Vencer program who, as we have seen in Chapter 6, face several obstacles to formal employment? To get an overall picture of former Vencer participants' economic capital formation and occupational attainment, Vencer survey participants are asked whether they are employed and, if so, where and how many hours per week. Sixty-three percent of survey respondents indicate that they work at the time of the survey (in 2009), whereas the remaining 37% report that they are unemployed. Of those who are in employment, 56% work more than 20 hours per week, while a further 23% work between 11 and 20 hours per week. Figure 7.1 lists the wide range of employment types reported by Vencer survey respondents. The most commonly reported occupations are administrative assistant, apprentice (e.g. at local NGOs), ICT teacher/technician and telemarketing operator.

Unfortunately, the Vencer survey data do not provide an in-depth picture of the *meanings* Vencer participants give to the nature of their employment situation and its consequences for their economic capital. The qualitative interviews are more instructive in this regard. Vencer coordinator Márcia notes that "there is a financial gain for some" through occupational attainment, which can enable participants to "rent or buy their own house and go to university; a change of perspective but also a very concrete change in lifestyle." In the previous chapters, former Vencer participants such as Marta, Carolina, Maria and Paulo describe the conversion of their newly acquired social and cultural capital into economic capital. Marta has a full-time

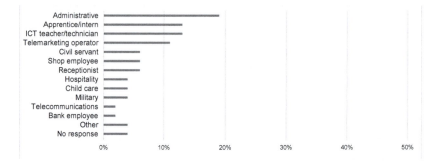

Figure 7.1 Types of employment of former Vencer participants.

job as a call center operator, having previously worked for a telemarketing company as part of her internship during Vencer. She argues that her current job gives her and her family more economic capital:

> When I first arrived [at Vencer] I hadn't done much with my life. I hadn't worked or done a course. The moment you start earning money you are able to become more independent, which is important. And it allows you to help your family, because my family doesn't have an income so I came to assist them. That's a very good thing.

Marta values the skills and knowledge she has developed during her participation in Vencer. However, she is adamant that she will need to keep studying in order to further enhance her cultural capital, which she believes would enable her to "open a better door for myself" in the future.

Maria's experience is broadly similar in this respect. Maria is a 19-year-old former Vencer participant who now works as a part-time assistant at a local NGO. In her view, there are few employment opportunities in her local community beyond those associated with the informal economy. This is her main motive for enrolling in Vencer, through which she receives intensive employability skills training and a four-month apprenticeship in the city. She describes how her participation in Vencer "helped me to obtain my first job; I gained new knowledge and now I am learning even more [in my new job]." For Maria, it is important that her job gives her a greater degree of financial independence: "My mother has never had a good financial situation and my stepfather has an income but spends it all. That's why I began to look at having my own things for my own endeavor, and not depend on them." Maria's experience indicates that the pressure to start working at an early age is not necessarily communicated by family members (as noted in Chapter 5). Rather, in Maria's case this pressure is very much self-imposed. As Vencer coordinator Ana remarks:

There is pressure to start working at an early age rather than to explore other opportunities. Bring money home. And it's not just the family that puts pressure on them. We say that as they grow older the toys become more expensive. They don't want to dress anymore using the same T-shirt their older brothers are using. They look around and want to be close to the reference group. This is the social pressure and consumer culture. Even if a person has a very strong family structure they cannot pay. So what are you going to do? Find a job. It's a kind of family pressure, social pressure, consumer pressure.

Indeed, young favela residents are very much aware of society's growing culture of consumerism and have a desire for cosmopolitan consumer goods despite having relatively few possibilities to realize this desire (Banck 1995; Dowdney 2003; Piccolo 2008). Like their middle-class counterparts, these youth endeavor to become individual cosmopolitan consumers to the best of their ability (Ireland 2010). In Maria's case, her salary allows her to "buy things I hadn't been able to afford, such as new clothes," and "go to the cinema and the shopping centre."

Other former Vencer participants report similar experiences with regard to the accumulation of economic capital. For example, Felipe, who is in his mid 20s, now works as a telemarketing operator in a middle-class neighborhood. During his participation in the Vencer program he worked as an apprentice at a private education institution. His former mentor Sandra describes Felipe's trajectory as follows: "His life has changed a lot. He works, earns more money and has become more motivated to study, to enrol in a university course. There are many people who don't have that perspective." Felipe himself acknowledges that "the Vencer program has helped me in every aspect [of my life]. It is because of the program that I gained my first job and I am still working there today." On a more critical note, however, Sandra recognizes that the issue of financial independence "is very complicated here" and that only a small minority of Vencer participants are likely to achieve this. She takes Felipe as an example:

A telemarketing operator, who earns a good wage, will get R$800 [$480] [per month]. For someone to be independent, that is, pay rent . . . that's difficult. There is certainly a financial improvement that sets a person in motion, which can generate more benefits in the long term. For example, Felipe earns well, around R$800. If he invests this in his education, a university degree, then eventually he will be financially independent. So people go on a pathway. Now, to be fully independent when the program finishes, that's difficult.

Sandra's remarks show that even though a significant number of Vencer participants are able to accumulate economic capital which considerably improves their financial situation in the short term, the volume of this capital is generally rather limited, particularly in the first few years of employment. The former Vencer participants who are currently employed earn between R$300 and R$2,400, with the vast majority earning well below R$1,000 ($600) on a monthly basis. Sandra's comments also indicate how it may be possible to convert one form of capital into another—in this case economic capital into institutionalized cultural capital, which in turn can increase one's future stock of economic capital. This process of conversion, she suggests, requires continuous effort by intelligent social agents in order to get ahead in the long term. However, there are several obstacles that hinder the accumulation of economic capital and the process of capital conversion. It is to these obstacles that I will now turn.

CONTEXTUAL AND INDIVIDUAL OBSTACLES TO ECONOMIC CAPITAL

In Chapters 4 to 6 we have seen how people's ability to acquire social and cultural capital in the sports context and to transfer these forms of capital to other spheres of life is affected by exogenous field effects, notably those emanating from the economy, education system, politics and family. These external field effects are also highly relevant with regard to economic capital. A common theme in the MG, Vencer and SSP studies is people's perceived shortage of opportunities to advance their occupational careers due to persistent unemployment or underemployment, poor preparation for the evolving knowledge economy in terms of educational qualifications and work experience and/or labor market discrimination. The Vencer program is a case in point. Chapter 6 shows how the limited work experience provided by Vencer can serve as a basis for the development of cultural capital. However, the conversion of this experience into post-program employment and hence into economic capital is often a difficult process. One of Vencer's key challenges has been to establish fruitful partnerships with public and private sector organizations to create job placements for Vencer participants. To date, approximately 71% of Vencer former participants have completed an internship or apprenticeship.

The Vencer survey results show that participants and staff consider job placement a vital component of the program, enabling participants to gain some professional work experience and credentials. For example, Vencer educator Edu argues:

> Job placement is important because it's a way to familiarize yourself with and investigate a certain environment, and to find out whether this is a path you would like to follow. I believe that nothing substitutes for practical experiences, going to a company and getting to know the work.

Although most Vencer participants seem to agree, as discussed in Chapter 6, some participants are critical of the extent to which job placements are available and/or translate into occupational attainment. Luisão, who is in his mid 20s, asserts that "youth don't have the experience and employers generally hire people with experience. But the majority of those searching for dignified and secure work are young people, so how are they going to find their first job if companies are not hiring them?" Luisão explains that he and his fellow Vencer participants

> were promised practical work experience, for example in a call center . . . but there were no job placements. They also said that when you complete the program, you would be employed almost straight away. But [a year later] we remain unemployed, so something needs to change.

Thus, Luisão contends, the program may create "a false expectation in many people." Sandra, who was one of Luisão's teachers at the Vencer program, is sympathetic to his criticism. She feels that "companies are not always open and willing to receive the young people" and points to the "highly competitive labor market" which makes it "very difficult for young people to succeed in this market." Sandra notes that "when they finish the program and don't have a job placement they may be stuck in the middle and not get a job. So it's very important to have partnerships with businesses, but it's not easy."

A number of Vencer staff and participants add to this the issue of labor market discrimination. Some residents of the communities being studied feel discriminated against by potential employers for being "slum dwellers" (favelados), which leads some of them to attempt to conceal their residential address during job applications. Prejudices and stereotypes held by potential employers may frustrate Vencer staff's efforts to establish partnerships with the private sector, as coordinator Ana confesses:

> We talk to people from big companies around here. I ask them how many of their employees come from this community. They say "just a few." Why? . . ."Oh, because in the favela we don't have qualified people" . . . [T]hey have the idea that "it's poor so nothing is good."

Furthermore, once in the labor market, favela residents may experience color-based wage discrimination, as the literature on labor market discrimination in Brazil clearly shows (Lovell 2000; Lovell and Wood 1998; Silva 2000). For example, Lovell and Wood (1998: 105–6) argue that "the fact that the wage differentials [between whites and non-whites] persist even after controlling for education and job experience suggests that urban labor markets in Brazil are characterized by color-based wage discrimination." Nelson do Valle Silva also finds that "the estimated effects of discrimination on income differences are still sizeable and significant" (Silva 2000:

26). According to Silva, in 1996 the monetary disadvantages suffered by nonwhites due to labor market discrimination amount to almost one-quarter of their group income, averaging about R$100 a month. This amount, he claims, is the "cost of not being white" in Brazil.

Some of the Vencer participants interviewed indeed report that they experience labor market discrimination. However, they nonetheless endeavor to be proactive in the process of accumulating economic capital through occupational attainment. For example, Juliana, a former participant in her 20s, describes how she feels discriminated against because she is black and lives in a favela, and that her family suffers from prejudice. She indicates that she would really like to change her life and that of her family, and that this desire stimulates her to engage in programs such as Vencer. Juliana notes:

> Discrimination exists. But I've learned that I have to believe in myself, and not think that I won't get a job because of my skin color or race. Doesn't matter whether there are ten people and I'm the only black one. You need to believe in yourself. You don't know what the profile of the company is, whether the employer is black or white, so you just have to show your best side. Many young people are still afraid. If you go to work in a shop they have to know where you live, and you cannot lie. They have to hire me based on who I am, not what I pretend to be.

Despite its qualitatively different social setting, a few MG participants also see labor market discrimination as an obstacle to occupational attainment. For instance, MG coach Roble asserts that "quite a few young Somali people are frustrated about their job opportunities, largely as a result of their fathers' situations [who mostly hold low-skilled jobs]. They are frustrated with the system, with the lack of opportunities. They often see this as being due to discrimination for being black, African, Muslim." However, as the story of former MG coach Mohamed described in Chapter 4 illustrates, some Somali youth take a proactive approach to overcoming discrimination. Thus, Mohamed argues that discrimination "says more about the person who discriminates than about the person who is discriminated against." He adds: "If you sit back and say 'I am discriminated against, I can't do nothing about it,' then that's when people discriminate against you because you're just too lazy to do something about it. If people discriminate against you, go up to them, invite them."

Another often-mentioned obstacle to the accumulation of economic capital in MG, Vencer and SSP is the judicial system. A few young MG players have dropped out of university or apprenticeships to take up taxi driving or find other ways to make money. For them, the road to qualifications is too long, too expensive and too uncertain in terms of securing a job at the end of the process. At the other end of the spectrum, some older MG participants have completed (higher) education in Somalia or in neighboring countries, but their qualifications are not officially recognized in Australia.

The lack of official recognition of higher education degrees hinders these individuals in their search for well-paid employment, often forcing them to go back to school or take up low-skilled jobs instead. Former MG president Abdirahman has experienced this dilemma firsthand. His business degree is not recognized in Australia, and he therefore decided to take up a job as a taxi driver to "feed my family." In the meantime, Abdirahman enrolled in tertiary education in Melbourne to enhance his cultural capital. After years of combining work and study, he earned a business degree from an Australian university which has enabled him to apply for competitive jobs. Abdirahman now works at a major bank. In retrospect, he describes the struggle to get his degree recognized and find a well-paid job as follows:

> People who are doing serious work and have good education, by the time we come [to Australia] there's that expectation, trying to do something . . . recognition of the university certificates, high school certificates. It took time but then later on some of the people got it; the major certificates from the universities particularly from medicine, engineering, accountancy. Transferring these documents into Australian standards was there for you . . . but the problem would be getting work through this. 'Cause even when these qualifications are approved in Australia . . . what do you know about Australia? If I came here three or four years ago I don't have that experience in Australia. Most of the people will knock you down.

In a similar vein, former MG secretary Bashir notes:

> This is where the disappointment comes in. People who come here with an educated background, they've got a diploma. Back home they'd be either doctors or lawyers or whatever, one of those big dream jobs. They come here and their qualification doesn't get recognized. . . . No one is going to put food on the table so they have to get a job like driving taxi.

The judicial field also affects SSP and Vencer participants' opportunities for the accumulation and conversion of economic and cultural capital. Chapter 2 discusses how the recent *Wet Investeren in Jongeren* impacts upon the SSP program and its participants. In the Netherlands, young people aged 18 to 27 are no longer entitled to social security benefits unless they work or are enrolled in education. This new legislation erodes the economic capital of unemployed young people who have dropped out of school, making it far more difficult for them to get by unless they accept the job or education offered to them by their municipal government. On the other hand, the legislation could have a positive impact on participants' commitment to and achievements in the SSP program, which in turn could enhance their cultural capital and occupational attainment in the longer term.

The same kind of ambivalence can be observed with regard to the impact of Brazilian labor laws on the Vencer program and its participants. Vencer coordinator Carolina notes that "the Brazilian economy is not very stable; it's complicated. Changes have an impact on the program, including law reforms." For example, recent changes to the *Lei do Estagio* (Internship Law) mean that employers now need to reimburse interns' travel costs and pay out recreational leave. Although these changes are generally beneficial for those who are in an internship, they have also caused several businesses to cut back on internships due to the increased costs which means that the number of available internships has diminished.

The analysis of contextual factors that affect people's ability to acquire economic, cultural and social capital by means of involvement in sports programs and activities reveals the interrelationships between sport and other social fields as well as the durability of external constraints in shaping their lives. These contextual factors may be seen to condition the aspirations, strategies and achievements of the social agents being studied by orienting their actions and inclinations through individual and collective habitus. As Young (1999: 202) notes, "social context not only directly shapes the capacity for individuals to access certain outcomes, but also the ability to first imagine those outcomes, thereafter determining whether they are legitimate or worthwhile pursuits." However, as argued in Chapter 1, these contextual factors neither strictly determine people's actions and inclinations nor do they necessarily reproduce the social inequalities with which they are confronted. Actors' dispositions are constantly subjected to a range of different experiences from which new forms and actions can arise. In this context, Bourdieu (1999: 340) argues that "pedagogical action can . . . open the possibility of an emancipation founded on awareness and knowledge of the conditionings undergone and on the imposition of new conditionings designed durably to counter their effects." In this book numerous examples have been given of individuals and families who develop and convert different types of capital through their participation in non-professional forms of sport, and who in some cases are strikingly successful in doing so, thereby increasing their prospects and possibilities for upward mobility and their influence over wider contextual factors.

Upholding the agency of the people being studied requires a move beyond structural constraints to incorporate into the analysis individual factors which affect the accumulation of economic capital, including motivation, drive, persistence, talent, skills and luck (cf. Perlman 2010: Chapter 9). The previous chapters provide ample illustration of the significance of these factors. For example, in Chapter 2 we have seen how SSP and Vencer coordinators regard personal motivation and persistence as key assets which can help participants navigate or even overcome certain structural constraints. Indeed, several research participants set goals for themselves and meet them, and they stress that people should have the right attitude and go after things they believe in rather than depending on others for their well-being. For these individuals, their pre-existing shortage of cultural capital is partly compensated for by their personal drive to succeed, resisting to some degree their present situation and proactively seeking to improve their socio-economic conditions (cf. Cain 2007). In this context, SSP coordinator Danny notes: "I find it admirable that some young people use that situation to say 'that's what I definitely don't want in life,' and use that background as a stimulus and motivation to walk a step faster to break free from that background." Although this view runs the risk of reinforcing the meritocracy myth (McNamee and Miller 2004), that is, the myth that the system distributes economic and cultural resources according to the merit of individuals, it is important in its emphasis on individual or group initiative as a gateway to social mobility. It is to the latter issue that I will now turn.

SOCIAL MOBILITY PATHS: OBJECTIVE INDICATORS

Mainstream social mobility research tends to measure individual mobility in terms of changes in occupational position at two or, at most, three fixed points: the job held by a parent (usually the father) at some point in the individual's lifetime, the first job of the respondent and the respondent's present occupation (Miller 1998: 147). Perceived in these terms, social mobility becomes synonymous with occupational status (and hence social class) which in turn is a main proxy of economic capital. This notion of social mobility, however, needs to be treated with care if it is to be analytically useful in each of the four social settings being studied. As shown earlier in this chapter, the present occupational status of research participants is a momentary snapshot that conceals the temporality and precarity of their employment experiences. In other words, the definition of fixed points compromises a process-based analysis of social mobility (Miller 1998: 147).

Moreover, determining which fixed points are most suitable for analytical purposes is a complex task. A "before-and-after" approach seems appropriate for the present purpose. This approach involves collecting information from participants prior to participation in the sports program or activity (i.e. a baseline study) and after they have been taking part for some time (Coalter 2008a: 30). However, while this approach may be feasible in the case of an official program with clearly demarcated timescales (i.e. SSP and Vencer), it is less suitable in situations where sports activities are engaged in for a longer, undetermined period of time (i.e. NCFL and MG). Finally, comparison between the job held by a parent and the respondent's present occupation as a measure of social mobility is somewhat skewed in the Vencer and MG cases due to the profound impact of structural mobility (i.e. rural-urban migration; Pastore 1982) and forced migration respectively, as discussed in Chapter 2. I should reiterate here that in this book the focus is on non-structural, intragenerational forms of social mobility since it is assumed that the impact of non-professional forms of sport on mobility is to be found principally at this level.

With these qualifications in mind, it is possible to analyze the extent and nature of intragenerational social mobility in the four settings being studied. Overall, participation in sports programs and activities certainly has the potential to bring about social advancement in people's lives through the accumulation and conversion of economic, cultural and social capital. In this chapter we have seen several illustrations of how such participation can facilitate occupational attainment either directly or indirectly via the conversion of social and cultural capital. Some research participants now work as sports coaches or stewards or in other sport-related professions, albeit usually on a part-time basis. Others have been able to use their social connections in the sports context to leverage job opportunities and/or to increase their cultural capital which enables them to gain a competitive advantage in the labor market or access certain jobs. For example, whereas the bonding and bridging social capital of NCFL volunteer Alex allows him to access jobs as a tradesman in northwest Victoria, former Vencer participant Carolina now holds a senior position in the Brazilian army and earns approximately six times the minimum wage.

The stories of Alex, Carolina and others are indicative of the ways in which participation in sports programs or activities facilitates the accumulation of resources to action, the composites of which may create paths for upward social mobility in each of the four settings under study. However, it is also clear from the preceding analysis that objective social mobility in terms of durable occupational advancement is not widespread and occurs only in a minority of cases. Moreover, where such advancement does take place it is at a personal and, to a lesser degree, family level rather than at any structural level. In other words, individual sports programs and activities are far more likely to stimulate personal change than effect any structural change.

These findings are consistent with the views of Vencer and SSP coordinators who emphasize not so much short-term economic improvements but rather the longer-term possibilities and prospects that flow from the personal and social development models they seek to engender, the outcomes of which may not yet be visible and cannot be seen in isolation from other spheres of participants' lives. For example, Vencer coordinator Bianca regards participation in Vencer as "a first yet significant step" toward improved educational and occupational attainment. In the same vein, Celi, who is the co-director of a local NGO, asserts: "It's a first step, seemingly a small step but I believe that it's a large step. I believe it's a door that can open other doors." Bianca and Celi both recognize that a sport-for-development program with an average duration of six months cannot fully compensate for major income and educational disadvantages. Nevertheless, Bianca estimates that approximately one-quarter of Vencer participants, notably those who have relatively large stocks of (institutionalized) cultural capital and are highly motivated, will experience upward social mobility in the short or longer term. These participants, Bianca argues, "just need one opportunity" to convert their cultural capital into occupational success:

> In this case it is Vencer, but it could also have been other opportunities, because they are very good. These ones will go to university and will get better jobs, for sure. So they will move with the opportunities we offer. What they have been lacking is the contacts to get the really good job opportunities. They found jobs but only informal, because that's the way things go here [in the local community]. That's the reality they know how to operate in. It is not because they are not very good, but because no one asks or gives them these resources and information.

Bianca believes that the majority of Vencer participants will experience more limited social advancement, such as "have a job or go to university or further study" or "rent or own a house." However, she also recognizes that even for those who do not achieve upward mobility in the objective sense, the development of social and cultural capital in Vencer can still be advantageous in a very real and important way: "to transform them from not being a citizen to being a citizen." Here Bianca refers to the sense of exclusion that many poor favela residents feel, a stance expressed in their complaint that they perceive that they are not seen as deserving human beings and therefore not as bearers of rights. Admittedly, the challenge this poses is enormous as it links into the struggle against need, disrespect and violence (Perlman 2010; Wheeler 2005). Also, it points to the potential discrepancies or contradictions between objective and subjective social mobility: improvements in the material conditions of life do not necessarily translate into perceived social mobility in the sense of increased agency and recognition, and vice versa.

Like most Vencer and SSP staff, Bianca views relationship building and skill development as longer-term, non-linear processes which are profoundly affected by events outside of the realm of the programs' influence and which can provide or obstruct future pathways to social mobility. As Crabbe et al. (2006: 15) note, this type of fractured progression story "should not be seen as a 'failure' but rather as the inevitable context in which work with participants occurs. In such circumstances the continued involvement of participants . . . represents a success in and of itself." In this context, SSP coordinator Danny argues:

> You notice that if they get a job or an apprenticeship that they really enjoy upon completion [of SSP], that's a huge gain and a major step forward. Because it's *theirs*, *they* achieve this. And for a large number of youth that's all they need, the rest will follow from that. But some

problems can resurface along the way. If they lose their job the chance of falling back is very high. That's why post-program support is very important, so they can come to you for support and reassurance.

Danny agrees with Bianca and Celi that participation in sport-for-development programs offers "a step forward" for young people who are what Young (1999: 224) calls "capital deficient" with respect to certain resources, networks and schemata of interpretation pertaining to the prospects and possibilities for upward social mobility.

SUBJECTIVE EXPERIENCES OF SOCIAL MOBILITY

The objective dimension of social mobility (i.e. changes in occupational status) of itself provides very limited insight into how changes in life chances are actually experienced and interpreted. It is therefore important to also take into consideration indicators of subjective awareness of social mobility, such as perceived changes in emancipation, personal development, skills and identity, as Bianca's comments clearly point out. How, then, do participants themselves articulate the prospects and possibilities for social mobility through sports activities or sport-for-development programs?

A number of former SSP participants give note of perceived social mobility. Sabrina, who is in her early 20s, expresses this as follows:

> I now study full-time to become a fully qualified security guard. I also work as a steward at Feyenoord games. That's quite a change for me. I had been sitting at home for a year and a half. When I came here [SSP] I suddenly had access to so much information and knowledge, which made it a lot easier for me to find my way. I feel that if I hadn't joined the program I probably wouldn't have started my studies at all. I was just sitting at home really, not knowing where to go or what to do. The program made me so positive about continuing my education. . . . And it has allowed me to obtain a diploma, which gives me a bit of a head start compared to other people who haven't done the program. And of course all the knowledge and experience you gain.

In a similar vein, 24-year-old former SSP participant Natasja notes:

> [SSP] has really helped me get ahead in life. I now have a full-time contract and am actually looking to start a new job as a prison officer. And I work part-time as a sport steward. If I compare my situation to how it was three or four years ago, I have to say that I am doing much better now. I've always dreamt of doing this type of work, but I never thought I could really achieve it. . . . I didn't have a job. I wanted to work, but one of the problems was that I am an immigrant, and initially I wasn't

allowed to work. That has been a problem for years. Now, at last, I have permanent residency and I am allowed to work. Program staff have helped me in many ways to get to where I am today: self-confidence, social skills, experience. And they have brought me into contact with employers who actually take me seriously.

As Sabrina's and Natasja's comments illustrate, the main avenues through which these perceived improvements are realized in relation to SSP include the institutional linkages facilitated by the program and affiliated organizations as well as the professional and social skills developed during the program, as discussed in Chapters 5 and 6.

Similar processes of subjective personal advancement can be observed in the Vencer program, particularly in relation to skill and knowledge development and the creation of institutional linkages. However, Vencer participants also place great emphasis on the importance of, on the one hand, meaningful social interaction and relationship building in threatening and unstable public contexts (i.e. the provision of a safe space) and, on the other, transferring the acquired capital to family members. For example, former Vencer participant Rosa, who is in her mid 20s, recognizes "the intimacy and intensity of the interaction" with peers in Vencer as a key aspect of her participation, which in her view is often absent in community life and at school. In addition, she experiences significant social advancement:

> The change [in my life] has been profound, not just a small step. Very positive. I've moved to a different neighborhood, so also residential mobility. I now have a continuing job in telemarketing and save money to pay for my studies. I have more financial independence but I spend a lot of my income on the pre-*vestibular* [university entry exam] course I'm doing. I have always wanted to do this but Vencer has helped me to focus my future plans, to encourage me and make it more real. My family also support my education but they don't have any experience with university so they cannot really help me with that. Vencer gave me more concrete opportunities and examples. I now also have a scholarship for an English language course. Vencer helped me apply for the scholarship.

Rosa acknowledges the process of social mobility she has experienced as a consequence of her participation in Vencer and subsequent vigorous work and study activities. At the same time, however, she emphasizes that this is part of, and a stepping stone for, a longer-term development process in which she aspires to complete a university degree. Rosa is one of several former Vencer participants who aim to invest their newly acquired economic and social capital in the accumulation of institutionalized cultural capital in the near or more distant future.

A common view among former Vencer participants is that although participation in Vencer increases their future mobility prospects, they have not yet achieved upward mobility. They tend to subscribe to the view that participation in Vencer constitutes "a first yet significant step" toward durable social advancement. Nilton, who is in his early 20s, expresses this as follows: "I think [in my case] it was the first degree of getting ahead. . . . I made the first step which was learning how it is to really enter the labor market, to have that knowledge and to prepare myself for that. It was a step ahead." Nilton's story suggests that progression is often fractured, inconsistent, and strongly influenced by external factors as well as personal drive, persistence and luck. In his case, significant contextual factors are his family's emotional support for his career aspirations, the poor quality of public schooling in his local community, labor market discrimination and the impact of violence. With regard to the latter, Nilton argues:

> I really want to take my mother out of the community. It's sad, sometimes when school finishes I cannot go home because of the shootouts, full of stray bullets, police everywhere. Sometimes I cannot sleep due to the shootouts. You have no peace, no freedom; you have to do what they want.

Nilton's experience highlights the relevance of the broad notion of subjective social mobility outlined in Chapter 1, which construes upward mobility in more philosophical terms as increased agency and control over one's own life. Moreover, his reference to the impact of violence reveals some of the contradictions and ambivalence in Vencer participants' pathways to social mobility: securing jobs with good pay can be a way to enhance control over their own lives and those of their families, but their prospects and possibilities for securing such jobs remain strongly affected by the durability of external constraints, which are also likely to diminish their sense of agency and autonomy. In such circumstances, it is hardly surprising that participants' narratives of *subir na vida* (getting ahead in life) are often fractured progression stories.

Compared to Vencer and SSP, respondents in the MG and NCFL studies infrequently articulate the impact of sport participation in their lives in terms of social mobility, which is consistent with their greater emphasis on participation in sport as a valued end in itself (see Chapter 3). However, we have also seen how participation in MG and NCFL as players or volunteers enables individuals to increase their portfolio of capital, particularly their social and cultural capital. The dominant themes that emerge from the MG fieldwork are sport's contribution to a sense of belonging, the (re)building of community networks and individual and family-level social and cultural capital. Although in most cases these themes do not translate into social mobility in the objective sense, MG participants nonetheless attach great meaning to them, particularly from the perspective of their social integration into Australian society and their knowledge of and interaction with "mainstream" society. As local community organizer Mohamed argues, sport "helps to integrate the community itself among its members. That's the first step of integration. The second step is that it brings us into the mainstream." For Mohamed, involvement in MG provides an important source of (bicultural) identity, belonging, peer support and mutual respect, all of which are indicators of subjective well-being (Correa-Velez et al. 2010). Thus, Mohamed contends, participation in MG can provide valuable resources for "successful settlement," better equipping participants for the challenges of "settling well" and "integrating" in a new country. The life history of MG secretary Samatar discussed at length in this book is one example of how access to such resources can create paths for upward mobility. However, Samatar's story also shows how the prospects and possibilities for social mobility are strongly influenced by a combination of contextual and individual factors, as noted earlier in this chapter and in Chapter 6.

The dominant themes that emerge from the NCFL study are slightly different from those reported in MG but similarly reveal the complex and dynamic interplay between agency and structure in the lives of participants. NCFL participants' emphasis on the role of local sports clubs and competitions in the construction of place identity, social connectedness, social support and inter-communal relations should be understood within the context of the changing demographics of small rural towns in northwest Victoria and the gaps in public service provision which have been increasingly filled by local volunteers including in the sports context. Nevertheless, participation in the NCFL is also a source of economic and cultural capital which can create paths for social advancement, particularly when it is linked to further employment and educational opportunities outside of the realm of sport. The stories of (former) NCFL officials Robin, Shane and Alex described in Chapter 6 are instructive in this regard. All three men report how their involvement in local sports clubs facilitates the development of new skills and knowledge which contribute to their ability to create and maintain new business ventures and opportunities outside of the sports context. Their stories indicate that while participation in the NCFL can facilitate individual social advancement, this tends to take place mainly as an unanticipated by-product of sports activities engaged in for expressive purposes. Moreover, where such advancement does occur it is usually experienced as a relatively "short-distance movement" (Pastore 1982) in the social space rather than any long-distance intragenerational class mobility.

THE PROCESS AND LONGEVITY OF SOCIAL MOBILITY: FINAL CONSIDERATIONS

The conclusions reported above regarding the nature and process of social mobility in the four settings being studied need to be qualified on two counts. First, even though the life stories presented in this book take a temporal, process-focused perspective that allows us to identify developments and changes over time, the multiple-case study upon which this book draws is not a longitudinal study (with the exception of the MG study). Indeed, a limitation of the multiple-case study design is that the bulk of data come from relatively short periods of intensive data collection at each of the research sites, which is inevitable given the constraints of time and resources. I have made every effort to overcome this limitation through a combination of long-term engagement with research participants, a more biographical interview approach, multiple trips to some of the sites and the development of an online research component which is less restricted by constraints of time and travel. Nonetheless, there may be a bias in the analysis toward short-term impacts of sport participation, with longer-term changes being under-explored. In other words, the longevity of the social mobility patterns examined in this chapter remains partly masked in the present analysis.

A longitudinal research project could rectify this imbalance. This involves selecting a group of participants at each of the research sites and following them through, administering interviews and questionnaires at intervals for as long as funding and participants' interest permit (Sapsford 1999: 83). The data presented in this book serve as a basis for future longitudinal research. Janice Perlman's (1976, 2010) longitudinal panel studies of poverty, durable inequality and citizenship in three poor communities in Rio de Janeiro are a noteworthy example. Perlman originally interviewed 750 favela residents in 1968–69 and, since 1999, has been conducting a re-study of the same people and communities, comparing within and across generations. Unfortunately, longitudinal studies of this kind are non-existent in sport-for-development research. As Collins et al. (1999: 10) already observed more than a decade ago, very few studies look at longer-term outcomes due to the difficulty of measuring such outcomes and/or the lack of data or resources over a long enough period to make a rigorous assessment. These concerns persist, and this book seeks to provide a major step forward through theory-driven, in-depth empirical investigation as well as sustained engagement with the communities and sports programs being studied.

The second qualification refers to the effect of *sport* in the processes of social mobility discussed in this chapter. Coalter (2008a: 30) rightly notes that other factors affecting individuals may explain at least some of the measured impacts. Indeed, it is difficult to disentangle the numerous mediating and moderating influences which affect the potential and actual benefits that accrue from participation in sport. In particular, isolating the influence of sport participation from other societal influences is a complex task (Verweel et al. 2005). This clearly hinders the identification of any "hard" causal relationship (direct or indirect) between sport participation and social mobility. Nonetheless, as I show in this book, close examination of people's encounters with sport and with others in the realm of sport, and of the wider contexts within which these encounters are situated, enables us to capture the complex and multi-faceted process through which individuals experience beneficial (or adverse) social outcomes from sport (see Kay 2009). In this respect, my approach aligns with that of Crabbe (2008), who argues that attempts to establish a quantified causal relationship between sport and singular outcomes ultimately fail to provide a valid and complete account of what is actually involved in the process. This issue will be explored further in the final chapter, with particular attention to the effect of sport in the accumulation of capital and the process of social mobility.

8 Sport and Social Outcomes
Contradictory Tendencies

The discussion contained in the preceding chapters reveals a series of conceptual couples and contradictory tendencies which capture the complex and multi-faceted processes through which individuals experience social outcomes from participation in non-professional forms of sport, and which are central to the theorizations of sport, capital and social mobility proffered in this book. In this final chapter, these themes are drawn upon to summarize and reflect on the main findings and conclusions.

With this purpose in mind, Table 8.1 delineates four inter-related sets of contradictory tendencies that shape, in conjunction, the extent to which and ways in which participation in non-professional forms of sport contributes to or inhibits social mobility. These contradictory tendencies are present in each of the four settings being studied. However, the nature, impact and direction of these tendencies as they operate in practice vary across space and time. In the final analysis, each social setting has its own unique "state of play" which has both resemblances and differences to other settings. This is consistent with a premise of this book that social relationships and behavior are constituted by social agents in specific socio-historical circumstances and with access to unequally distributed assets. Within each social setting, different social agents can be said to engage in the struggles ongoing within that setting as bearers of different volumes and combinations of capital, some yielding greater advantages within that particular setting than others.

Table 8.1 Four Inter-related Sets of Contradictory Tendencies

Unit of analysis	Contradictory tendencies	
social system	social change ⇔ social reproduction	
governance	social welfare ⇔ social control	
group life	social inclusion ⇔ social exclusion	
individual	autonomy ⇔ constraint	

Conceptualizing the relationship between sport participation and social mobility in these terms enables a nuanced understanding of not only the challenges, opportunities and obstacles that particular individuals and groups face in their search for social advancement but also the homologies and idiosyncrasies of different fields and how these bear upon individuals' portfolios of capital and their prospects and possibilities for upward mobility. As shown in the preceding chapters, although sport is a relatively autonomous social field which produces its own distinctive capital, the social, cultural and economic resources generated in the realm of sport are to a high degree transferable to other fields, whereas, at the same time, exogenous field effects strongly influence individuals' ability to get ahead in life through participation in non-professional forms of sport.

SOCIAL CHANGE AND SOCIAL REPRODUCTION

The contradictory tendencies identified in Table 8.1 serve to de-mythologize the "power of sport" discourse discussed in the Introduction by revealing the myriad of often ambiguous and inconsistent processes which shape the social impacts of participation in non-professional sport. At the level of social systems, the main themes that emerge from the comparative analysis are *social change* and *social reproduction*. I have sought to show how even though the durability of the external constraints that affect the lives of the people being studied should not be underestimated, the individual or group initiatives they undertake can counter at least some of the effects of structural constraints. A Bourdieuian framework has been instructive for making sense of these themes.

As noted in Chapter 1, Bourdieu (1990) argues that individuals act within socially constructed ranges of possibilities durably inscribed within them as well as within the social world in which they move. He regards habitus as an open concept since actors' dispositions are constantly subjected to a range of different experiences from which new forms and actions may arise. Nonetheless, Bourdieu anticipates that most experiences will serve to reinforce habitus since people are more likely to encounter situations and interpret them according to their pre-existing dispositions rather than to modify their inclinations (Bourdieu and Wacquant 1992: 133). Although the accounts and life stories presented in this book reveal greater tension and instability in social reproduction than Bourdieu seems to allow, his focus on the structural-processual positionings of social groups and how these orient people's actions and inclinations is nevertheless key to understanding the broader social influences that affect people's experiences of sport, as well as their ability to accumulate and access capital in and outside of the field of sport.

Locating people's experiences within their wider social, economic and political contexts alerts us to the fact that the structural causes of deprivation and disadvantage, and of inequality of opportunity in sport, are largely absent from the "power of sport" discourse. The pathways to social mobility explored in Chapter 7 are a case in point. While upward social mobility can result from individual improvement and successes (i.e. non-structural mobility), it may also have its basis in structural mobility stemming from processes of (post)industrialization and urbanization which tend to generate changes in the class distribution of a society. Moreover, where social mobility through sport does take place in the case studies that constitute this research, it is at a personal and, to a lesser degree, family level rather than at any structural level, which lies largely beyond the realm of programs' influence. Having said this, it should also be noted that in the settings under study non-structural mobility is at least equally prominent. As Pastore (1982: 102) already observed two decades ago with reference to Brazil, "experience, on-the-job training, urban life, increase in contacts, schooling, and aspirations should act as powerful actors in circulation mobility in the coming decades." It is in these areas that the impact of programs such as Vencer and SSP is most felt and valued. However, it is also clear from the preceding analysis that access to these "powerful actors" continues to be unequally distributed and affected to a considerable degree by a person's social origins. This ambiguity points to the co-existence of, and tension between, processes of social transformation and reproduction.

GOVERNING SPORT: SOCIAL WELFARE AND SOCIAL CONTROL

At the level of governance, the discussion contained in the preceding chapters highlights an interesting paradox that problematizes the view of sport as an inherently wholesome and benevolent force: while sports programs aimed at wider social objectives are typically highly valued by their participants, such programs tend to operate in a wider political-ideological context focused on the regulation and disciplining of the target groups rather than on enhancing their agency and autonomy. This paradox is captured in the inter-related themes of *social welfare* and *social control*. With regard to the former, the case studies analyzed in this book lend further weight to the argument that participation in non-professional forms of sport can have significant beneficial social outcomes, with a particular emphasis on the accumulation of social, cultural and economic capital as a potential pathway to upward social mobility. In addition, the narratives of research participants reveal a number of emergent themes which may be less tangible and accrue mainly as an unanticipated by-product of engagement with sports activities, such as a sense of belonging, identity and subjective well-being. These themes are highly context-specific of course and offer possibilities of future research to examine their import in the nexus of individual empowerment and sports participation.

Contrary to the view of sport as an inherently beneficial and wholesome force, this book has shown that the notion of sport as social welfare is imbued not only with humanistic motives but also with control and regulation motives. As discussed in Chapter 3, sport is used directly or indirectly as a form of social control by state and other institutions aimed principally at those individuals deemed to be "at risk" and "potentially troublesome." This category, which is variously defined across the four settings, is targeted through programs which use sport as a vehicle to alleviate social problems, enhance community cohesion and generate social order. The ways in which such initiatives are framed, implemented and experienced are dependent on the particular social and political contexts in which they operate. In all instances, however, they reveal the tension between freedom and control. Although sport is one sphere of life over which people are believed to exercise considerable autonomy and freedom, in practice sports activities are imbued with discipline and regulation efforts exerted top-down or bottom-up in formal or informal ways. These efforts co-exist and may clash with the notions of sport as social welfare and play (ludus).

Social control in and through sport manifests itself in a multiplicity of forms (Eitzen 2000). In the political and educational contexts discussed in this book, social control usually takes the form of "subtle oppression" through encouraging certain individuals and groups to fit into accepted social roles, changing their behaviors or suppressing their individuality in less obvious ways (cf. Blakemore and Griggs 2007). Although social control may be benign and/or socially desirable to some degree, it has the potential to significantly diminish the autonomy of individuals labelled "at-risk" as well as undermine open and democratic participation and respectful relationships in the sports context. Building and sustaining long-term positive relationships in the field of sport means enabling participants and their significant others to contribute to the activities or programs with ideas, knowledge and resources; that is, to cultivate a sense of ownership and voice (cf. Donnelly and Coakley 2002). This then allows them to act not merely as recipients but as contributors and educators in their own right, hence fostering a broader forum for community engagement and non-paternalistic participatory education. By focusing on issues of ownership, participation and (bottom-up) partnership, sport-for-development programs in particular can engender social outcomes which are both substantive in scale and lasting in time. In such conditions, good governance in community sport means to be participatory, transparent, responsive, equitable, reflexive and inclusive.

SOCIAL INCLUSION AND EXCLUSION:
THE DUALITY OF CAPITAL

Few proponents of the "power of sport" movement would disagree with these principles of good governance in sport. However, it is clear from the preceding analysis that sports, as sites for meaningful social interaction and socialization experiences, exhibit contradictions and ambiguities which the notion of good governance may neglect or trivialize. The conceptualization of social and cultural capital in this book serves to reveal some of these ambiguities by highlighting two mutually constitutive processes that operate principally at the level of group life and interpersonal interaction: *social inclusion* and *social exclusion*. Social and cultural capital are defined not only in terms of their actual or potential benefits, but also as a basis for exclusion from such benefits. Thus, group membership and access to network resources for some implies social exclusion for others. The comparative analysis shows how social and cultural capital operate in part through a range of exclusionary mechanisms in each of the communities being studied, albeit in different forms and to varying degrees. Processes of social exclusion that occur within the sports context manifest themselves, *inter alia*, in talent/ability barriers, gender inequalities, racial discrimination and rivalries between opposing teams. Also relevant to sport's contribution to social mobility are wider exclusionary processes which relate to the classed nature of education systems, labor market and residential discrimination, public service provision (or lack thereof), social violence and so forth.

There is a further dimension to the theme of inclusion/exclusion which requires us to reflect upon the social-cultural constructions of sports and how these affect people's ability to access the social and cultural resources associated with different sports. Sports are attractive, popular activities which play a significant role in the social life of the communities being studied, but as socio-cultural products some sports are more attractive and culturally appropriate than others (e.g. Van Bottenburg 2001). The concentration on football in Vencer, SSP and MG is explained by the extremely high levels of local interest and, to a lesser extent, the low skill entry levels and basic facility and equipment costs. In contrast, in the NCFL a broader range of team sports are widely practiced, most notably Australian football, netball, cricket and hockey. The provision of culturally relevant sports activities makes sense from the perspective of building and sustaining long-term commitment and relationships based on the needs and aspirations of diverse people in local communities (e.g. Hylton and Totten 2008). However, to determine what sports "work" in terms of facilitating access to social, cultural and economic capital, it is of great import to recognize that such access is shaped in part by broader social factors. It is instructive to reflect on this issue in terms of how habitus defines the meaning conferred on and the social profits expected from sports activities.

The probability of practicing a particular sport depends in part on an individual's economic and cultural capital (Bourdieu 1978, 1984). In this context, Bourdieu (1978: 837) distinguishes between *popular* sports which usually require practically no economic or cultural capital and "are tacitly associated with youth," and *bourgeois* sports which are "mainly practised for their functions of physical maintenance and for the social profit they bring" and tend to have significant hidden entry requirements (e.g. family tradition, early training, obligatory clothing). The significance of this argument lies not only in its emphasis on inequalities in access to different sports, but also in its recognition that bourgeois sports may be better endowed with the kinds of capital that are relevant for social advancement than popular sports. As Bourdieu (1978: 839) notes, bourgeois sports activities may be a "mere pretext" for select and exclusive encounters which enable the accumulation and reproduction of social capital among high status groups. In contrast, encounters in popular team sports such as those analyzed in this book may contain fewer high status resources. In other words, the field of sport is itself highly differentiated in terms of the distribution of high status cultural signals used for social and cultural exclusion, and sports activities may therefore maintain and reinforce social inequalities rather than resist or subvert them.

The above processes of social exclusion should not be viewed as fully determining or impeding people's ability to accumulate multiform capital through participation in non-professional forms of sport. Indeed, the preceding chapters clearly show how despite the presence of exclusionary mechanisms and structural constraints which profoundly affect the distribution of and access to capital, significant social, cultural and economic benefits do accrue, in certain circumstances, even to those participants who are capital deficient with regard to certain resources, networks and schemata of interpretation pertaining to the possibilities for social advancement. We should thus take into account both inclusionary and exclusionary processes as they influence in conjunction people's interaction with others in and outside of the realm of sport in order to grasp how social interaction, socialization and other forms of collective experience create access or barriers to capital, which in turn can act as both a resource and a liability to upward mobility (Young 1999: 224). This approach also enables us to assess which kinds of capital sport participants are more or less likely to acquire, differentiating between those resources that help them to navigate their more immediate life circumstances and to get by, and those that facilitate getting ahead in the larger social world. Thus, while capital certainly acts as a basis for exclusion, this is not its only effect, as shown in research participants' stories of sport as a site for meaningful social interaction, shared experience, community cohesion, identity and belonging.

AUTONOMY, CONSTRAINT AND THE
ADDED VALUE OF SPORT

The contradictory tendencies at the levels of social systems, governance and group life affect the actions, inclinations and aspirations of individuals, revealing themselves in the relationship between *autonomy* and *constraint*. In this book, the concept of habitus is used to show how people's dispositions are durably oriented yet constantly subjected to different experiences from which new forms and actions can arise, thus incorporating both reproduction and possibilities for resistance and change. The potential malleability of habitus has been addressed in two ways: firstly, through in-depth empirical investigation of the accumulation of social, cultural and economic capital through participation in sport, and, secondly, by analyzing the impact of pedagogical action in the field of sport. We have seen how and under which conditions participation in non-professional forms of sport enables individuals to develop, convert and transfer capital. Access to and command of these resources can put individuals in positions of greater status and power, enhance their sense of autonomy and agency and, in some cases, produce considerable, if not life-altering, social advancement.

The themes of autonomy and constraint direct our attention to the effects of sport in this process of capital formation. The preceding chapters associate the experiences and outcomes reported by research participants not simply with *playing* sport but with a range of issues and processes that take place in and around sports clubs and sport-for-development programs, notably the provision of access to social spaces and resourceful social institutions and the acquisition of several funds of knowledge through skills training or volunteering. These findings imply that sport should be regarded as a *site* for socialization experiences rather than a *cause* of specific socialization outcomes (Coakley et al. 2009: 120). As Coalter (2008b: 48) rightly notes, "*sport* in any simply sense rarely achieves the variety of desired outcomes attributed to it" and "issues of process and context . . . are key to understanding its developmental potential." The comparative analysis proffered in this book demonstrates that the most profound benefits tend to accrue to individual participants in situations where sport is undertaken within a personal and social developmental model (cf. Crabbe et al. 2006: 19), particularly for those who are confronted with persistent social and economic disadvantages.

As sites for meaningful social interaction, the sports activities analyzed in this book have value beyond their intrinsic appeal to (prospective) participants. The narratives of research participants are remarkably consistent on this issue across the four settings, indicating that sport has at least three characteristics that make it a suitable context for the development of social and cultural capital.

Firstly, sport can engage people in culturally and physically relevant ways, including those who may be hard to reach through other social institutions.

Sports activities are seen as attractive and enjoyable for many people, providing spaces in which people can temporarily escape their wider troubles, participate in social life and develop new relationships, skills and aspirations. Sport-for-development programs such as Vencer and SSP tap into this passion and enthusiasm for sport. However, as noted, the meanings associated with specific sports are strongly influenced by the particular socio-cultural contexts in which they are played and consumed. For example, while football is the most popular and prestigious sport in three of the four settings under study (Vencer, SSP and MG), in small rural towns in north-west Victoria it is far less popular in terms of participation and spectating. In this context, NCFL coach Jim argues that in his local community "soccer tends to be seen as an immigrant sport . . . while [Australian football] is seen as a truly native game. There is generally less exposure to other ['foreign' sporting] cultures here." Moreover, it should be kept in mind that in the absence of an inclusive and supportive sporting environment, playing sport can actually turn out to be an "additional alienating experience" (Crabbe et al. 2006: 19), as the exclusionary mechanisms described earlier clearly indicate.

Second, sport is seen to have certain qualities for fostering social relationships which underpin several of the social outcomes discussed in this book (see also Kay 2010). Research participants emphasize how playing sport enables them to develop a commitment toward others, co-receptive trust and respect, and social skills involving co-operation, responsibility and discipline (cf. Crabbe et al. 2006: 17). In several cases, the relationships that develop among participants during the sports activities spread to other aspects of their lives. However, these perceived qualities of sport need to be qualified on the points that social interaction in sport may be experienced differently by different people according to their socio-cultural locations (in terms of gender, class, social status, ethnicity, age and ability) and that loose bridging ties created in the sports context are more likely to be restricted to the sports activity itself (Elling 2004), even though practitioners in all four settings seek to create an inclusive sporting environment in which all participants have the opportunity to engage.

A third quality of sport reported in all four settings is that it provides a suitable context for informal learning and for supporting and delivering educational content in an experiential way (cf. Kay 2010; Spaaij, in press). Sports activities generate valuable teaching and learning moments, not only in terms of effective co-operation and decision-making skills but also in relation to dealing with conflict and competition. In the Vencer and SSP programs sport is also used to deliver educational messages directly, which are carried over to classroom activities. At MG, some parents use football as a specific incentive for young people to attend and succeed at school in order to be allowed to play on weekends.

These three characteristics are of course not unique to sport. Certain non-sporting activities, including (certain types of) arts and music, can also generate the "added value" discussed above (Crabbe et al. 2006; White 1998). Some of the people interviewed for this book explicitly raise this issue. Samir, a former SSP participant in his 20s, argues:

> They should create a music centre here in the community. Just as the people here [at SSP] have this project, you should also have music and dance, and maybe even attach an education program to it. That would be a way to also attract other people, who are not interested in sport. There are plenty of women who sing [mainly rap and hip-hop] in the neighborhood. Plenty of talent.

Samir's argument resonates with that of Vencer participants who describe their enthusiasm for various forms of Brazilian music and dance, while young Somalis in Melbourne similarly identify with rap and hip-hop music. Samir's reference to the need for non-sporting activities is also reflected in the account of Jane, a shopkeeper in one of the small towns in the NCFL:

> Sport is crucial to the community, especially its social aspect. But at the same time you need to provide facilities for those who are not interested in sport in order to enable them to establish similar social networks. Otherwise you exclude those people from social networks. Our [regional] arts group plays such a role and provides socializing for people interested in arts.

Jane's and Samir's remarks emphasize the importance of identifying and catering to people's differential leisure interests and preferences. Put differently, when it comes to providing a suitable context for the development of multiform capital, the ability to find activities (sport or otherwise) that attract and engage the target group is key.

In the social settings analyzed in this book, sports clearly meet this criterion. In each of these settings sport is a significant social institution which facilitates meaningful social interaction and engagement and generates opportunities for individuals (and their families) to accumulate different types of capital. The ability of sports activities to realize wider social outcomes is also closely linked to their role as public spaces and their contribution to community development. As we have seen, this ability is influenced by a myriad of processes which jointly shape the multi-faceted social impacts of participation in non-professional sport.

Notes

1 Private communication with Professor Tess Kay, 2009–2010.
2. The fictitious name Melbourne Giants is used to preserve the anonymity of respondents and to prevent any potential damage to the club or the community under study.
3. This argument is corroborated by Griffiths (2002), who reports in his research with Somali refugees in the United Kingdom that all his Somali respondents spoke English and that there was no need for interpreters.
4. Pseudonyms are used to preserve the anonymity of the participants.
5. It should be noted, however, that there have been significant changes to the composition of the NCFL since the Second World War, including the disbanding of one football club, the amalgamation and disintegration of another and the transfer of three clubs to the NCFL from other leagues.
6. The "Midnight Basketball" programs in the United States during the 1990s are a noteworthy example. These programs sought to reduce crime by young African-American males in impoverished urban neighborhoods with high levels of recorded youth crime (Hartmann 2001). The programs offered supervised basketball matches during the so-called "high crime" hours (between 10 p.m. and 2 a.m.). Similar programs aimed at reducing youth crime and delinquency have been initiated in a range of countries (Nichols 2007; Morris et al. 2003).
7. The notion of cultural intermediary is used here to highlight a cultural axis that is different from, for example, that in Bourdieu's (1984) work. See Crabbe (2005).
8. Some members of staff are also critical. For example, Vencer coordinator Márcia says: "I have to confess that I don't have good experiences with the mentors. We have only had a couple of good mentors. Many mentors don't have the connection with the students. . . . I don't see the return or the feedback. In theory it's really good, but here in Brazil somehow it doesn't work."
9. For a historical analysis of power relations in the favelas, see for example Valladares (2005), Dowdney (2003), Arias (2006), Leeds (1996) and Zaluar and Alvito (1998).
10. The significance of the home environment to the SSP program is discussed in Chapter 5.
11. Clearly, the focus in this book on non-professional forms of sport precludes exploration of macro-level economic impacts of major sporting events.

References

Abdullahi, M.D. (2001) *Culture and Customs of Somalia*, Westport, CT: Greenwood Press.

Abramovay, M., Castro, M.G., Pinheiro, L., Lima, F.S. and Martinelli, C.C. (2002) *Juventude, violência e vulnerabilidade social na América Latina: Desafios para políticas públicas*, Brasília: UNESCO.

Alexander, D. (2008) 'Crossing Boundaries: Local Government Amalgamations and Inter-Community Relations in Buloke Shire', in T. Marjoribanks (ed.) *Reimagining Sociology Conference Proceedings*, Melbourne: The Australian Sociological Association, pp. 1–16.

Alston, M. (2005a) 'Gender Perspectives in Australian Rural Community Life', in C. Cocklin and J. Dibdin (eds) *Sustainability and Change in Rural Australia*, Sydney: University of New South Wales Press, pp. 139–156.

Alston, M. (2005b) 'Social Exclusion in Rural Australia', in C. Cocklin and J. Dibdin (eds) *Sustainability and Change in Rural Australia*, Sydney: University of New South Wales Press, pp. 157–170.

Alston, M. and Kent, J. (2004) *Social Impacts of Drought*, Wagga Wagga: Charles Sturt University.

Amara, M. (2008) 'An Introduction to the Study of Sport in the Muslim World', in B. Houlihan (ed.) *Sport and Society*, 2nd edn, London: Sage, pp. 532–552.

Amara, M., Aquilina, D., Argent, E., Betzer-Tayar, M., Green, M., Henry, I., Coalter, F. and Taylor, J. (2004) *The Roles of Sport and Education in the Social Inclusion of Asylum Seekers and Refugees: An Evaluation of Policy and Practice in the UK*, Loughborough: Loughborough University.

Anheier, H., Gerhards, J. and Romo, F. (1995) 'Forms of Capital and Social Structure in Cultural Fields: Examining Bourdieu's Social Topography', *American Journal of Sociology*, 100(4): 859–903.

Araújo, T.P. and Lima, R.A. (2005) 'Public Employment Policies as Tools for the Reduction of Poverty and Inequality in Brazil', in A. Cimadamore, H. Dean and J. Siqueira (eds) *The Poverty of the State*, Buenos Aires: CLACSO, pp. 179–198.

Arias, E.D. (2004) 'Faith in Our Neighbors: Networks and Social Order in Three Brazilian Favelas', *Latin American Politics and Society*, 46(1): 1–38.

Arias, E.D. (2006) *Drugs and Democracy in Rio de Janeiro: Trafficking, Social Networks, and Public Security*, Chapel Hill, NC: University of North Carolina Press.

Arias, E.D. and Rodrigues, C.D. (2006) 'The Myth of Personal Security: Criminal Gangs, Dispute Resolution, and Identity in Rio de Janeiro's Favelas', *Latin American Politics and Society*, 48(4): 53–81.

Arneil, B. (2006) *Diverse Communities: The Problem with Social Capital*, Cambridge: Cambridge University Press.

Atherley, K.M. (2006) 'Sport, Localism and Social Capital in Rural Western Australia', *Geographical Research*, 44(4): 348–360.

Australian Bureau of Statistics (2006) *Census of Population and Housing*, Canberra: ABS.

Bailey, D. (2005) 'Evaluating the Relationship between Physical Education, Sport and Social Inclusion', *Educational Review*, 57(1): 71–90.

Baillergeau, E. and Duyvendak, J.W. (2001) 'Tussen aanpassing en ontplooiing: Sociale integratie en de jeugd van toen en tegenwoordig', in J.W. Duyvendak and L. Veldboer (eds) *Meeting point Nederland*, Amsterdam: Boom, pp. 122–138.

Baillergeau, E. and Schaut, C. (2001) 'Social Work and the Security Issue in the Netherlands and Belgium', *European Journal on Criminal Policy and Research*, 9: 427–446.

Balibar, E. and Wallerstein, I. (1991) *Race, Nation, Class: Ambiguous Identities*, London: Verso.

Banck, G. (1995) 'Mass Communication and Urban Contest in Brazil: Some Reflections on Lifestyle and Class', *Bulletin of Latin American Research*, 13(1): 45–60.

Barros, R.P., Henriques, R. and Mendonça, R. (2000) 'Desigualdade e pobreza no Brasil', *Revista Brasileira de Ciências Sociais*, 15: 123–142.

Bartlett, S. and Straume, S. (2008) *Sports-for-Development Monitoring and Evaluation Consultancy: Final Report*, Washington, DC: Inter-American Development Bank.

Berlinck, M.T. and Hogan, D. (1979) 'Social Marginality or Class Relations in the City of São Paulo', in N. Aguiar (ed.) *The Structure of Brazilian Development*, New Brunswick, NJ: Transaction Books, pp. 167–202.

Bertaux, D. (1974) 'Mobilité sociale biographique: Une critique de l'approche transversale', *Revue française de sociologie*, 15(3): 329–362.

Bertaux, D. (1977) *Destins personnels et structure de classe*, Paris: PUF.

Bertaux, D. (1980) 'L'approche biographique: Sa validité méthodologique, ses potentialités', *Cahiers internationaux de sociologie*, 69: 197–225.

Bertaux, D. (ed.) (1981) *Biography and Society: The Life History Approach in the Social Sciences*, London: Sage.

Bertaux, D. (1983) 'The Bakers of France', *History Today*, 33(6): 33–37.

Bertaux, D. and Thompson, P. (1997) 'Introduction', in D. Bertaux and P. Thompson (eds) *Pathways to Social Class: A Qualitative Approach to Social Mobility*, Oxford: Clarendon Press, pp. 1–31.

Beutler, I. (2008) 'Sport Serving Development and Peace: Achieving the Goals of the United Nations through Sport', *Sport in Society*, 11(4): 359–369.

Bigelow, M. (2007) 'Social and Cultural Capital at School: The Case of a Somali Teenage Girl with Limited Formal Schooling', in N.R. Faux (ed.) *Low-Educated Adult Second Language and Literacy Acquisition: Proceedings of Inaugural Symposium*, Richmond, VA: Literacy Institute at Virginia Commonwealth University, pp. 7–22.

Bigelow, M. (2008) 'Somali Adolescents' Negotiation of Religious and Racial Bias in and out of School', *Theory into Practice*, 47(1): 27–34.

Bjork, S. (2007) 'Modernity Meets Clan: Cultural Intimacy in the Somali Diaspora', in A. Kusow and S. Bjork (eds) *From Mogadishu to Dixon: The Somali Diaspora in a Global Context*, Trenton, NJ: The Red Sea Press, pp. 135–155.

Black, A., Duff, J., Saggers, S. and Baines, P. (2000) *Rural Communities and Rural Social Issues: Priorities for Research*, Canberra: Rural Industries Research and Development Corporation.

Black, D. (2009) 'The Ambiguities of Development: Implications for "Development through Sport"', *Sport in Society*, 13(1): 121–129.

Blackshaw, T. and Crabbe, T. (2004) *New Perspectives on Sport and 'Deviance'*, London: Routledge.

Blakemore, K. and Griggs, E. (2007) *Social Policy: An Introduction*, 3ʳᵈ edn, Buckingham: Open University Press.

Blokland, T. (2002) 'Waarom de populariteit van Putnam zorgwekkend is: Een bespreking van Robert Putnams benadering van sociaal kapitaal', *Beleid en Maatschappij*, 29(2): 101–109.

Blokland, T. and Savage, M. (2008) 'Social Capital and Networked Urbanism', in T. Blokland and M. Savage (eds) *Networked Urbanism*, Aldershot: Ashgate, pp. 1–20.

Bloyce, D. and Smith, A. (2010) *Sport Policy and Development: An Introduction*, London: Routledge.

Booth, D. and Tatz, C. (2000) *One-Eyed: A View of Australian Sport*, Sydney: Allen & Unwin.

Bourdieu, P. (1978) 'Sport and Social Class', *Social Science Information*, 17: 819–840.

Bourdieu, P. (1980) 'Le capital social: Notes provisoires', *Actes de la Recherche en Sciences Sociales*, 31: 2–3.

Bourdieu, P. (1984) *Distinction: A Social Critique of the Judgement of Taste*, London: Routledge.

Bourdieu, P. (1986) 'The Forms of Capital', in J. Richardson (ed.) *Handbook of Theory and Research for the Sociology of Education*, New York: Greenwood, pp. 241–258.

Bourdieu, P. (1990) *The Logic of Practice*, Stanford, CA: Stanford University Press.

Bourdieu, P. (1993) *Sociology in Question*, London: Sage.

Bourdieu, P. (1999) 'Scattered Remarks', *European Journal of Social Theory*, 2(3): 334–340.

Bourdieu, P. (2002) 'Habitus', in J. Hillier and E. Rooksby (eds) *Habitus: A Sense of Place*, Aldershot: Ashgate, pp. 27–34.

Bourdieu, P. and Passeron, J.-C. (1977 [1970]) *Reproduction in Education, Society and Culture*, Beverly Hills, CA: Sage.

Bourdieu, P. and Passeron, J.-C. (1979 [1964]) *The Inheritors*, Chicago, IL: University of Chicago Press.

Bourdieu, P. and Wacquant, L. (1992) *An Invitation to Reflexive Sociology*, Chicago, IL: University of Chicago Press.

Bourke, L. (2001) 'Rural Communities', in S. Lockie and L. Bourke (eds) *Rurality Bites: The Social and Environmental Transformation of Rural Australia*, Annadale: Pluto Press, pp. 118–128.

Brandão, A.A. (2004) *Miséria da periferia: Desigualdades raciais e pobreza na metrópole do Rio de Janeiro*, Rio de Janeiro: Pallas.

Brasset-Grundy, A. (2004) 'Family Life and Learning: Emergent Themes', in T. Schuller, J. Preston, C. Hammond, A. Brasset-Grundy and J. Bynner (eds) *The Benefits of Learning*, London: Routledge Falmer, pp. 80–98.

Breen, R. and Goldthorpe, J. (1999) 'Class Inequality and Meritocracy: A Critique of Saunders and an Alternative Analysis', *British Journal of Sociology*, 50: 1–27.

Briceño-León, R. (2010) 'The Five Dilemmas of Latin American Sociology', in S. Patel (ed.) *The ISA Handbook of Diverse Sociological Traditions*, Los Angeles, CA: Sage, pp. 177–188.

Briggs, X. de Souza (1998) 'Brown Kids in White Suburbs: Housing Mobility and the Multiple Faces of Social Capital', *Housing Policy Debate*, 9(1): 177–221.

Brough, M., Gorman, D., Ramirez, E. and Westoby, P. (2003) 'Young Refugees Talk about Well-being: A Qualitative Analysis of Refugee Youth Mental Health from Three States', *Australian Journal of Social Issues*, 38(2): 193–208.

Brubaker, R. (1993) 'Social Theory as Habitus', in C. Calhoun, E. LiPuma and M. Postone (eds) *Bourdieu: Critical Perspectives*, Chicago, IL: University of Chicago Press, pp. 212–234.

Brubaker, R. (2004) 'Rethinking Classical Theory: The Sociological Vision of Pierre Bourdieu', in D. Swartz and V. Zolberg (eds) *After Bourdieu: Influence, Critique, Elaboration*, Dordrecht: Kluwer, pp. 25–64.

Bruce, A. (2003) 'The Un-making of the World: Mental Health and Resettled Refugees from the Horn of Africa', in D. Barnes (ed.) *Asylum Seekers and Refugees in Australia: Issues of Mental Health and Wellbeing*, Sydney: Transcultural Mental Health Centre, pp. 102–134.

Bryman, A. (2001) *Social Research Methods*, Oxford: Oxford University Press.

Buchmann, C. and Hannum, E. (2001) 'Education and Stratification in Developing Countries: A Review of Theories and Research', *Annual Review of Sociology*, 27: 77–102.

Budge, T. (2007) 'The Changing Dynamics of Small Towns', in Department of Sustainability and Environment *Towns in Time 2001 Analysis*, Melbourne: Victorian Government, pp. 45–61.

Burnett, C. (2006) 'Building Social Capital through an Active Community Club', *International Review for the Sociology of Sport*, 41(3): 283–294.

Cain, A. (2007) *Social Mobility of Ethnic Minorities in the Netherlands: The Peculiarities of Social Class and Ethnicity*, Delft: Eburon.

Calhoun, C. (1993) 'Habitus, Field, and Capital: The Question of Historical Specificity', in C. Calhoun, E. LiPuma and M. Postone (eds) *Bourdieu: Critical Perspectives*, Chicago, IL: University of Chicago Press, pp. 61–88.

Calhoun, C. (2000) 'Pierre Bourdieu', in G. Ritzer (ed.) *The Blackwell Companion to Major Social Theorists*, Oxford: Blackwell, pp. 696–730.

Castro, M.G. and Abramovay, M. (2002) 'Jovens em situação de pobreza, vulnerabilidades sociais e violências', *Cadernos de Pesquisa*, 116: 143–176.

Centrum voor Onderzoek en Statistiek (2008) *Feitenkaart inkomensgegevens op deelgemeente- en buurtniveau*, Rotterdam: Gemeente Rotterdam.

Clyne, M. and Kipp, S. (2005) 'On the Somali Language in Melbourne', *Migration Action*, 27(1): 19–22.

CMY (2007) *Playing for the Future: The Role of Sport and Recreation in Supporting Refugee Young People to 'Settle Well' in Australia*, Melbourne: Centre for Multicultural Youth.

Coakley, J., Hallinan, C., Jackson, S. and Mewett, P. (2009) *Sports in Society: Issues and Controversies in Australia and New Zealand*, North Ryde: McGraw-Hill.

Coalter, F. (2002) *Sport and Community Development: A Manual*, Edinburgh: Sportscotland.

Coalter, F. (2007) *A Wider Social Role for Sport: Who's Keeping the Score?* London: Routledge.

Coalter, F. (2008a) *Sport-in-Development: A Monitoring and Evaluation Manual*, London: UK Sport.

Coalter, F. (2008b) 'Sport-in-Development: Development for and through sport?', in M. Nicholson and R. Hoye (eds) *Sport and Social Capital*, Oxford: Elsevier Butterworth-Heinemann, pp. 39–67.

Coalter, F., Allison, M. and Taylor, J. (2000) *The Role of Sport in Regenerating Deprived Areas*, Edinburgh: The Stationery Office.

Coleman, J. (1988) 'Social Capital in the Creation of Human Capital', *American Journal of Sociology*, 94: 95–120.

Coleman, J. (1990) *Foundations of Social Theory*, Cambridge: The Belknap Press of Harvard University Press.

Collins, J. (2009) 'Social Reproduction in Classrooms and Schools', *Annual Review of Anthropology*, 38: 33–48.

Collins, M., Henry, I., Houlihan, B. and Buller, J. (1999) *Sport and Social Exclusion: A Report to the Department of Culture, Media and Sport*, Loughborough: Loughborough University.

Collins, M. and Kay, T. (2003) *Sport and Social Exclusion*, London: Routledge.

Connell, R. (2007) *Southern Theory: The Global Dynamics of Knowledge in Social Science*, Sydney: Allen & Unwin.

Correa-Velez, I., Gifford, S. and Barnett, A. (2010) 'Longing to Belong: Social Inclusion and Wellbeing among Youth with Refugee Backgrounds in the First Three Years in Melbourne, Australia', *Social Science & Medicine*, 71: 1399–1408.

Cortis, N. (2009) 'Social Inclusion and Sport: Culturally Diverse Women's Perspectives', *Australian Journal of Social Issues*, 44(1): 91–106.

Costa Ribeiro, C.A. (2003) *Estrutura de classe e mobilidade social no Brasil*, São Paulo: EDUSC-ANPOCS.

Covey, S. (1998) *The 7 Habits of Highly Effective Teens*, New York: Fireside.

Crabbe, T. (2000) 'A Sporting Chance? Using Sport to Tackle Drug Use and Crime', *Drugs: Education, Prevention and Policy*, 7(4): 381–391.

Crabbe, T. (2005) *Getting to Know You: Engagement and Relationship Building*, London: Home Office.

Crabbe, T. (2008) 'Avoiding the Numbers Game: Social Theory, Policy and Sport's Role in the Art of Relationship Building', in M. Nicholson and R. Hoye (eds) *Sport and Social Capital*, Oxford: Elsevier Butterworth-Heinemann, pp. 21–37.

Crabbe, T., Bailey, G., Blackshaw, T., Brown, A., Choak, C., Gidley, B., Mellor, G., O'Connor, K., Slater, I. and Woodhouse, D. (2006) *Knowing the Score: Positive Futures Case Study Research. Final Report*, London: Home Office.

DaMatta, R. (1985) *A casa e a rua: Espaço, cidadania, mulher e morte no Brasil*, São Paulo: Brasiliense.

Danish, S.J., Taylor, T.E. and Fazio, R.J. (2003) 'Enhancing Adolescent Development through Sports and Leisure', in G.R. Adams and M.D. Berzonsky (eds) *Blackwell Handbook of Adolescence*, Oxford: Blackwell, pp. 92–108.

Danso, R. (2001) 'From "There" to "Here": An Investigation of the Initial Settlement Experiences of Ethiopian and Somali Refugees in Toronto', *GeoJournal*, 55: 3–14.

Darnell, S. (2010) 'Power, Politics and "Sport for Development and Peace": Investigating the Utility of Sport for International Development', *Sociology of Sport Journal*, 27(1): 54–75.

DeFilippis, J. (2001) 'The Myth of Social Capital in Community Development', *Housing Policy Debate*, 12(4): 781–806.

Dempsey, K. (1990) *Smalltown: A Study of Social Inequality, Cohesion and Belonging*, Melbourne: Oxford University Press.

Dempsey, K. (1992) *A Man's Town: Inequality between Men and Women in Rural Australia*, Melbourne: Oxford University Press.

Department of Planning and Community Development (2008) *Towns in Time: Spatial Analysis and Research*, Melbourne: Victorian Government.

Devereux, S. (1993) ' "Observers are Worried": Learning the Language and Counting the People in Northeast Ghana', in S. Devereux and J. Hoddinott (eds) *Fieldwork in Developing Countries*, Boulder, CO: Lynne Rienner, pp. 43–56.

Devine, F. (2004) *Class Practices: How Parents Help Their Children Get Good Jobs*, Cambridge: Cambridge University Press.

Doherty, A. and Misener, K. (2008) 'Community Sport Networks', in M. Nicholson and R. Hoye (eds) *Sport and Social Capital*, Oxford: Elsevier Butterworth-Heinemann, pp. 113–141.

Domínguez, S. and Watkins, C. (2003) 'Creating Networks for Survival and Mobility: Social Capital among African-American and Latin-American Low-Income Mothers', *Social Problems*, 50(1): 111–135.

Donnelly, P. and Coakley, J. (2002) 'The Role of Recreation in Promoting Social Inclusion', Working Paper, Toronto: Laidlaw Foundation.

Donnelly, P., Darnell, S., Wells, S. and Coakley, J. (2007) 'The Use of Sport to Foster Child and Youth Development and Education', in Sport for Development and Peace International Working Group (ed.) *Literature Reviews on Sport for Development and Peace*, Toronto: SDP IWG, pp. 7–47.

Dowdney, L. (2003) *Children of the Drug Trade*, Rio de Janeiro: 7 Letras.

Driscoll, K. and Wood, L. (1999) *Sporting Capital: Changes and Challenges for Rural Communities in Victoria*, Melbourne: RMIT.

Duncan, G.J. and Brooks-Gunn, J. (eds) (1997) *Consequences of Growing Up Poor*, New York: Russell Sage.

Durkheim, E. (1964 [1893]) *The Division of Labor in Society*, New York: Free Press.

Dykes, J. and Olliff, L. (2007) *Sport and Recreation as a Tool for Social Inclusion: The Experiences of Refugee and Migrant Young People*, Melbourne: CMY.

Edwards, B. and Foley, M. (1997) 'Social Capital and the Political Economy of our Discontent', *American Behavioral Scientist*, 40: 669–678.

Edwards, R. (2004a) 'Present and Absent in Troubling Ways: Families and Social Capital Debates', *The Sociological Review*, 52(1): 1–21.

Edwards, R. (2004b) 'Social Capital in the Field: Introduction to Researchers' Tales', in R. Edwards (ed.) *Social Capital in the Field: Researchers' Tales*, London: London South Bank University, pp. 3–7.

Eisenhardt, K. (1989) 'Building Theories from Case Study Research', *Academy of Management Review*, 14(4): 532–550.

Eitle, T. and Eitle, D. (2002) 'Race, Cultural Capital, and the Educational Effects of Participation in Sports', *Sociology of Education*, 75(2): 123–146.

Eitzen, D.S. (2000) 'Social Control and Sport', in J. Coakley and E. Dunning (eds) *Handbook of Sports Studies*, Los Angeles, CA: Sage, pp. 370–381.

Eitzen, D.S. (2006) *Fair and Foul: Beyond the Myths and Paradoxes of Sport*, 3rd edn, Lanham, MD: Rowman & Littlefield.

Eitzen, D.S. and Sage, G.H. (2003) *Sociology of North American Sport*, 7th edn, Boston, MA: McGraw-Hill.

Elias, N. (1987) *Involvement and Detachment*, Oxford: Blackwell.

Elias, N. and Scotson, J.L. (1965) *The Established and the Outsiders*, London: Frank Cass.

Elling, A. (2002) *'Ze zijn er (niet) voor gebouwd': In- en uitsluiting in de sport naar sekse en etniciteit*, Nieuwegein: Arko Sports Media.

Elling, A. (2004) ' "We zijn vrienden in het veld": Grenzen aan sociale binding en "verbroedering" door sport', *Pedagogiek*, 24(4): 342–360.

Engbersen, G., Snel, E. and Weltevrede, A. (2005) *Sociale herovering in Amsterdam en Rotterdam: Één verhaal over twee wijken*, The Hague: WRR.

Esping-Andersen, G. (2007) 'Investing in Children and their Life Chances', Paper prepared for the Fundación Carolina International Workshop Welfare State and Competitivity, Madrid, 26–27 April.

Evans, P. (1996) 'Government Action, Social Capital and Development: Reviewing the Evidence on Synergy', *World Development*, 24(6): 1119–1132.

Feldman, M., Bell, J. and Berger, M. (2003) *Gaining Access: A Practical and Theoretical Guide for Qualitative Researchers*, New York: Altamira.

Field, J. (2005) *Social Capital and Lifelong Learning*, Bristol: Policy Press.

Field, J. (2008) *Social Capital*, 2nd edn, London: Routledge.

Fine, B. (2001) *Social Capital versus Social Theory: Political Economy and Social Science at the Turn of the Millennium*, London: Routledge.

Fine, B. (2006) 'Social Capital', in D.A. Clark (ed.) *The Elgar Companion to Development Studies*, Cheltenham: Edward Elgar, pp. 559–563.

Fleming, S. (2009) *Eleven. Making Lives Better: 11 Stories of Development through Football*, Durrington: Pitch.

Freire, P. (1972) *Pedagogy of the Oppressed*, New York: Penguin.

Freire, P. (1973) *Education for Critical Consciousness*, New York: Continuum.
Freire, P. and Macedo, D.P. (1987) *Literacy: Reading the Word and the World*, South Hadley, MA: Bergin & Garvey.
Friedmann, J. (2002) 'Placemaking as Project? Habitus and Migration in Transnational Cities', in J. Hillier and E. Rooksby (eds) *Habitus: A Sense of Place*, Aldershot: Ashgate, pp. 299–316.
Fuchs, C. (2003) 'Some Implications of Pierre Bourdieu's Works for a Theory of Social Self- Organization', *European Journal of Social Theory*, 6(4): 387–408.
Gacitúa Marió, E. and Woolcock, M. (eds) (2008) *Social Exclusion and Mobility in Brazil*, Washington: World Bank.
Gallie, D. and Paugam, S. (2002) *Social Precarity and Social Integration*, Brussels: European Commisson.
Gans, H. (1962) *The Urban Villagers*, New York: Free Press.
Gasparini, W. and Vieille-Marchiset, G. (2008) *Le sport dans les quartiers*, Paris: PUF.
Gemeente Rotterdam (2003) *Rotterdam zet door: Op weg naar een stad in balans*, Rotterdam: Gemeente Rotterdam.
Gemeente Rotterdam (2005) *Werkloze jongeren in Rotterdam*, Rotterdam: Dienst Sociale Zaken en Werkgelegenheid.
Gemeente Rotterdam (2007) *Jeugdveiligheidsindex 2007*, Rotterdam: Gemeente Rotterdam.
Gemeente Rotterdam (2008a) *Rotterdam sociaal gemeten: Eerste meting door de Sociale Index*, Rotterdam: Gemeente Rotterdam.
Gemeente Rotterdam (2008b) *Wijkanalyse Delfshaven*, Rotterdam: Gemeente Rotterdam.
Giddens, A. and Diamond, P. (eds) (2005) *The New Egalitarianism*, Cambridge: Polity.
Gijsberts, M. and Dagevos, J. (2005) *Uit elkaars buurt: De invloed van etnische concentratie op integratie en beeldvorming*, The Hague: Social and Cultural Planning Office.
Gittell, R. and Vidal, A. (1998) *Community Organizing: Building Social Capital as a Development Strategy*, London: Sage.
Giulianotti, R. (1999) *Football: A Sociology of the Global Game*, Cambridge: Polity.
Giulianotti, R. (2005) *Sport: A Critical Sociology*, Cambridge: Polity.
Goffman, E. (1961) *Encounters: Two Studies in the Sociology of Interaction*, Indianapolis, IN: Bobbs-Merrill.
Goldstein, D. (2003) *Laughter Out of Place: Race, Class, Violence, and Sexuality in a Rio Shantytown*, Berkeley, CA: University of California Press.
Granovetter, M. (1973) 'The Strength of Weak Ties', *American Journal of Sociology*, 78(6): 1360–1380.
Griffiths, D. (2002) *Somali and Kurdish Refugees in London: New Identities in the Diaspora*, Aldershot: Ashgate.
Gunn, S. (2005) 'Translating Bourdieu: Cultural Capital and the English Middle Class in Historical Perspective', *British Journal of Sociology*, 56(1): 49–64.
Hallinan, C., Hughson, J. and Burke, M. (2007) 'Supporting the "World Game" in Australia: A Case Study of Fandom at National and Club Level', *Soccer & Society*, 8(2): 283–297.
Hammersley, M. and Atkinson, M. (2007) *Ethnography: Principles in Practice*, 3rd edn, London: Routledge.
Hargreaves, J. (1986) *Sport, Power and Culture: A Social and Historical Analysis of Popular Sports in Britain*, Cambridge: Polity.
Harriss, J. and De Renzio, P. (1997) 'An Introductory Bibliographic Essay: "Missing Link" or Analytically Missing? The Concept of Social Capital', *Journal of International Development*, 9(7): 919–937.

Hartmann, D. (2001) 'Notes on Midnight Basketball and the Cultural Politics of Recreation, Race, and At-Risk Urban Youth', *Journal of Sport and Social Issues*, 25(1): 39–71.

Hasenbalg, C. (2003a) 'A distribuição de recursos familiares', in C. Hasenbalg and N.V. Silva (eds) *Origens e destinos*, Rio de Janeiro: Topbooks, pp. 55–83.

Hasenbalg, C. (2003b) 'A transição da escola ao mercado de trabalho', in C. Hasenbalg and N.V. Silva (eds) *Origens e destinos*, Rio de Janeiro: Topbooks, pp. 147–172.

Hasenbalg, C. and Silva N.V. (eds) (2003) *Origens e destinos: Desigualdades sociais ao longo da vida*, Rio de Janeiro: Topbooks.

Hay, R. (2009) 'No Single Pattern: Australian Migrant Minorities and the Round Ball Code in Australia', *Soccer & Society*, 10(6): 823–842.

Healy, T. and Côté, S. (2001) *The Well-being of Nations: The Role of Human and Social Capital*, Paris: OECD.

Hinch, T. and Higham, J. (2001) 'Sport Tourism: A Framework for Research', *International Journal of Tourism Research*, 3(1): 45–58.

Hogan, D. and Owen, D. (2000) 'Social Capital, Active Citizenship and Political Equality in Australia, in I. Winter (ed.) *Social Capital and Public Policy in Australia*, Melbourne: Australian Institute of Family Studies, pp. 74–104.

Hopkins, G. (2006) 'Somali Community Organizations in London and Toronto: Collaboration and Effectiveness', *Journal of Refugee Studies*, 19(3): 361–380.

Horst, C. (2002) 'Vital Links in Social Security: Somali Refugees in the Dadaab Camps, Kenya', *Refugee Survey Quarterly*, 21(1): 242–259.

Horst, C. (2006) *Transnational Nomads: How Somalis Cope with Refugee Life in the Dadaab Camps of Kenya*, Oxford: Berghahn Books.

Horst, C. (2007) 'The Somali Diaspora in Minneapolis: Expectations and Realities', in A. Kusow, A. and S. Bjork (eds) *From Mogadishu to Dixon: The Somali Diaspora in a Global Context*, Trenton, NJ: The Red Sea Press, pp. 275–294.

Houlihan, B. (2008) 'Introduction', in B. Houlihan (ed.) *Sport and Society*, 2nd edn, London: Sage, pp. 1–8.

Hylton, K. and Bramham, P. (eds) (2008) *Sports Development*, London: Routledge.

Hylton, K. and Totten, M. (2008) 'Community Sports Development', in K. Hylton and P. Bramham (eds) *Sports Development*, London: Routledge, pp. 77–117.

Inter-American Development Bank (2003) *Football and Team Sports Partnership Model for Youth Employability: A Ganar (Vencer in Brazil)*, Washington DC: Inter-American Development Bank.

International Labour Organization (2008) *Decent Work and Youth–Latin America*, Lima: ILO.

International Sport for Development and Peace Association (2010) 'Sport for Development and Peace: Defining the Field through Theory and Practice', Power of Sport Summit, 10–12 June, Boston, MA: Northeastern University.

Ireland, R. (2005) 'Fragile Synergies for Development: The Case of Jardim Oratório SP, Brazil', in A. Cimadamore, H. Dean and J. Siqueira (eds) *The Poverty of the State*, Buenos Aires: CLACSO, pp. 241–262.

Ireland, R. (2010) 'Citizenship and Democratisation in Brazil's Favelas: The End of the Dream?', Paper presented at the Association of Iberian and Latin American Studies of Australasia Conference 'Independence! Two Centuries of Struggle', Canberra, July.

Israel, G., Beaulieu, L. and Hartless, G. (2001) 'The Influence of Family and Community Social Capital on Educational Achievement', *Rural Sociology*, 66: 43–68.

Ivo, A.B.L. (2005) 'The Redefinition of the Social Issue and the Rhetoric on Poverty during the '90s', in A. Cimadamore, H. Dean and J. Siqueira (eds) *The Poverty of the State*, Buenos Aires: CLACSO, pp. 65–90.

Jacobi, P. (2006) 'Public and Private Responses to Social Exclusion among Youth in São Paulo', *The Annals of the American Academy of Political and Social Science*, 606: 216–230.

Janssens, J. (ed.) (2004) *Education through Sport: An Overview of Good Practices in Europe*, Nieuwegein: Arko Sports Media.

Jary, D. and Jary, J. (2000) *Collins Dictionary of Sociology*, 3rd edn, Glasgow: Harper Collins.

Jenkins, R. (1992) *Pierre Bourdieu*, London: Routledge.

Jupp, J. (2001) *The Australian People*, Cambridge: Cambridge University Press.

Kalmijn, M. and Kraaykamp, G. (2003) 'Dropout and Downward Mobility in the Educational Career: An Event-History Analysis of Ethnic Schooling Differences in The Netherlands', *Educational Research and Evaluation*, 9(3): 265–287.

Kay, T. (2006) 'Daughters of Islam: Family Influences on Muslim Young Women's Participation in Sport', *International Review for the Sociology of Sport*, 41(3): 339–355.

Kay, T. (2009) 'Developing through Sport: Evidencing Sport Impacts on Young People', *Sport in Society*, 12(9): 1177–1191.

Kay, T. (2010) 'The Reported Benefits of Sport: Local Voices from Brazil', *Leisure Studies Association Newsletter*, 85: 34–40.

Kay, T. and Bradbury, S. (2009) 'Youth Sport Volunteering: Developing Social Capital?', *Sport, Education and Society*, 14: 121–140.

Kay, T. and Spaaij, R. (in press) 'The Mediating Effects of Family on Sport in International Development Contexts', *International Review for the Sociology of Sport*, 46.

Kay, T., Welford, J., Jeanes, R., Morris, J. and Collins, S. (2008) *The Potential of Sport to Enhance Young People's Lives: Sport in the Context of International Development*, Loughborough: Loughborough University.

Kidd, B. (2008) 'A New Social Movement: Sport for Development and Peace', *Sport in Society*, 11(4): 370–380.

Kingsbury, D. (2004) 'Community Development', in D. Kingsbury, J. Remenyi, J. McKay and J. Hunt (eds) *Key Issues in Development*, Houndmills: Palgrave Macmillan, pp. 221–242.

Kolb, D.A. (1984) *Experiential Learning*, Englewood Cliffs: Prentice-Hall.

Krouwel, A., Boonstra, N., Duyvendak, J.W. and Veldboer, L. (2006) 'A Good Sport? Research into the Capacity of Recreational Sport to Integrate Dutch Minorities', *International Review for the Sociology of Sport*, 41(2): 165–180.

Kusow, A.M. (2004) 'Beyond Indigenous Authenticity: Reflections on the Insider/Outsider Debate in Immigration Research', *Symbolic Interaction*, 26: 591–599.

Lamba, N. and Krahn, H. (2003) 'Social Capital and Refugee Resettlement: The Social Networks of Refugees in Canada', *Journal of International Migration and Integration,* 4(3): 335–360.

Lambert, J. (2007) 'A Values-based Approach to Coaching Sport in Divided Societies', in J. Sugden and J. Wallis (eds) *Football for Peace?* Oxford: Meyer & Meyer Sport, pp. 13–33.

Lamont, M. and Lareau, A. (1988) 'Cultural Capital: Allusions, Gaps and Glissandos in Recent Theoretical Developments', *Sociological Theory*, 6: 153–168.

Lareau, A. and Weininger, E. (2004) 'Cultural Capital in Educational Research: A Critical Assessment', in D. Swartz and V. Zolberg (eds) *After Bourdieu*, Dordrecht: Kluwer, pp. 105–144.

Lawrence, G. (2005) 'Globalisation, Agricultural Production Systems and Rural Restructuring', in C. Cocklin and J. Dibdin (eds) *Sustainability and Change in Rural Australia*, Sydney: University of New South Wales Press, 2005, pp. 104–120.

Laws, S., Harper, C. and Marcus, R. (2003) *Research for Development: A Practical Guide*, London: Sage.

Leeds, E. (1996) 'Cocaine and Parallel Polities on the Brazilian Urban Periphery: Constraints on Local Level Democratization', *Latin American Research Review*, 31(3): 47–83.

Leeds, E. (2007) 'Rio de Janeiro', in K. Koonings and D. Kruijt (eds) *Fractured Cities: Social Exclusion, Urban Violence and Contested Spaces in Latin America*, London: Zed Books, pp. 23–35.

Leonard, W. and Reyman, J. (1988) 'The Odds of Attaining Professional Athlete Status: Refining the Computations', *Sociology of Sport Journal*, 5: 162–169.

Leslie, H. and Storey, D. (2003) 'Entering the Field', in R. Scheyvens and D. Storey (eds) *Development Fieldwork: A Practical Guide*, London: Sage, pp. 119–138.

Lever, J. (1983) *Soccer Madness*, Chicago, IL: University of Chicago Press.

Levermore, R. (2008) 'Sport: A New Engine of Development', *Progress in Development Studies*, 8(2): 183–190.

Levermore, R. and Beacom, A. (eds) (2009a) *Sport and International Development*, Houndmills: Palgrave Macmillan.

Levermore, R. and Beacom, A. (2009b) 'Sport and Development: Mapping the Field', in R. Levermore and A. Beacom (eds) *Sport and International Development*, Houndmills: Palgrave Macmillan, pp. 1–25.

Lin, N. (2001) *Social Capital: A Theory of Social Structure and Action*, Cambridge: Cambridge University Press.

Loizos, P. (2000) 'Are Refugees Social Capitalists?', in S. Baron, J. Field and T. Schuller (eds) *Social Capital: Critical Perspectives*, Oxford: Oxford University Press, pp. 124–141.

Long, J. (2008) 'Sport's Ambiguous Relationship with Social Capital: The Contribution of National Governing Bodies of Sport', in M. Nicholson and R. Hoye (eds) *Sport and Social Capital*, Oxford: Elsevier Butterworth-Heinemann, pp. 207–232.

Long, J. and Sanderson, I. (2001) 'The Social Benefits of Sport: Where's the Proof?', in C. Gratton and I. Henry (eds) *Sport in the City*, London: Routledge, pp. 187–203.

Lopez, N. (2003) *Hopeful Girls, Troubled Boys: Race and Gender Disparity in Urban Education*, New York: Routledge.

Lovell, P.A. (2000) 'Gender, Race, and the Struggle for Social Justice in Brazil', *Latin American Perspectives*, 27(6): 85–102.

Lovell, P.A. and Wood, C.H. (1998) 'Skin Color, Racial Identity, and Life Chances in Brazil', *Latin American Perspectives*, 25(3): 90–109.

Lyle, J. (2008) 'Sports Development and Sports Coaching', in K. Hylton and P. Bramham (eds) *Sports Development*, London: Routledge, pp. 214–235.

MacAloon, J. (2006) 'Muscular Christianity after 150 Years', *International Journal of the History of Sport*, 23(5): 687–700.

Machado da Silva, L.A. (2006) 'Favela, crime violento e política no Rio de Janeiro', in F. Lopes de Carvalho (ed.) *Observatório da Cidadania n°10–Arquitetura da exclusão*, Rio de Janeiro: IteM/Ibase, pp. 76–81.

Maguire, J. (1988) 'Doing Figurational Sociology: Some Preliminary Observations on Methodological Issues and Sensitising Concepts', *Leisure Studies*, 7(2): 187–193.

Maguire, J. (2005) *Power and Global Sport: Zones of Prestige, Emulation and Resistance*, London: Routledge.

Marcus, G. (1995) 'Ethnography in/of the World System: The Emergence of Multi-sited Ethnography', *Annual Review of Anthropology*, 24: 95–117.

Marsh, P., Rosser, E. and Harré, R. (1978) *The Rules of Disorder*, London: Routledge.

Martin, J. (2007) 'The Study of Small Towns in Victoria Revisited', in Department of Sustainability and Environment *Towns in Time 2001 Analysis*, Melbourne: Victorian Government, pp. 62–70.

McCann, P. and Ewing, M. (2006) 'Motivation and Outcomes of Youth Participation in Sport', in S. Spickard Prettyman and B. Lampman (eds) *Learning Culture through Sports*, Toronto: Rowman & Littlefield Education, pp. 35–49.

McIlwaine, C. and Moser, C.O.N. (2001) 'Violence and Social Capital in Urban Poor Communities: Perspectives from Colombia and Guatemala', *Journal of International Development*, 13: 965–984.

McKenzie, F. (1994) 'Population Decline in Non-Metropolitan Australia', *Urban Policy and Research*, 12: 253–263.

McManus, P. and Pritchard, B. (2000) 'Introduction', in B. Pritchard and P. McManus (eds) *Land of Discontent: The Dynamics of Change in Rural and Regional Australia*, Sydney: University of New South Wales Press, pp. 1–13.

McMichael, C. (2003) 'Narratives of Forced Migration: Conducting Ethnographic Research with Somali Refugees in Australia', in P. Allotey (ed.) *The Health of Refugees*, Oxford: Oxford University Press, pp. 185–199.

McMichael, C. and Ahmed, M. (2003) 'Family Separation: Somali Women in Melbourne', in M. Leach and F. Mansouri (eds) *Critical Perspectives on Refugee Policy in Australia*, Burwood: Deakin University, pp. 131–150.

McMichael, C. and Manderson, L. (2004) 'Somali Women and Well-being: Social Networks and Social Capital among Immigrant Women in Australia', *Human Organization*, 63(1): 88–99.

McNamee, S.J. and Miller, R.K. (2004) *The Meritocracy Myth*, Lanham, MD: Rowman & Littlefield.

McPherson, B., Curtis, J.E. and Loy, J.W. (1989) *The Social Significance of Sport: An Introduction to the Sociology of Sport*, Champaign, IL: Human Kinetics.

Meier, M. and Saavedra, M. (2009) 'Esther Phiri and the Moutawakel Effect in Zambia: An Analysis of the Use of Female Role Models in Sport-for-Development', *Sport in Society*, 12(9): 1158–1176.

Melo, M. (1999) *Consultations with the Poor: Brazil—National Synthesis Report*, Washington, DC: World Bank.

Merton, R.K. (1968) *Social Theory and Social Structure*, 2nd edn, New York: Free Press.

Mewett, P. (2003) 'Sport', in R. Jureidini and M. Poole (eds) *Sociology: Australian Connections*, 3rd edn, Sydney: Allen & Unwin, pp. 443–467.

Miller, R. (1998) 'The Limited Concerns of Social Mobility Research', *Current Sociology*, 46(4): 145–163.

Miller, R. (2001) *Researching Social Mobility: New Directions*, Kuala Lumpur: National University of Malaysia.

Ministry of Health, Welfare and Sport (2005) *Tijd voor sport*, The Hague: Ministerie van VWS.

Ministry of Health, Welfare and Sport (2008) *The Power of Sport*, The Hague: Ministerie van VWS.

Moore, R. (2008) 'Capital', in M. Grenfell (ed.) *Pierre Bourdieu: Key Concepts*, Stocksfield: Acumen, pp. 101–117.

Morgan, D. (1988) *Focus Groups as Qualitative Research*, London: Sage.

Morris, L., Sallybanks, J. and Willis, K. (2003) *Sport, Physical Activity and Antisocial Behaviour in Youth*, Canberra: Australian Institute of Criminology.

Morrow, V. (2001) 'Young People's Explanations and Experiences of Social Exclusion: Retrieving Bourdieu's Concept of Social Capital', *International Journal of Sociology and Social Policy*, 21: 37–63.

Morrow, V. (2004) 'Networks and Neighbourhoods: Children's Accounts of Friendship, Family and Place', in C. Phillipson, G. Allian and D. Morgan (eds) *Social Networks and Social Exclusion: Sociological and Policy Perspectives*, Aldershot: Ashgate, pp. 50–71.

Mosely, P. (1997) 'Soccer', in P. Mosely, R. Cashman, J. O'Hara and H. Weatherburn (eds) *Sporting Immigrants*, Crow's Nest: Walla Walla Press, pp. 155–173.

Narayan, D. (1999) *Bonds and Bridges: Social Capital and Poverty*, Washington, DC: World Bank.

Nascimento, E. Arantes do, with Duarte, O. and Bellos, A. (2006) *Pelé: The Autobiography*, London: Simon & Schuster.

Nicholls, S. (2009) 'On the Backs of Peer Educators: Using Theory to Interrogate the Role of Young People in the Field of Sport-in-Development', in R. Levermore and A. Beacom (eds) *Sport and International Development*, Houndmills: Palgrave Macmillan, pp, 156–175.

Nichols, G. (2007) *Sport and Crime Reduction*, London: Routledge.

Nicholson, M. and Hoye, R. (eds) (2008) *Sport and Social Capital*, Oxford: Elsevier Butterworth-Heinemann.

Noleto, M.J. and Werthein, J. (eds) (2003) *Pobreza e desigualdade no Brasil*, Brasília: UNESCO.

Noordhoff, F. (2008) *Persistent Poverty in the Netherlands*, Amsterdam: Amsterdam University Press.

Nsubuga-Kyobe, A. and Dimock, L. (2002) *African Communities and Settlement Services in Victoria*, Melbourne: Australian Multicultural Foundation.

Nunn, A. et al. (2007) *Factors Influencing Social Mobility*, London: Department for Work and Pensions.

O'Hare, G. and Barke, M. (2002) 'The Favelas of Rio de Janeiro: A Temporal and Spatial Analysis', *GeoJournal*, 56: 225–240.

Omar, Y.S. (2005) 'Young Somalis in Australia: An Educational Approach to Challenges and Recommended Solutions', *Migration Action*, 27(1): 6–18.

Omar, Y.S. (2009) 'Somali Youth in Diaspora: A Comparative Study of Gender Perceptions of Further Studies and Future Career (Case Study: Somali Youth Melbourne, Australia)', *Bildhaan: International Journal of Somali Studies*, 8(1): 52–95.

Onyx, J. and Bullen, P. (2000) 'Measuring Social Capital in Five Communities', *Journal of Applied Behavioral Science*, 36(1): 23–42.

Onyx, J., Edwards, M. and Bullen, P. (2007) 'The Intersection of Social Capital and Power: An Application to Rural Communities', *Rural Society*, 17(3): 215–230.

Overton, J. and Van Diermen, P. (2003) 'Using Quantitative Techniques', in R. Scheyvens and D. Storey (eds) *Development Fieldwork: A Practical Guide*, London: Sage, pp. 37–56.

Palmer, C. (2009) 'Soccer and the Politics of Identity for Young Muslim Refugee Women in South Australia', *Sport in Society*, 10(1): 27–38.

Panferov, S.K. (2002) 'Exploring the Literacy Development of Russian and Somali ESL Learners: A Collaborative Ethnography', Unpublished PhD Thesis, Columbus, OH: Ohio State University.

Pastore, J. (1982) *Inequality and Social Mobility in Brazil*, Madison, WI: University of Wisconsin Press.

Pastore, J. (2004) 'Falta muita educação.' Online. Available http://www.josepastore.com.br/ artigos/ed/ed_037.htm (accessed 19 May 2009).

Pastore, J. and Silva, N.V. (2000) *Mobilidade Social no Brasil*, São Paulo: Makron.

Patriksson, G. (1995) 'Scientific Review Part 2', in I. Vuori, P. Fentem, B. Svoboda, G. Patriksson, W. Andreff and W. Weber (eds) *The Significance of Sport for Society: Health, Socialisation, Economy*, Strasbourg: Council of Europe Press, pp. 111–134.

Peillon, M. (1998) 'Bourdieu's Field and the Sociology of Welfare', *Journal of Social Policy*, 27(2): 213–229.

Perlman, J. (1976) *The Myth of Marginality: Urban Poverty and Politics in Rio de Janeiro*, Berkeley, CA: University of California Press.

Perlman, J. (2005) 'The Chronic Poor in Rio de Janeiro: What has Changed in 30 Years?', in M. Keiner, M. Koll-Schretzenmayr and W.A. Schmid (eds) *Managing Urban Futures*, Aldershot: Ashgate, pp. 165–186.

Perlman, J. (2006) 'The Metamorphosis of Marginality: Four Generations in the Favelas of Rio de Janeiro', *The Annals of the American Academy of Political and Social Science*, 606: 154–177.

Perlman, J. (2010) *Favela: Four Decades of Living on the Edge in Rio de Janeiro*, Oxford: Oxford University Press.

Pernice R. and Brook, J. (1996) 'Refugees' and Immigrants' Mental Health: Association of Demographic and Post-Immigration Factors', *Journal of Social Psychology*, 136: 511– 519.

Piccolo, F.D. (2006) 'Sociabilidade e conflito no *morro* e na *rua*', Unpublished PhD thesis, Rio de Janeiro: Federal University of Rio de Janeiro.

Piccolo, F.D. (2008) 'Os jovens entre o morro e a rua: reflexões a partir do baile funk', in G. Velho (ed.) *Rio de Janeiro: cultura, política e conflito*, Rio de Janeiro: Zahar, pp. 30–58.

Pinheiro, P.S. (2000) 'Democratic Governance, Violence, and the (Un)rule of Law', *Daedalus*, 129: 119–143.

Pino, J.C. (1997) *Family and Favela: The Reproduction of Poverty in Rio de Janeiro*, Westport, CT: Greenwood.

Poli, R. (2010) 'African Migrants in Asian and European Football: Hopes and Realities', *Sport in Society*, 13(6): 1001–1011.

Pooley, J.C. (1976) 'Ethnic Soccer Clubs in Milwaukee: A Study of Assimilation', in M. Hart (ed.) *Sport in the Socio-Cultural Process*, 2nd edn, Dubuque, IA: W.C. Brown, pp. 475–492.

Portes, A. (1998) 'Social Capital: Its Origins and Applications in Modern Sociology', *Annual Review of Sociology*, 24(1): 1–24.

Portes, A. (2000) 'The Two Meanings of Social Capital', *Sociological Forum*, 15(1): 1–12.

Portes, A. and Landolt, P. (1996) 'The Downside of Social Capital', *The American Prospect*, 26: 18–22.

Portes, A. and Landolt, P. (2000) 'Social Capital: Promise and Pitfalls of its Role in Development', *Journal of Latin American Studies*, 32: 529–547.

Portes, A. and Zhou, M. (1993) 'The New Second Generation: Segmented Assimilation and its Variants', *The Annals of the Academy of Political and Social Science*, 530: 74–96.

Prefeitura da Cidade do Rio de Janeiro (2008) *Índice de Desenvolvimento Social– comparando as realidades microurbanas da cidade do Rio de Janeiro*, Rio de Janeiro: Instituto Pereira Passos.

Preteceille, E. and Valladares, L. (2000) 'A desigualdade entre os pobres—favela, favelas', in R. Henriques (ed.) *Desigualdade e pobreza no Brasil*, Rio de Janeiro: IPEA, pp. 459–485.

Putnam, R. (1993) 'The Prosperous Community: Social Capital and Public Life', *The American Prospect*, 13: 35–42.

Putnam, R. (1995) 'Bowling Alone: America's Declining Social Capital', *Journal of Democracy*, 6(1): 65–78.

Putnam, R. (2000) *Bowling Alone: The Collapse and Revival of American Community*, New York: Simon & Schuster.

Putzel, J. (1997) 'Accounting for the Dark Side of Social Capital: Reading Robert Putnam on Democracy', *Journal of International Development*, 9(7): 939–949.

Reay, D. (1998) 'Cultural Reproduction: Mothers' Involvement in Their Children's Primary Schooling', in M. Grenfell, D. James, P. Hodkinson, D. Reay and D. Robbins *Bourdieu and Education: Acts of Practical Theory*, London: Falmer, pp. 55–71.

Reed-Danahay, D. (2005) *Locating Bourdieu*, Bloomington, IN: Indiana University Press.

Ribeiro, L.C.Q. and Telles, E.E. (2000) 'Rio de Janeiro: Emerging Dualization in a Historically Unequal City', in P. Marcuse and R. van Kempen (eds) *Globalizing Cities*, Oxford: Blackwell, pp. 78–94.

Rijpma, S. and Meiburg, H. (1989) 'Sports Policy Initiatives in Rotterdam: Targeting Disadvantaged Groups', in P. Bramham, I. Henry, H. Mommaas and H. van der Poel (eds) *Leisure and Urban Processes*, London: Routledge, pp. 141–155.

Riley, E., Fiori, J. and Ramirez, R. (2001) 'Favela Bairro and a New Generation of Housing Programmes for the Urban Poor', *Geoforum*, 32(4): 521–531.

ROA (2009) *Schoolverlaters tussen onderwijs en arbeidsmarkt 2008*, Maastricht: Researchcentrum voor Onderwijs en Arbeidsmarkt.

Roble, A. and Rutledge, D. (2008) *The Somali Diaspora: A Journey Away*, Minneapolis, MN: University of Minnesota Press.

Rubio, M. (1997) 'Perverse Social Capital: Some Evidence from Colombia', *Journal of Economic Issues*, 31(3): 805–816.

Rural and Regional Services and Development Committee (2004) *Inquiry into Country Football: Final Report*, Melbourne: Parliament of Victoria.

Rural and Regional Services and Development Committee (2006) *Inquiry into Retaining Young People in Rural Towns and Communities*, Melbourne: Parliament of Victoria.

Rutten, E., Stams, G.J., Biesta, G., Schuengel, C., Dirks, E. and Hoeksma, J. (2007) 'The Contribution of Organized Youth Sport to Antisocial and Prosocial Behavior in Adolescent Athletes', *Journal of Youth and Adolescence*, 36: 255–264.

Saavedra, M. (2009) 'Dilemmas and Opportunities in Gender and Sport-in-Development' in R. Levermore and A. Beacom (eds) *Sport and International Development*, Houndmills: Palgrave Macmillian, pp. 124–155.

Sack, A.L. and Thiel, R. (1979) 'College Football and Social Mobility: A Case Study of Notre Dame Football Players', *Sociology of Education*, 52(1): 60–66.

Sale, J., Lohfeld, L. and Brazil, K. (2002) 'Revisiting the Quantitative-Qualitative Debate: Implications for Mixed-Methods Research', *Quality & Quantity*, 36(1): 43–53.

Samatar, A.I. (2007) 'Somalia's Post-Conflict Economy: A Political Economy Approach', *Bildhaan: International Journal of Somali Studies*, 7: 126–168.

Sandford, R., Armour, K. and Warmington P. (2006) 'Re-engaging Disaffected Youth through Physical Activity Programmes', *British Educational Research Journal*, 32: 251–271.

Sansone, L. (2003) 'Jovens e oportunidades: as mudanças na década de 1990', in C. Hasenbalg and N.V. Silva (eds) *Origens e destinos*, Rio de Janeiro: Topbooks, pp. 245–279.

Sapsford, R. (1999) *Survey Research*, London: Sage.

Savage, M. (1997) 'Social Mobility and the Survey Method: A Critical Analysis', in D. Bertaux and P. Thompson (eds) *Pathways to Social Class*, Oxford: Clarendon, pp. 299–325.

Savage, M., Warde, A. and Devine, F. (2005) 'Capitals, Assets, and Resources: Some Critical Issues', *British Journal of Sociology*, 56(1): 31–47.

Schuller, T., Baron, S. and Field, J. (2000) 'Social Capital: A Review and Critique', in S. Baron, J. Field and T. Schuller (eds) *Social Capital: Critical Perspectives*, Oxford: Oxford University Press, pp. 1–38.

Seippel, Ø. (2006) 'Sport and Social Capital', *Acta Sociologica*, 49(2): 169–183.

Sen, A. (1999) *Development as Freedom*, Oxford: Oxford University Press.

Sennett, R. (2003) *Respect in a World of Inequality*, New York: W.W. Norton.

Sherry, E. (2010) '(Re)engaging Marginalized Groups through Sport: The Homeless World Cup', *International Review for the Sociology of Sport*, 45(1): 59–71.

Silva, J.S. (2003) '*Por que uns e não outros?*' *Caminhada de jovens pobres para a universidade*, Rio de Janeiro, 7 Letras.

Silva, N.V. (2000) 'A Research Note on the Cost of Not Being White in Brazil', *Studies in Comparative International Development*, 35(2): 18–27.

Soares, L.E., Bill, M.V. and Athayde, C. (2005) *Cabeça de porco*, Rio de Janeiro: Objetiva.

Sociaal Platform Rotterdam (2007) *De kracht van sport in de wijk*, Rotterdam: SPR.

Sorokin, P. (1959) *Social Mobility*, Glencoe, IL: Free Press.

Souza, M.L. (2008) *Fobópole: O medo generalizado e a militarização da questão urbana*, Rio de Janeiro: Bertrand Brasil.

Spaaij, R. (2009a) 'Sport as a Vehicle for Social Mobility and Regulation of Disadvantaged Urban Youth: Lessons from Rotterdam', *International Review for the Sociology of Sport*, 44(2): 247–264.

Spaaij, R. (2009b) 'The Glue that Holds the Community Together? Sport and Sustainability in Rural Australia', *Sport in Society*, 12(9): 1124–1138.

Spaaij, R. (in press) 'Building Social and Cultural Capital among Young People in Disadvantaged Communities: Lessons from a Brazilian Sport-based Intervention Program', *Sport, Education and Society*, 16.

Spaaij, R. and Anderson, A. (2010) 'Psychosocial Influences on Children's Identification with Sports Teams: A Case Study of Australian Rules Football Supporters', *Journal of Sociology*, 46(3): 299–315.

Sport England (1999) *The Value of Sport*, London: Sport England.

Sposito, M.P., Silva, H.H.C. and Souza, N.A. (2006) 'Juventude e poder local: Um balanço de iniciativas públicas voltadas para jovens em municípios de regiões metropolitanas', *Revista Brasileira de Educação*, 11(32): 238–257.

Stanton-Salazar, R.D. (1997) 'A Social Capital Framework for Understanding the Socialization of Racial Minority Children and Youths', *Harvard Educational Review*, 67(1): 1–40.

Stanton-Salazar, R.D. and Spina, S.U. (2005) 'Adolescent Peer Networks as a Context for Social and Emotional Support', *Youth & Society*, 36: 379–417.

Stanton-Salazar, R.D., Vàsquez, O. and Mehan, H. (2000) 'Engineering Academic Success through Institutional Support', in S. Gregory (ed.) *The Academic Achievement of Minority Students*, Lanham, MD: University Press of America, pp. 213–247.

Stayner, R. (2005) 'The Changing Economies of Rural Communities', in C. Cocklin and J. Dibdin (eds) *Sustainability and Change in Rural Australia*, Sydney: University of New South Wales Press, pp. 121–138.

Strauss, A.L. (1971) *The Contexts of Social Mobility: Ideology and Theory*, Chicago, IL: Aldine.

Sugden, J. and Wallis, J. (eds) (2007) *Football for Peace? The Challenges of Using Sport for Co-existence in Israel*, Oxford: Meyer & Meyer Sport.

Tacon, R. (2007) 'Football and Social Inclusion: Evaluating Social Policy', *Managing Leisure*, 12: 1–23.

Talbot, L. and Walker, R. (2007) 'Community Perceptions on the Impact of Policy Change on Linking Social Capital in a Rural Community', *Health & Place*, 13: 482–492.

Taylor, P., Crow, I., Irvine, D. and Nichols, G. (1999) *Demanding Physical Activity Programmes for Young Offenders under Probation Supervision*, London: Home Office.

Telles, E.E. (2004) *Race in Another America: The Significance of Skin Color in Brazil*, Princeton, NJ: Princeton University Press.

Thompson, J.B. (1991) 'Editor's Introduction', in P. Bourdieu *Language and Symbolic Power*, Cambridge: Polity, pp. 1–31.

Thomson, P. (2008) 'Field', in M. Grenfell (ed.) *Pierre Bourdieu: Key Concepts*, Stocksfield: Acumen, pp. 67–81.

Tolsma, J., Coenders, M. and Lubbers, M. (2007) 'De onderwijskansen van allochtone and autochtone Nederlanders vergeleken: een cohort-design', *Mens & Maatschappij*, 82(2): 133–154.

Tonts, M. (2000) 'The Restructuring of Australia's Rural Communities', in B. Pritchard and P. McManus (eds) *Land of Discontent: The Dynamics of Change in Rural and Regional Australia*, Sydney: University of New South Wales Press, pp. 52–72.

Tonts, M. (2005a) 'Competitive Sport and Social Capital in Rural Australia', *Journal of Rural Studies*, 21(2): 137–149.

Tonts, M. (2005b) 'Government Policy and Rural Sustainability', in C. Cocklin and J. Dibdin (eds) *Sustainability and Change in Rural Australia*, Sydney: University of New South Wales Press, pp. 194–211.

Townsend, M., Moore, J. and Mahoney, M. (2002) 'Playing Their Part: The Role of Physical Activity and Sport in Sustaining the Health and Well-being of Small Rural Communities', *Rural and Remote Health*, 2: 109.

Trueba, H.T. (2002) 'Multiple Ethnic, Racial and Cultural Identities in Action: From Marginality to a New Cultural Capital in Modern Society', *Journal of Latinos and Education*, 1: 7–28.

Uitermark, J. and Duyvendak, J.W. (2008) 'Civilising the City: Populism and Revanchist Urbanism in Rotterdam', *Urban Studies*, 45: 1485–1503.

UNDP (2001) *Relatório de Desenvolvimento Humano do Rio de Janeiro 2001*, Brasília: United Nations Development Program.

UNHCR (2010) 'Somalia—Thousands Fleeing Deadly Clashes in Mogadishu', Press release 12 March, Geneva: UNHCR. Online. Available http://www.unhcr.se/en/News/press10 /press_100312_ somalia.html (accessed 8 September 2010).

UNICEF (2006) *Sport for Development in Latin America and the Caribbean*, Panama: UNICEF Regional Office for Latin America and the Caribbean.

UNICEF (2009) *O direito de aprender: potencializar avanços e reduzir desigualdades*, Brasília: UNICEF.

United Nations Inter-Agency Task Force on Sport for Development and Peace (2003) *Sport as a Tool for Development and Peace: Towards Achieving the United Nations Millennium Development Goals*, New York: UN.

Valladares, L. (2005) *A invenção da favela*, Rio de Janeiro: Editora FGV.

Van Bottenburg, M. (2001) *Global Games*, Champaign, IL: University of Illinois Press.

Van den Berg, M. (2007) *'Dat is bij jullie toch ook zo?' Gender, etniciteit en klasse in het sociaal kapitaal van Marokkaanse vrouwen*, Amsterdam: Aksant.

Van Ginkel, F., Veenbaas, R. and Noorda, J. (2007) *Jongerenwerk: Stand van zaken en perspectief*, Amsterdam: SWP.

Veldboer, L., Duyvendak, J.W., Kleinhans, R. and Boonstra, N. (2007a) *In beweging brengen en richting geven: Herstructurering en sociale stijging in Hoogvliet*, Rotterdam: Deelgemeente Hoogvliet.

Veldboer, L., Boonstra, N. and Krouwel, A. (2007b) 'Eenheid en verdeeldheid op het veld: De januskop van sport', in L. Veldboer, J.W. Duyvendak and C. Bouw (eds) *De mixfactor: Integratie en segregatie in Nederland*, Amsterdam: Boom, pp. 71–80.

Velho, G. (2008) 'Metrópole, cultura e conflito', in G. Velho (ed.) *Rio de Janeiro: cultura, política e conflito*, Rio de Janeiro: Zahar, pp. 7–29.

Verweel, P. (2007) *Respect in en door sport*, Amsterdam: SWP.

Verweel, P., Janssens, J. and Roques, C. (2005) 'Kleurrijke zuilen: Over de ontwikkeling van sociaal kapitaal door allochtonen in eigen en gemengde sportverenigingen', *Vrijetijdsstudies*, 23(4): 7–21.

VICSEG (1997) *VICSEG Cultural Profile: Somalia and the Somalis*, Melbourne: Victorian Co-operative on Children's Services for Ethnic Groups.

Victorian Government (2005) *Regional Matters: An Atlas of Regional Victoria*, Melbourne: Victorian Government Printing Office.

Victorian Multicultural Commission (2007) *Victorian Community Profiles: 2006 Census—Somalia-born*, Melbourne: VMC.

Vuori, I. and Fentem, P. (1995) 'Scientific Review', in I. Vuori, P. Fentem, B. Svoboda, G. Patriksson, W. Andreff and W. Weber (eds) *The Significance of Sport for Society*, Strasbourg: Council of Europe Press, pp. 19–87.

Wacquant, L. (1998) 'Negative Social Capital: State Breakdown and Social Destitution in America's Urban Core', *Netherlands Journal of Housing and the Built Environment*, 13(1): 25–40.

Wacquant, L. (2004) *Body and Soul: Notebooks of an Apprentice Boxer*, Chicago, IL: University of Chicago Press.

Wacquant, L. (2008a) 'Pierre Bourdieu', in R. Stones (ed.) *Key Sociological Thinkers*, 2nd edn, Basingstoke: Palgrave Macmillan, pp. 261–277.

Wacquant, L. (2008b) 'The Militarization of Urban Marginality: Lessons from the Brazilian Metropolis', *International Political Sociology*, 2: 56–74.

Walseth, K. (2008) 'Bridging and Bonding Social Capital in Sport: Experiences of Young Women with an Immigrant Background', *Sport, Education and Society*, 13(1): 1–17.

Walseth, K. and Fasting, K. (2004) 'Sport as a Means of Integrating Minority Women', *Sport in Society*, 7(1): 109–129.

Walvin, J. (1995) *Passion of the People? Football in South America*, London: Verso.

Waring, A. and Mason, C. (2010) 'Opening Doors: Promoting Social Inclusion through Increased Sports Opportunities', *Sport in Society*, 13(3): 517–529.

Weiss, R.S. (1994) *Learning from Strangers*, New York: Free Press.

Wheeler, J.S. (2005) 'Rights Without Citizenship? Participation, Family and Community in Rio de Janeiro', in N. Kabeer (ed.) *Inclusive Citizenship: Meanings and Expressions*, London: Zed Books, pp. 99–113.

White, R. (1998) *Public Spaces for Young People: A Guide to Creative Projects and Positive Strategies*, Canberra: Commonwealth Attorney-General's Department.

White, R., Perrone, S., Guerra, C. and Lampugnani, R. (1999) *Ethnic Youth Gangs in Australia: Do They Exist? Report No. 4: Somalian Young People*, Melbourne: Australian Multicultural Commission.

Williams, L. (2006) 'Social Networks of Refugees in the United Kingdom: Tradition, Tactics and New Community Spaces', *Journal of Ethnic and Migration Studies*, 32(5): 865– 879.

Winterstein, P. (2009) 'Brazil Best Place to Invest Among BRICS, Mauldin Says.' Online. Available http://www.bloomberg.com/apps/news?pid=newsarchive&sid=asTBbZ084 2FM (accessed 3 August 2010).

Woolcock, M. (1998) 'Social Capital and Economic Development: Towards a Theoretical Synthesis and Policy Framework', *Theory and Society*, 27: 151–208.

Woolcock, M. (2001) 'The Place of Social Capital in Understanding Social and Economic Outcomes', *Isuma: Canadian Journal of Policy Research*, 2(1): 1–17.

World Bank (2001) *Attacking Brazil's Poverty*, Washington, DC: World Bank.

WRR (2009) *Vertrouwen in de school: Over de uitval van 'overbelaste' jongeren*, The Hague: Wetenschappelijke Raad voor het Regeringsbeleid.

Yin, R.K. (1994) *Case Study Research: Design and Methods*, 2nd edn, Thousand Oaks, CA: Sage.

Yin, R.K. (2004) 'Introduction', in R.K. Yin (ed.) *The Case Study Anthology*, Thousand Oaks, CA: Sage, pp. xi–xix.

Young, A. (1999) 'The (Non)Accumulation of Capital: Explicating the Relationship of Structure and Agency in the Lives of Poor Black Men', *Sociological Theory*, 17(2): 201–226.

Zaluar, A. (2004) 'The Paradoxes of Democratization and Violence in Brazil', Paper prepared for the Conference 'Brazil and the Extended European Union', Federal University of Rio de Janeiro, September.

Zaluar, A. (2007) 'Unfinished Democratization: The Failure of Public Safety', *Estudos Avançados*, 21: 31–49.

Zaluar, A. and Alvito, M. (eds) (1998) *Um século de favela*, Rio de Janeiro: Editora FGV.

Index

An environmentally friendly book printed and bound in England by www.printondemand-worldwide.com